CONCENTRATE Q&A
HUMAN RIGHTS
& CIVIL LIBERTIES

CONCENTRATE Q&A HUMAN RIGHTS
& CIVIL LIBERTIES

Dr Steve Foster

Principal Lecturer in Law, Coventry University

SECOND EDITION

OXFORD
UNIVERSITY PRESS

Great Clarendon Street, Oxford, OX2 6DP,
United Kingdom

Oxford University Press is a department of the University of Oxford.
It furthers the University's objective of excellence in research, scholarship,
and education by publishing worldwide. Oxford is a registered trade mark of
Oxford University Press in the UK and in certain other countries

First edition 2016

Impression: 1

Public sector information reproduced under Open Government Licence v3.0
(http://www.nationalarchives.gov.uk/doc/open-government-licence/open-government-licence.htm)

Published in the United States of America by Oxford University Press
198 Madison Avenue, New York, NY 10016, United States of America

British Library Cataloguing in Publication Data
Data available

Library of Congress Control Number: 2018948469

ISBN 978–0–19–881989–9

Printed in Great Britain by
Ashford Colour Press Ltd, Gosport, Hampshire

Contents

Guide to the book

Every book in the Concentrate Q&A series contains the following features:

Are you ready to face the exam? This box at the start of each chapter identifies the key topics and cases that you need to have learned, revised, and understood before tackling the questions in each chapter.

Demonstrating your knowledge of the crucial debates is a sure-fire way to impress examiners. These at-a-glance boxes help remind you of the key debates relevant to each topic, which you should discuss in your answers to get the highest marks.

Each question represents a typical essay or problem question so that you know exactly what to expect in your exam.

Don't fall into any traps! This feature points out common mistakes that students make, and which you need to avoid when answering each question.

Not sure where to begin? Clear diagram answer plans at the start of each question help you see how to structure your answer at a glance, and take you through each point step-by-step.

What makes a great answer great? Our authors show you the thought process behind their own answers, and how you can do the same in your exam. Key sentences are highlighted and advice is given on how to structure your answer well and develop your arguments.

Don't settle for a good answer—make it great! This feature gives you extra points to include in the exam if you want to gain more marks and make your answer stand out.

TAKING THINGS FURTHER

Really push yourself and impress your examiner by going beyond what is expected. Focused further reading suggestions allow you to develop in-depth knowledge of the subject for when you are looking for the highest marks.

Guide to the online resources

Every book in the Concentrate Q&A series is supported by additional online materials to aid your study and revision: www.oup.com/uk/qanda/

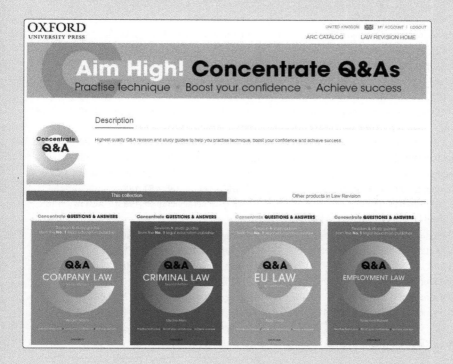

- Extra essay and problem questions.
- Bonus questions to help you practise and refine your technique. Questions are annotated, highlighting key terms and legal issues to help you plan your own answers. An indication of what your answers should cover is also provided.

- Online versions of the diagram answer plans.
- Video guidance on how to put an answer plan together.
- Flashcard glossaries of key terms.

Table of cases

Table of legislation

Exam Skills for Success in Human Rights and Civil Liberties Law

1

Dos and don'ts during exams

Answering: pointers common to both essays and problems

- Spelling and general literariness *will* be rewarded, so at the very least make sure you can spell key words and phrases, such as 'proportionality', 'prescribed by law' (not proscribed by law') correctly. Similarly, cite and spell key statutes correctly: do not call the Human Rights Act 1998 the Human Right Act. If you have 'good cause' for any writing or spelling difficulties, then inform your law school.

- Cite authority for your propositions. As ever in law exams, the more relevant authority you cite properly, the better your answer will be. For cases, the principles and their application to the facts and decision (and other cases) are the most important aspects; remember names if you can, and include dates if the date is significant, e.g. for modernity. Underline, or otherwise emphasise, the name. If you cannot remember the name, use some such phrase as 'in a decided case' or 'in the recent detention without trial case'.

- Spell out the name of a statute the first time you use it (**'Human Rights Act 1998'**, but use 'HRA' thereafter). Try to recall the section numbers if you can, particularly the key ones (e.g. **s.4 of the Human Right Act 1998**), and if the exam is open book; otherwise indicate that you know what the section provides—'the HRA allows courts to declare legislation incompatible . . .'.

Answering: essays

- Essay questions are often chosen by students who prefer to revise and provide more detail and analysis, rather than display the law's practical application in problem questions. Alternatively, students with good problem-solving skills and technique prefer these questions as the same amount of knowledge may be deployed to greater effect in a problem question.

- Always analyse and answer the question: use your knowledge in the manner required by the question, i.e. if the question is: **'The recent case law of the European Court of Human Rights displays a widening of the doctrine of the margin of appreciation. Discuss'**, then there are few marks to be had for discussing the general procedure of bringing claims before the Court. Answer the question set—use recent case examples to show how the Court has respected state law and sovereignty—not the question you wish had been set—'what is the procedure followed by the European Court in deciding cases brought against Member States?'.

● Base your analysis and criticism on the academic materials you have been studying, and show an appreciation of leading academic views. If the essay question attributes a view to someone or something prominent, e.g. a textbook or a recent Law Commission, ensure that you are aware of those views, show them respect, and challenge that view only if you have reliable evidence.

● Use PEA—Point, Evidence, Analysis—for each paragraph. Each point you make in your essay should be followed up with evidence and analysis (this book will use this method to structure the answers to essay questions).

● Say what you are going to say, say it, and say what you have said. This is employed in coursework—introductions, the main body, and conclusions—but adapt this technique in exams to ensure that introductions and conclusions are more succinct.

Answering: problems

● Use ISAC—Identify (the relevant area of law and how it relates to the facts: 'the first issue is whether the statement made by Tony is defamatory'); State (the relevant law—definition of a defamatory comment/relevant case or other authority); Apply (the law (definition/authority) to the facts of the problem); Conclude. This will be used throughout this book to structure answers to problem questions.

● Note the question, i.e. what you are being asked to do with the data. Often, it will be to advise one or more of the parties; e.g. would she succeed in her application for an injunction or damages? The answer may well be qualified—examiners like their creations to be evenly balanced and you will be required to consider the strengths of both claims. So too the relevant point of law may be unclear, as might its application to the declared facts—this is very common in cases such as has X's privacy been unjustifiably intruded upon, or did Y's imprisonment amount to degrading treatment? Debate the issues—do not just raise them.

● Make sure that you have grasped the legal significance of the factual scenario—most of the information provided will be relevant to your answer—that X was a celebrity, that X has publicised affairs before. If your initial analysis leaves parts of the story untouched, read them again. You could use a highlighting pen for this purpose, thus giving you a cumulative visual check. The examiner will have chosen the facts very carefully, not only so that you can raise obvious points and apply general principles, but that you can also spot slight variations from similar cases and can explore how those variations will shape your answer.

● Deal with each legal and factual area in turn, after you have set the scene—this scenario raises the question whether X can bring a claim for breach of **article 8 ECHR**, and whether Y may defend that action by claiming that **article 10** outweighs X's claim.

● So far as choice of sequence is concerned, usually deal with them in the order in which the facts appear in the question or how the relevant law appears in the statute or the case authority. Another way, particularly if you are running out of time, is to deal first with those points which are worth the most marks.

Human rights law exams in particular

● Questions on human rights and civil liberties involve the explanation and understanding of *law*; you have to be familiar with the relevant legal rules and the hard case law. The student cannot, therefore, answer a question on press freedom and privacy without knowing the relevant domestic law on confidentiality and privacy, and the application of the Human Rights Act 1998 and the European Convention on Human Rights. You cannot *simply* argue for the public right to know, or the privacy rights of the celebrity, however articulate those arguments are. Those social and philo-sophical arguments, although relevant, can only be presented once the law has been understood and explained appropriately.

● However, your answers also require you to comprehend and contribute to the arguments sur-rounding the protection and restriction of human rights and civil liberties. Thus, answers should combine knowledge of the relevant substantive law with a critical appreciation of the arguments for and against the protection of human rights and civil liberties and an awareness of the effect on the subject of constitutional principles such as the rule of law, the separation of powers, the inde-pendence of the judiciary, and democracy. In addition, when studying international human rights, students must appreciate doctrines such as cultural relativism, state sovereignty, and the margin of appreciation.

● The student needs to be able to incorporate case law and statutory and treaty provisions into their answers so as to *enhance* their answers. Equally, the student needs to avoid simply giv-ing a bare account of the law; you must be able to articulate arguments about whether those legal rules are compatible with human rights norms, and that will require an appreciation of *established and objective* principles of fairness, such as legality, necessity, proportionality, and concepts such as the rule of law and democracy. For example, the question 'To what extent does the domestic law of defamation strike a correct balance between freedom of speech and the protection of reputation?' cannot be answered by simply relating the general rules on the law of defamation. First, the student needs to establish what specific aspects of defamation law have human rights implications on free speech, individual privacy, press freedom, and the public right to know. Only if you appreciate the potential effect of defamation law on principles of free speech and privacy will you be able to pinpoint the actual dilemmas that the law faces and attempts to resolve.

● It is essential that you are up-to-date and include the most recent legal and other developments in the area. Human rights law changes frequently and there are fresh developments every week—during your studies and revision keep your eye on media items, recent development sites, and journals.

● Be aware of the potential for mixed-topic questions. It is common for questions to be set that re-quire a knowledge of both defamation and privacy, or free speech values and freedom of assembly. Further, areas such as prisoners' rights or terrorism and human rights require a knowledge of a variety of human rights.

● Be knowledgeable of and sensitive to various human rights theories and arguments—this is especially true where you are asked to write about areas that raise constitutional or political matters (e.g. human rights and terrorism raise issues about the separation of powers, government autonomy, and the role of the courts) or the balancing of two human rights (privacy and press freedom).

- Be prepared to make use of reports produced by government agencies or human rights groups to illustrate various arguments on the law's application or efficiency. There is more scope for this in essays, but you can mention them briefly in problem questions.

- Ensure that you at least appreciate the liberal principles and viewpoints about human rights. You do not always have to take a liberal viewpoint yourself, or always side with human rights, but at the very least show an appreciation of the values and importance of human rights.

- For domestic law, ensure that you not only know the content and wording of relevant statutory provisions (e.g. Human Rights Act 1998 or Public Order Act 1986) but that you are aware of the reason for their implementation and the human rights concerns they raise.

- European and international provisions. You should be knowledgeable of relevant provisions of the **European Convention on Human Rights (ECHR) 1950**, and of some EU law, and of international treaties such as the **International Covenant on Civil and Political Rights (1966)**. Refer to them in your answers when appropriate and always ensure that you understand the relationship between those provisions. Be sure you know the relevant legal status of these international provisions in domestic law and their effect in international law. Do not confuse European Convention law with EU law (often they are related, but they are not the same) or the European Court of Human Rights with the ECJ.

Nature and Enforcement of Human Rights and Civil Liberties

2

ARE YOU READY?

In order to attempt questions in this chapter, which cover the theory of human rights and the methods for their enforcement and restriction, you will need to have acquired a sound knowledge of the areas listed below during the course and your revision programme:

- A range of questions have been included to reflect the fact that different courses assess different aspects of theory and enforcement; these theories and mechanisms will then be vital to answering questions in substantive areas of human rights law, such as the right to life and freedom of expression.
- The theoretical basis of individual human rights: where such rights come from, what values they promote, whether such rights are democratically justifiable, and how such rights should be balanced with other rights and interests.
- The key institutions responsible for making and enforcing human rights law.
- The manner in which such rights are enforced, both domestically and internationally: the various mechanisms for recognising human rights, the efficacy of those methods, and the variety of constitutional, legal, and moral dilemmas that arise from those methods.
- The essential elements of legality in controlling the violation of human rights, such as necessity and proportionality.

KEY DEBATES

This area of human rights is a matter of constant theoretical and legal debate. Although the basic theories are well-established, the debate surrounding the role of international human rights law and the most effective and democratic method of protecting them at the domestic level are informed by new political and moral ideas. In particular, the current government's plans to repeal the Human Rights Act 1998 is founded on its approach to balancing human rights with other social interests and reducing the weight of human rights claims.

ⓔ

Debate: Nature of Human Rights

This debate concerns the meaning of human rights and the dilemmas in upholding them. For example, a recent dilemma facing national and international law includes the position relating to refugees and asylum seekers. Evaluating the tensions between refugees' human rights and governments' resistance to accommodating refugees has been a hot topic during the Syrian crisis and also informs other issues on immigration, expulsion, and human rights. Further debates include the question over the legitimacy of the death penalty in international law and how human rights are affected by the global and national threat of terrorism. Each issue raises questions of financial resources, state sovereignty and cultural relativism, and how such matters affect the enjoyment of human dignity and liberty.

Debate: Relationship between Courts and the State

This debate concerns the advantages of a 'democratic dialogue' between the courts and Parliament whereby both work together to ensure the observance of human rights within the separation of powers; and whether it is working in the UK constitution. There is an ongoing debate about the proper democratic role of the courts in safeguarding human rights and whether such a role conflicts with parliamentary sovereignty and government autonomy. This matter has been raised in the issue of the right to die; whether it is appropriate for the courts to question legislation which restricts a person's right to assisted suicide. Further issues of dialogue exist between international courts—such as the European Court of Human Rights—and domestic courts and legislatures on issues such as deportation and whether prisoners should be entitled to vote.

Debate: A Bill of Rights for the UK; Reform of the Human Rights Act 1998

These debates concern recent proposals for a Bill of Rights for the UK and the Conservative government's plans to repeal the Human Rights Act 1998 (HRA) using arguments of national sovereignty and utilitarianism; at the time of writing these plans have been shelved to allow the government time to concentrate on BREXIT. Such a proposal raises questions of parliamentary sovereignty and the extent to which it is appropriate for the courts to decide the balance between rights and other interests, such as public safety and national security. The effect of this on international human rights obligations, especially the UK's relationship with the Council of Europe, is also relevant. Although BREXIT may release the government from its obligations under EU law, its continued membership of the Council of Europe requires our law to be compatible with the European Convention on Human Rights (ECHR).

QUESTION | 1

What do we mean by the terms 'human rights' and 'civil liberties'? Explain and analyse the leading theories on human rights protection and describe how those theories are implemented in national and international human rights documents.

CAUTION!

- This question *does not* require a *detailed* knowledge of the theory of human rights or of the variety of national and international instruments; instead display a sound understanding of both.

- You should concentrate on explaining how human rights theory is reflected in their enforcement and appreciate the importance of rights protection.
- The question does not require an exposition of the substantive law, but it is acceptable to work in examples of substantive rights to illustrate the importance of rights.

 DIAGRAM ANSWER PLANS

> Define human rights and civil liberties, stressing their status and importance

> Provide examples of both rights and liberties

> Explain the leading theories on rights and liberty

> Illustrate their recognition and status in domestic law (bills of rights)

> Illustrate their universal recognition and status in international treaties

A   **SUGGESTED ANSWER**

[1] The essay starts with a clear identification of the essential characteristics of fundamental rights and what they uphold, together with simple examples: this provides a good basis from which to proceed.

Human rights and civil liberties are those rights or moral claims that are regarded as fundamental to either the individual's liberty—such as freedom of movement, freedom from torture, and freedom of expression—or basic needs, such as shelter, food, and clothing.[1] Although individuals should respect each other's rights, they refer to those basic rights that are owed by the state to its own (or other states') citizens. Accordingly, each state should respect these rights and its legal and constitutional system should ensure that individuals are provided with such rights and that they are protected from encroachment. Human rights and civil liberties thus represent the way in which states should treat individuals with respect to their basic liberty, humanity, and worth.

The term 'human rights' often refers to the state's obligation to provide the individual with the basic needs of human life. These are often referred to as social and economic rights—including rights such as food, shelter, clothing, and employment. However, 'human rights' can be used in an 'umbrella' sense—referring to both civil and political and social and economic rights. Equally, documents such as the European Convention refer to 'Human Rights and Fundamental Freedoms', and also makes some mention of social and economic rights, such as the right to education. The term 'civil liberties' on the other hand is employed in domestic law and largely refers to civil and political rights which are contained in documents such as the **European Convention on Human Rights**. They impose an obligation on the state *not to interfere* with the individual's basic freedoms, and include the right to life, privacy, free speech, freedom from slavery and torture, and due process and freedom from arbitrary arrest.

The basis of civil liberties is entrenched in the idea of the liberty of the individual and protection from the acts of arbitrary government. Each state should recognise and protect the individual citizen's basic rights to life, liberty, and property, contained in both domestic bills of rights throughout the world and in international treaties. This need to be free from state interference came to prominence in the so-called 'Age of Enlightenment', in order to control the acts of arbitrary and oppressive governments. Philosophers such as John Locke devised the 'social contract', which has since formed the basic justification for the constitutional protection of civil rights. These liberties are bolstered by international treaties and thus are regarded globally as fundamental, and superior to other rights or interests. For example, the democratic rights to free speech and freedom of assembly will be regarded as more important than the 'right' to be free from the inconvenience of demonstrations.[2] Although the latter interest might, in some circumstances, override our fundamental right, there is no argument that the 'right' to (shop) has a fundamental status and is, therefore, worthy of inclusion in domestic or international bills of rights.

Such protection can be justified on a number of grounds. First, under the 'social contract', expounded by such writers as Locke and Rawls, every individual is said to enter into a contract with the state under which the latter agrees to protect the fundamental rights of each citizen. Here the citizen's promise of allegiance to the state is conditional on the retention of fundamental claims. Rawls imagines a hypothetical social contract, whereby each individual, not yet knowing his or her ultimate destination or choices, seeks to achieve a society that will best allow him or her to achieve those individual goals. This position may not find favour with the utilitarian view expounded by those such as Jeremy Bentham,[3] which condones individual liberty being sacrificed for the greater public good if necessary. This philosophy has been expressed recently by those who support the repeal of the UK's **Human Rights Act 1998**.

Secondly, human rights uphold the basic dignity of the individual as a human being. Thus, every human being is deserving of humane treatment, and should not, for example, be subject to torture or to slavery. Consequently, states violate human dignity when committing any of these acts, and the restriction of an individual's right of choice, such as freedom of expression, is regarded as an attack on human worth and dignity. This justification also ensures that states do not violate the standards of civilised society.

Thirdly, human rights are based on the idea of equality and freedom from discrimination. Ronald Dworkin believes that every state has a duty to treat all of its citizens with equal concern and respect.[4]

[2] The essay uses a practical and simple example to illustrate the importance of rights (in this case democracy) and their superior status over basic rights (such as the general right of the peaceful enjoyment of recreation or not to be disturbed).

[3] The recent concerns over the repeal of the HRA is used to illustrate the principle of utilitarianism, thus showing an appreciation of the principle and an awareness of recent events: this is expected of human rights students and will often separate the excellent answers from the good ones.

[4] A respected theorist is used to explain the basis of equality and human rights, which is then supplemented by an explanation of how that theory is incorporated into various human rights law—which is the basis of the question.

This will ensure that every person, particularly those who espouse unpopular views, enjoy these fundamental rights. International treaties and domestic bills of rights insist that rights are enjoyed free from discrimination on grounds such as sex, race, national origin, and religion (**article 14 ECHR**). Thus, domestic laws will be passed to ensure that individuals and groups are not subject to unlawful discrimination.

Fourthly, the protection of individual liberty and rights can be supported with reference to the rule of law. Law should be open, clear, and prospective, and government should not interfere with people's rights in an arbitrary fashion. The rule of law also insists on the equal application of the law to all classes, including government officials, and on due process. This will include the principles of a fair trial, the presumption of innocence and the guarantee of judicial impartiality and independence, contained in article 6 ECHR. The rule of law also provides a public good, and society benefits from the application of 'due process' rights such as the right to liberty and security of the person and the right to a fair trial, both of which uphold the principles of legality, the rules of natural justice, and the independence and impartiality of the judiciary. Consequently, anti-terrorism provisions have been subject to challenge on the basis that they departed from fundamental principles of liberty and justice (*A v Secretary of State for the Home Department* [2005] 2 AC 68).[5]

> [5]A well-known and relevant example of an unlawful infringement of the rule of law is provided in illustration: this displays a knowledge and appreciation of the principles and the important case law in the area.

Fundamental rights and liberties are contained in both domestic and international instruments; protecting rights such as the right to life, the right to property, the right to a fair trial, and freedom of expression. Equally, basic needs such as food, shelter, clothing, and the right to education will be accommodated in both the state's legal and constitutional framework, and will be recognised and protected by a variety of international treaties and measures.

With respect to civil and political rights, treaties such as the **European Convention on Human Rights 1950** and the **International Covenant on Civil and Political Rights 1966** adopt the above theories and give a special status to individual freedom and rights. Such rights are given the status of 'fundamental' rights, assuming that they are *normally* more important than the enjoyment of other rights or interests and can only be overridden in exceptional circumstances and under certain prescribed conditions. Thus, International treaties impose on the state a burden to prove that any interference is legal, necessary, and proportionate;[6] For example, **article 10** ECHR and the case law of the European Court of Human Rights insist that any interference with freedom of expression has to be prescribed by law and be necessary in a democratic society for the protection of a legitimate aim (*Handyside v United Kingdom* (1976) 1 EHRR 737).

> [6]An example from a treaty, together with case authority, is provided to illustrate the requirements of a lawful and proportionate interference with a human right.

Equally, a domestic bill of rights will provide special constitutional recognition and elevate them above regular rights so as to protect them from arbitrary interference. This gives the right the characteristic of an immunity, which should then ensure that the individual's right will start from the strongest position possible, thus normally trumping other rights and interests.

With respect to the protection of social and economic human rights, domestic and international treaties tend not to offer the same degree of legal protection that is available with respect to civil and political rights. Consequently, these treaties are not generally policed by a judicial body capable of making legally binding decisions on alleged violations of such rights. Nevertheless, treaties, such as the **International Covenant on Economic, Social and Cultural Rights 1966** and the **European Social Charter 1961** represent global and regional concern for such rights and the need to ensure their provision in each state. Similarly, the domestic law will pass specific protective law in the fields of social welfare and employment protection. Alternatively, it will link the violation of such rights with legally enforceable civil and political rights, such as the right to enjoyment of private life or freedom from inhuman and degrading treatment (*R (Limbuela) v Secretary of State for the Home Department* [2004] 3 WLR 561).

[7]The conclusion neatly summarises the essential points and displays an understanding of the question and the primary, though not exclusive, status of rights.

In conclusion, although social and economic rights may be enforced differently, and perhaps less effectively, both sets of rights share the quality of being fundamental.[7] Consequently, both domestic and international law will recognise that status and will attempt to ensure their observance in all but the most exceptional circumstances. This stance will reflect the above theories of rights protection and give such claims the status of 'trump' rights.

LOOKING FOR EXTRA MARKS?

- Clearly explain and display an appreciation of the various theories, and the underlying values of particular classifications of human rights and civil liberties (e.g. how the political right of free speech promotes democracy).
- Stress their importance and weight in political and legal debate.
- Use various examples of how both national and international law recognises and protects such rights and their values, displaying your critical skills in commenting on their purpose and potential effectiveness.

QUESTION | 2

What remedies are available in international law to those whose human rights have been violated? How effective are those remedies and to what extent is it realistic to expect human rights to be protected at a universal level?

CAUTION!

- You require an overall knowledge of various international mechanisms for protecting rights, but appraise the *effectiveness* of those systems.

- Appreciate that certain treaties are enforced via judicial means, others rely on state reporting and visits, and that some are purely aspirational, and comment on the effectiveness of each.

- Be aware of the doctrines of state sovereignty and cultural relativism and their impact on enforcement.

- Although the question is in two parts, take a critical approach throughout when considering the various mechanisms and then assess overall effectiveness at the end.

DIAGRAM ANSWER PLANS

Explanation of the international human rights movement, including the various international treaties and other measures offering protection against and redress for human rights violations

⬇

Explanation of the various techniques employed in international law for such protection and redress

⬇

Critical analysis of the efficacy of such treaties and measures (taking into account the aims of international human rights law)

⬇

Overall analysis of the difficulties facing international law and its machinery in providing such universal protection and the expectations of international law in this area

SUGGESTED ANSWER

[1] The essay begins with a simple statement justifying the establishment of international human rights law and the need to monitor state practice.

The post-Second World War movement to provide international recognition of human rights and effective protection against human rights violations gave human rights a global significance[1] and provided a mechanism by which all states can agree universal standards on human rights. This movement recognises the limitations of domestic law and that a general standard of rights needs to be subject to some form of international policing.

The first formal recognition of human rights in the international order was the **United Nations Charter 1945**, **article 1** stating that one of the purposes of the United Nations is to promote and encourage respect for human rights and for fundamental freedoms for all without distinction as to race, sex, language, or religion.

² The initial treaties are used to illustrate the overall purpose of international human rights law and the last sentence provides an update of the enforcement mechanism.

These declarations are no more than aspirational, yet they support principles of liberty and individual freedom that subsequently formed the content of specific rights treaties.² More specifically, **article 68** provides that the Economic and Social Council of the United Nations shall set up commissions for, inter alia, the promotion of human rights. The Council established the Commission on Human Rights (replaced by the Human Rights Council in 2006), who in turn drafted the **Universal Declaration of Human Rights 1948**.

The 1948 Declaration listed a full range of both civil and political and economic and social rights and established the UN Commission on Human Rights. The Commission could consider communications revealing a consistent pattern of gross violations of human rights. In addition, it was concerned with the promotion and encouragement of human rights, including undertaking investigations into the position of human rights in particular countries. This enforcement procedure departed from the principle that such law should not interfere in the domestic affairs of each state. This in turn led to the **International Covenant on Civil and Political Rights** and the **International Covenant on Economic, Social and Cultural Rights**.

The **International Covenant on Civil and Political Rights 1966** contains rights similar to those found in the **ECHR** and is monitored by the Human Rights Committee. This Committee, established under **article 28**, can receive and study reports submitted by the state parties on how they have given effect to the rights recognised in the Covenant (**article 40**). It may also receive communications from other state parties alleging that a state party is not fulfilling its obligations (**article 41**). This latter process requires a declaration from the relevant state recognising the competence of the Committee to receive and consider such complaints. The Committee has no power to make binding judgments, although it may use its powers to achieve a friendly settlement between the parties.

More controversially, the Committee may receive communications from individuals claiming to be a victim of a violation of their rights by a state party (**Optional Protocol to the Covenant, article 1**). Communications can be received by an individual claiming to be a victim and the Committee must be satisfied that the complainant has exhausted all available domestic remedies and that the complaint is not being considered by any other international procedure. The state has the opportunity to forward its views on the allegations, and if it finds against the state, the Committee has no power to enforce the finding and must leave it to the state to take any remedial action.

The **International Covenant on Economic, Social and Cultural Rights 1966, article 1** states that all peoples have the right of self-determination and the right to pursue their economic, social, and cultural development. **Article 3** then provides that the state parties undertake to ensure the equal right of men and women to enjoy the rights laid down in the Covenant. The Covenant then includes such rights as the right to work, including the right to just and favourable conditions of work (**articles 6 and 7**); to form trade unions (**article 8**); to social security (**article 9**); to an adequate standard of living (**article 11**); the right to education (**article 13**); and the right to take part in cultural life (**article 14**). These rights impose a general duty to attempt to ensure the conditions whereby such rights might be realised. This reflects the nature of economic and social rights, which impose a positive obligation on the state to provide resources for enforcement, dependent on the economic resources of each individual state. This is reflected in the enforcement mechanism, which is based on the principle of self-monitoring and regulation. Under **article 16,** the state parties agree to submit (to the UN Committee on Economic, Social and Cultural Rights) reports on the measures that they have adopted and the progress made in achieving the observance of such rights.

There also exist a number of regional human rights documents, which attempt to regulate the recognition and enforcement of human rights in a particular region. These include, the **European Convention on Human Rights 1950**, the **African Charter on Human and People's Rights 1981**, and the **American Convention on Human Rights 1969.** These member states share a reasonably common set of values, particularly with respect to the identification and protection of human rights and fundamental freedoms.[3] The most famous and arguably effective is the **European Convention on Human Rights and Fundamental Freedoms 1950**, which applies to members of the Council of Europe (and not just to members of the European Union). Its central aim is to effect incorporation of the Convention and its principles into the domestic law of member states. Thus, **article 1** of the Convention provides that the High Contracting Parties undertake to secure to everyone within their jurisdiction the rights and freedoms set out in **Section One**.

The most striking feature of the European Convention relates to the machinery for judicial enforcement.[4] Thus, the European Court of Human Rights has the power to receive applications from individuals claiming to be victims of a violation at the hands of a member state (**articles 34 and 35**). Further, it may make judicial declarations on the Convention, which are then binding in international law on any relevant state party who has accepted the Court's compulsory jurisdiction. This includes the power to award remedies, including compensation, in the form of 'just satisfaction' under **article 41** of the Convention. Several judgments have resulted in a state changing its law and practice so as to comply with the Court's judgment. For example, the UK Parliament passed the

[3] The essay uses the European Convention as an example of how regional treaties can draw on common values.

[4] It then uses the Court as the most well-known example of judicial enforcement.

Interception of Communications Act 1985 following the Court's decision in *Malone v United Kingdom* **(1984) 7 EHRR 14**, which held that unregulated telephone tapping was in violation of **article 8** of the Convention. However, the Court has no power to enforce its judgments directly, as evidenced by the 'pilot' judgment in *MT and Greens v United Kingdom*, *The Times*, **24 November 2010**, which was ignored by the UK government with respect to prisoner enfranchisement until very recently.

However, a more cautious and less confrontational procedure is usually available in international law. For example, the **United Nations Charter** lacks any machinery for the enforcement of the rights it espouses and relies purely on declaring the importance of such rights and their protection by each member state. This method is bolstered by a body that is responsible for the promotion of particular fundamental rights, thus encouraging greater awareness and international support. Thus, in 2006, the Human Rights Council, which supersedes the Commission, has new powers, including the undertaking of periodic reviews of the state's human rights obligations. Further, such treaties as the **International Covenants on Civil and Political Rights** and **Economic, Social and Cultural Rights** place a duty on each member state to make periodic reports of the measures adopted within their jurisdiction. This will allow the international body to review and comment critically on those measures. A more proactive method of international enforcement is the one adopted under the **European Convention on the Prevention of Torture 1987**. Under this Convention the European Committee for the Prevention of Torture is charged with the duty to make visits to various places where individuals are detained, for the purpose of assessing whether the conditions of such detention constitute torture or inhuman or degrading treatment or punishment. This appears more effective than the general **UN Convention against Torture**, which lacks these specific monitoring processes.

[5] The essay neatly illustrates the inevitable limitations in enforcing such rights, together with some factual data on the relevant mechanisms.

Although these methods are, arguably, less effective than the method employed under the **European Convention**, they do promote international recognition and respect for fundamental rights, often informing domestic law and practice in this area. Further, the European Convention model does not concentrate on addressing or avoiding human rights violations, although it might be said that a finding by the European Court will force it to improve its standards.[5]

Some instruments were never intended to be subject to adjudication, but instead aim to raise awareness of particular rights or specific groups such as women, refugees, prisoners, and children. Thus, treaties such as **UN Minimum Standards on the Treatment of Prisoners 1987** are primarily intended to offer guidance to states on the standard treatment of prisoners. Further, the standards identified by such measures might have persuasive force in other formal judicial proceedings.

Many methods also highlight caution in expecting international law to provide full and effective protection against human rights violations. The protection of human rights at international level raises the state's right to self-determination, and consequently a balance must be maintained between the right of each state to its individual autonomy and the protection of fundamental human rights.[6] There may, therefore, be difficulty in achieving a consensus among states on what rights should be included and the extent that they are protected and limited. This is, particularly so with respect to economic and social rights where the state may not have the financial and other resources to comply.

[6] The essay highlights the practical limitations of international human rights law enforcement and of the countervailing argument of state autonomy.

Further, the state's autonomy and cultural and social differences will need to be accommodated. Thus, international human rights law will need to accommodate the principle of cultural relativism so that certain practices—such as the death penalty—may be allowed in certain states even though contrary to other states' practice. Further, a treaty might allow states to make reservations when ratifying a treaty, or to derogate from its obligations in time of war or other emergency (**article 4 of the International Covenant on Civil and Political Rights**). This will be attractive to states that do not enjoy the political, social, and constitutional stability needed to provide stable fundamental rights and will thus act as an incentive for such states to subscribe to international standards. Equally, the international machinery for enforcing these fundamental rights must allow each member state a certain margin of appreciation or margin of error in how they achieve a proper balance between the protection of human rights and the achievement of other social or individual interests (***Handyside v United Kingdom* (1976) 1 EHRR 737**).

In conclusion, international and regional human rights measures aimed at the recognition and protection of fundamental rights exist for the purpose of globalising human rights and offering effective protection against their abuse by individual states. However, because of social, economic, and constitutional differences, international law can only hope to set globally agreed minimum standards and it would be unrealistic to expect those standards to be rigid.[7]

[7] The essay finishes on a cautious note which identifies the constant problems of enforcement and neatly concludes the answer to the second part of the question.

LOOKING FOR EXTRA MARKS?

- Clearly explain and display an appreciation of the aims of international human rights law and the limits of the various mechanisms and their aspirations.

- Be aware of recent political debates in this area and of any recent reforms or proposals for change.

- Show your awareness of the diplomatic, cultural, and legal problems regarding expectations and enforcement—such as cultural relativism.

QUESTION | 3

What purpose do national bills of rights serve in the protection of human rights and civil liberties? In your opinion, are such documents damaging to the public interest and anti-democratic?

CAUTION!

■ This question does *not* require you to provide a detailed analysis of any particular constitutional bill of rights, or of the Human Rights Act 1998, although you can use those instruments in illustration.

■ You should explain why such documents exist and what *purpose* they achieve with respect to the recognition and protection of rights.

■ The central aspect of the question is to address the danger of such documents to the public interest and democracy; you thus need to be aware of the constitutional and democratic arguments for and against special (judicial) protection of such rights; using in particular the current debates surrounding the possible repeal of the UK Human Rights Act 1998.

DIAGRAM ANSWER PLANS

> Explain how domestic law usually enshrines the fundamental rights of its citizens in a bill of rights and provide examples of such

▼

> Explain the purpose of such a method and the constitutional and legal effects of such

▼

> Explain the advantages of such a method to both the state and the individual

▼

> Explore the constitutional and democratic concerns regarding this method, providing examples of potentially undemocratic and unconstitutional practice

▼

> Conclude using pro- and anti-bills of rights arguments and illustrations

SUGGESTED ANSWER

A state's written constitution will make express provision for the enjoyment of human rights within a 'bill of rights'. This will contain a number of rights and liberties that are regarded as common to the notion of individual liberty and human worth, and whose enjoyment are central to the control of arbitrary government. Such documents usually cover rights which protect life, liberty, and property (**American and French Declarations**). This document will recognise and protect rights[1] such as the right to life, freedom from torture and slavery, liberty of the person, and freedom of expression.

[1] Give a simple example of the content of such documents after explaining the basic principle behind bills of rights.

The legal system will then need to decide how and to what extent such rights are to be protected, and in particular what status is to be afforded to them *vis-à-vis* their relationship with other rights and interests. Central to this question will be the extent to which the courts possess power to question or set aside administrative or legislative acts which are incompatible with their enjoyment. One method might be to identify the rights and liberties as central to the constitution of the state, thereby giving them some special constitutional standing. This declaration may be merely aspirational in that the constitution does not provide any mechanism for the *legal* enforcement of these rights or liberties, with the state then left to decide how those rights should be protected within the law.

[2] The principle of judicial enforcement and supremacy, and its effect, is introduced at an early stage: this is the most controversial aspect of bills of rights and requires a clear explanation.

However, many bills of rights are given legal support by bestowing the ultimate power of interpretation and enforcement to the courts, thereby restricting the power of lawmakers and executive government to violate these rights.[2] This 'constitutional' method of protection is evident in the **United States Constitution**, under which the courts have the ultimate power to interpret both the Constitution and the **Bill of Rights** and are allowed to declare legislative acts unconstitutional. For example, in *Madison v Malsbury* **1 Cranch 137 (1803)**, the US Supreme Court declared state law that criminalised abortion was in violation of the right to private life and thus unconstitutional.

[3] To answer the question, and defend your thesis, you need to provide clear and strong justifications for bills of rights, stressing their benefit to the public and not just to the individual.

Such bills of rights achieve a number of aims.[3] First, such documents reflect common interests in concepts such as democracy, the rule of law, and the control of excessive and arbitrary government. Their protection, therefore, is seen as an essential element of the state's and society's constitutional beliefs. Thus, freedom of expression not only recognises the public's belief in individual self-autonomy, but also promotes the common good in press freedom, democracy, and the public right to know. Secondly, they can reflect notions of individual liberty as expressed in theories such as the social contract and the right to equality. A bill of rights will ensure that each and every individual enjoys basic rights of liberty, and this will reflect a common belief in individual freedom and equality. Thirdly, bills of rights are capable of protecting minorities, who might otherwise have their fundamental rights abused by government and the majority. Consequently, they are often relied on by 'vulnerable' groups, such as prisoners, children, women, and immigrants, who might otherwise be left unprotected by the regular law. Fourthly, they allow domestic law to reflect the international obligations of that state and thus to incorporate those treaties into its domestic law. Thus, a bill of rights can often exist side by side with such international treaties, allowing the courts to employ international human rights norms in the adjudication of domestic disputes.

However, bills of rights are seen by some as damaging to society and, specifically, anti-democratic.[4] First, such documents may be seen as inconsistent with the main aims of a state's constitution and government: to secure the greatest happiness for the greatest number of people in that state. Under this utilitarian approach no one person's liberty should be allowed to frustrate the pursuit of the common good. Thus, individual rights should be enjoyed within the context of attaining the greatest benefit for the majority. Accordingly, to allow the enjoyment of the right to free expression over the protection of national security or public morals could be viewed as damaging to the principal interests of society. Equally, the prohibition of ill-treatment might be seen as protecting the individual's human dignity at the expense of achieving a greater good, such as obtaining intelligence information from terrorist suspects.

More specifically, some believe that it is damaging to democracy to make the courts the final arbiters of the law's compatibility with fundamental human rights. Under legally entrenched bills of rights the legislative and the executive are disentitled from passing or executing provisions that are inconsistent with such rights. Accordingly, the courts are left with the final say as to the interpretation and application of the bill of rights and what weight should be attached to such rights. This may be regarded as breaching the separation of powers, as the courts can rule on the compatibility of the law or administrative practice with the enjoyment of fundamental rights. Thus, where a court decision is in conflict with the express wishes of a democratically elected legislature there may be allegations of anti-democratic practice. As an example, witness the recent dispute concerning prisoners' voting rights in the UK.[5]

Another concern is that they are used by unpopular and divisive groups. Such documents can thus be seen as a 'rogues' charter', there to protect those who have transgressed society's laws or morals, or who otherwise pose a threat to its security and well-being. For example, great public and political debate has surrounded decisions not to remove convicted or suspected individuals from the country on the grounds that it would conflict with their basic rights.[6]

These concerns led the last Conservative government to establish a commission to consider a British Bill of Rights: 'Do we need a UK Bill of Rights?' (2011), and to consider the repeal of the Human Rights Act 1998 (*Protecting Human Rights in the UK* (2014)); although the present government has shelved any such proposals, pending BREXIT. Are these concerns justified?[7] First, many bills of rights do not relinquish

[4] The answer provides a clear account of the objections to bills of rights, without committing to the validity of those views. The author presents them objectively, in preparation of countering them later in the essay.

[5] The answer is enhanced by highlighting the constitutional concerns and dilemmas of judicial enforcement of human rights by a simple clear reference to basic constitutional doctrines.

[6] The author provides a topical and controversial example—deportation of criminals and suspects—to illustrate public concern. This shows an awareness of recent events and an ability to weave them into an academic essay.

[7] The author provides evidence from recent political and legal debates surrounding the disadvantages of bills of rights, and then begins to consider the validity of those concerns.

ultimate legal power to the courts, allowing the government the ultimate power to interfere with fundamental rights. For example, under the **Canadian Charter of Fundamental Rights**, the legislature is allowed to pass legislation with a 'notwithstanding' clause. Here legislation remains legitimate notwithstanding the fact that it is inconsistent with the fundamental rights in the Charter. Under some systems, such as the ones adopted by New Zealand and the UK, the judiciary is merely given the power to interpret legislation, wherever possible, in conformity with fundamental rights. Here the legislature retains the power to pass legislation that is clearly inconsistent with such rights. In this way, parliamentary sovereignty is retained and the democratically elected government remains the ultimate arbiter on questions relating to the protection of human rights and civil liberties.

Secondly, whatever system is adopted, all legal systems will need to provide for circumstances where it is permissible to violate, or compromise, fundamental rights. This can be done by placing express exceptions to the scope of a particular right: for example, that the right to life is to be subject to the lawful implementation of the death penalty, or by allowing interferences, provided they possess the characteristics of legitimacy and reasonableness. Further, in the **European Convention on Human Rights**, restrictions on freedom of speech are permissible provided they are prescribed by law and necessary in a democratic society for the protection of a legitimate aim, such as national security or public morals (*Handyside v United Kingdom* **(1976) 1 EHRR 737**). In addition, fundamental rights can be limited by judicial interpretation. For example, the first amendment to the American Constitution provides that no law shall be passed which abridges freedom of speech. However, the American courts have limited the enjoyment of freedom of expression by deciding either that certain speech is not within the ambit of the article (*New York v Ferber* **485 US 747 (1982)**) or that it can be compromised for certain legitimate reasons.

[8] The author defends bills of rights from attack by pointing out the limitations of judicial power and rights enforcement as well as the advantages of rights protection.

Thirdly, bills of rights can be defended against allegations that they are anti-democratic.[8] As we have seen, the rights recognised by such documents are central to the tenets of democracy and individual freedom, based on beliefs shared by all citizens. Thus, rights such as free speech and peaceful assembly actively promote democracy in that they inform the public and offer a means to challenge government. Further, a bill of rights might allow individual interests to be compromised on grounds such as national security and public morality provided there is a pressing need to restrict individual freedom. This is particularly so where there exists an emergency such as war or terrorism, when it is legitimate to further restrict such rights in the name of safety and security. Finally, although bills of rights might allow the courts the final say, a 'democratic dialogue' will exist between the courts and government with respect to the amount of deference that should be shown by judges when challenging the political judgement of government officials. This is particularly so when such acts have been given direct authority from the democratically elected legislative.

In conclusion, one might use the opinions of Lord Bingham in *A v Secretary of State for the Home Department* **[2005] 2 AC 68** to support the proposition that judicial enforcement of human rights is neither socially divisive nor anti-democratic. His Lordship stressed that, although judges were not elected, the function of independent judges charged to interpret and apply the law was a cardinal feature of the modern democratic state. Thus, constitutional bills of rights bestow on the courts a specific constitutional role: to uphold the rule of law and to safeguard the fundamental and democratic rights of its citizens.[9] Provided that is done in good faith, and due weight is attached to competing social interests, then the protection of such rights by a bill of rights should not be regarded as harmful or anti-democratic.

[9] A strong conclusion is provided, using a judicial pronouncement that respects the anti-bill of rights argument, but ultimately justifies the pro-bill of rights stance.

LOOKING FOR EXTRA MARKS?

- Show a clear *appreciation of the need for the special protection* of human rights at the domestic level, stressing how they give greater weight to such rights and how they reflect international human rights standards.

- Explore the constitutional and democratic advantages and disadvantages of these instruments *vis-à-vis* democratic accountability, the separation of powers, and the need to uphold the rule of law.

- Provide judicial and political examples to support the above arguments: relevant case law and recent public debates, prevalent in the UK surrounding the repeal of the Human Rights Act, regarding the supremacy of rights over the public interest.

TAKING THINGS FURTHER

- Blom-Cooper, L, 'The Commission on a Bill of Rights: An English Approach to a UK Bill of Rights' [2013] PL 209
  A critical analysis of the recent proposals for a Bill of Rights in the UK

- Feldman, D, *Civil Liberties and Human Rights in England and Wales*, 2nd edn (OUP 2002), chs. 1 and 2
  An expert analysis of human rights theories and values

- Harvey, C, 'Talking about Human Rights' [2004] 5 EHRLR 500
  A discussion of values of human rights and benefits of their protection

Harvey, C, *Human Rights Law in Perspective; Humanity and Legality* (Hart 2014)
Examination of dilemmas facing international human rights law, especially in the area of refugees

Slowe, R, 'The Conservatives' Proposals for a British Bill of Rights' [2015] 4 EHRLR 372
Explanation and critical analysis of the present government's plans to scrap the Human Rights Act 1998

Smith, R, *Textbook on International Human Rights*, 7th edn (OUP 2016), ch. 1
Overview of the purpose and scope of international human rights law

Waldron, J, *The Law* (Routledge 1990), ch. 5
A thought-provoking debate on rights and their balance with social interests

Young, A, 'Is Democratic Dialogue Working?' [2011] PL 773
An examination of the balance of power between domestic courts and Parliament

Online Resources

www.oup.com/uk/qanda/

Go online for extra essay and problem questions, a glossary of key terms, online versions of all the answer plans and audio commentary on how selected ones were put together, and a range of podcasts which include advice on exam and coursework technique and advice for other assessment methods.

3 The European Convention on Human Rights

ARE YOU READY?

In order to attempt questions in this chapter, which covers the machinery for enforcement under the European Convention and the underlying principles of human rights adjudication employed by the European Court of Human Rights, you will need to have acquired a sound knowledge of the areas listed below during the course and your revision programme:

- A range of questions have been included to reflect the fact that different courses concentrate on different aspects of the Convention: such as its history, machinery for enforcement, its underlying principles, its relationship with domestic law, and the reform of the Convention and the European Court of Human Rights.
- The history of the Convention and the European human rights movement and an appreciation of its relationship with, and distinction from, EU Law.
- The key institutions of the Convention, particularly the role played by the European Court of Human Rights in enforcing the rights under the Convention.
- The manner in which such rights are adjudicated upon by the European Court, employing basic principles of legality and reasonableness together with the doctrines of state authority and the margin of appreciation.
- The controversies surrounding the Convention with respect to the Court's role and the effect of the Convention on domestic law, together with a knowledge of any necessary reforms.

 ## KEY DEBATES

Debate: The Role and Reform of the European Court of Human Rights

This aspect of the European Convention is the centre of legal and diplomatic debates concerning the proper role and status of the Convention. The Court has been the subject of several reforms over the years; both to increase its powers and to reduce its workload. Cases have included the right to a fair

▶

trial (and its balance with the successful prosecution of crime), the deportation of criminals or suspects, prisoners' rights and the balance between free speech and other rights and interests, including national security and public safety. There is an ongoing debate about the future of the Convention and the Court and its role in safeguarding human rights in Europe: should the Convention machinery stay, or should it be replaced by a system where the Court gives greater deference to national legal systems?

Debate: The Relationship between the European Court of Human Rights and Domestic Law

This area is the subject of much political, constitutional, diplomatic, and legal debate, largely concerned with the relationship between the European Convention and domestic law and the power of the European Court to override national law and domestic judicial decisions. Accordingly, the student should be aware of papers and journal articles on the reform of the Convention and the Court and the possible repeal of the Human Rights Act 1998 in the UK. More specifically, there is a debate as to the importance of the case law of the Court and its possible conflict with decisions of the national courts; when interpreting and applying Convention rights, should domestic courts follow the Strasbourg Court or the decisions of superior national courts?

QUESTION   1

Why was the European Convention on Human Rights drafted and ratified? Critically evaluate the machinery established by the Convention for the enforcement of human rights and its effectiveness in protecting human rights in Europe.

! CAUTION!

- This question does *not* require an analysis of the *rights* contained in the Convention; a general knowledge of the types of rights will suffice and can be mentioned briefly where relevant.

- You should explain why the Convention was drafted and ratified and what aims it intended to achieve, both in Europe generally and in the domestic law of its member states.

- The question does *not* require a *detailed* examination of the Convention and the European Court's process, but rather an evaluation of the effectiveness of that system given the original aims of the Convention.

DIAGRAM ANSWER PLANS

> History of the setting up of the Council of Europe and the drafting of the Convention

> Analysis of the aims and objectives of the European Convention

Explanation of the machinery under the Convention, notably the role of the Court

▼

Critical examination of effectiveness in protecting rights within the Council of Europe

SUGGESTED ANSWER

The **European Convention on Human Rights and Fundamental Freedoms 1950** was drafted by the Council of Europe to achieve unity among its members in matters such as the protection of fundamental human rights. It was drafted in the light of the atrocities that took place before and during the Second World War and in its preamble refers to the common heritage of political traditions, ideals, freedom, and the rule of law shared by the member states.

[1] The essay begins by outlining the main aims of the Convention, thus allowing the author to contextualise further information and debate with respect to those aims.

The aims of the Convention were threefold.[1] First, Part One of the Convention identified a number of (mainly) civil and political rights that were felt central to any democratic and civilised society. These include the right to life (**article 2**), freedom from torture and inhuman and degrading treatment (**article 3**), liberty and security of the person (**article 5**), the right to a fair trial (**article 6**), and democratic rights such as the right to free speech (**article 10**), and peaceful assembly (**article 11**).

Secondly, the Convention imposed an obligation on each Contracting Party to secure those rights within their own jurisdiction (**article 1**), thus creating within each state a culture of human rights protection that is consistent with the ideals of the Convention. Thirdly, and most controversially, the Convention established its own machinery for the enforcement of these rights. This includes the power to receive individual and state applications and the establishment of a Court of Human Rights, empowered to make binding judicial decisions. This process reflects the intention of the Convention that states would be subject to a degree of international judicial control.

The Convention established three enforcement bodies. First, the European Commission of Human Rights would consider the admissibility and merits of any application made to it, a task now carried out by the full-time European Court, below. Secondly, the Committee of Ministers, consisting of politicians of each state, is charged under **article 46** with supervising the execution of the European Court's judgments. **Protocol No. 14** enables the Committee to bring proceedings before the Court where a state refuses to comply with the judgment[2] (see the UK's persistent refusal to accept the Court's judgment in *MT and Greens v United Kingdom* (2011) 53 EHRR 21 with respect to prisoner enfranchisement). Thirdly, **article 19** gives the European Court a judicial role to 'ensure observance of the engagements undertaken by the High Contracting Parties in the Convention

[2] The author uses the topical issue of prisoner enfranchisement to illustrate the power, and limitations, of the Convention and the European Court.

and the Protocols'. Thus, the European Court decides whether there has been a violation of one of its substantive rights and whether any and sufficient justification existed for any violation.

The Court consists of Committees, who consider the initial admissibility of applications and have the power (under **article 28**) to strike out cases from its list. It also includes Chambers of the Court, who decide on the admissibility and merits of the application. In addition, the Convention has now established the Grand Chamber, which has the power to determine applications relinquished to it by a Chamber of the Court (**article 31**). This is where the case raises a serious question affecting the interpretation or application of the Convention or a serious issue of general importance (see *A v United Kingdom* **(2009) 49 EHRR 29**, on the issue of the detention of terrorist suspects). Further, under **article 43** the Grand Chamber acts as an appeal court by considering requests by the parties to a case for referral within three months of the decision. It may also consider requests for advisory opinions under **article 47**, and can give 'pilot' judgments covering class actions, as shown in the recent case considering prisoner enfranchisement (*MT and Greens*).

Applications can either be brought by member states on behalf of individual victims of breaches by another High Contracting Party (**article 33**), for example *Ireland v United Kingdom* **(1978) 2 EHRR 25**, or from individual applicants (**article 34**). State applications must comply with some of the admissibility criteria in **article 35** in that states must exhaust all domestic remedies and applications must be made within six months of the last decision, unless there is a continuing breach (*De Becker v Belgium* **(1979–80) 1 EHRR 43**).

Article 34 provides that the Court may receive applications from any person, non-governmental organisation, or group of individuals claiming to be a victim of a violation by one of the High Contracting Parties.[3] A person includes companies, but does not include an unborn child (*Vo v France* **(2005) 40 EHRR 12**). The applicant must normally be affected by the alleged violation (*Klass v Germany* **(1978) 2 EHRR 214**), although it is possible for family and other representatives of the victim to bring proceedings (*Keenan v United Kingdom* **(2001) 33 EHRR 38**). **Article 34** allows the Court to declare an application inadmissible if it is anonymous, an abuse of the right of petition, or substantially the same as one already investigated under the Convention or other international machinery. Further it can be declared inadmissible as 'manifestly ill founded', in other words where the alleged violation is clearly lawful under the Convention. **Article 38** allows the European Court of Human Rights to effect a friendly settlement between the applicant and the defendant state and to strike the case out; either on the basis that the state agrees to amend the relevant law or practice (*Sutherland v United Kingdom*, *The Times*, 13 April 2001), or without any admission of liability (*Amekrane v United Kingdom* **(1974) 44 CD 101**).

[3] The author provides what has to be a descriptive account of certain information, but keeps it concise and relevant to the nature of the question.

The decisions of the European Court of Human Rights are binding in international law on those states that have accepted the compulsory jurisdiction of the Court and place a duty on the state to comply with the judgment. However, the absence of direct application and effect can cause difficulties if the state refuses to accept the judgment, as evidenced in the recent dilemma over prisoner enfranchisement (*MT and Greens*). Under **article 41** the European Court is empowered to award just satisfaction, to place the victim into the position had the violation not occurred. Any such award can include pecuniary damages to compensate for any direct financial loss, and non-pecuniary loss, where the applicant has suffered because of the nature of the violation, for example, for physical or mental distress (*Smith and Grady v United Kingdom* (2000) 29 EHRR 493). In some cases, the Court will regard the judgment itself as just satisfaction and offer no damages award (*Firth v United Kingdom*, **Application No. 48874/09**). The Court can also compensate for legal costs and expenses 'actually, necessarily and reasonably incurred'.[4]

With respect to the effectiveness of the Convention and its machinery, the creation of a full-time Court via **Protocol No. 11** is testimony to the success of that machinery. Indeed, the Convention may have become a victim of its own success.[5] **Protocol No. 14** deals with the increasing caseload by allowing a single judge to decide on admissibility in certain cases, and three-man committees to decide on admissibility in the case of repeated violations. In addition, the 'pilot' judgment procedure should assist in this respect. Further, cases can be declared inadmissible where the applicant has not suffered a serious disadvantage and where respect for human rights does not require the court to examine the merits of the case. This addresses the concern that the Court is now acting as an international court of appeal, conflicting with the original intent of the Convention that the Court would only be used as a last resort after effective state protection had failed. **Protocol No. 15**, which refers specifically to the principle of 'subsidiarity', also addresses this concern.

The decisions of the European Court have had an enormous impact on the protection of the human rights of certain groups such as prisoners[6] (*Golder v United Kingdom* (1975) 1 EHRR 524), those facing expulsion from the state (*Soering v United Kingdom* (1989) 11 EHRR 439), children (*A v United Kingdom* (1999) 27 EHRR 611), and sexual minorities (*Dudgeon v United Kingdom* (1982) 4 EHRR 149 and *Goodwin v United Kingdom* (2002) 35 EHRR 18). These cases have highlighted human rights abuses of such groups, and have provided the victim with a remedy that would not have been available in domestic law.

The decisions of the Court have also had a considerable influence on the establishment of international human rights norms. Thus, the Court has established firm principles of legality and proportionality with respect to the death penalty (*Ocalan v Turkey* (2003) 37 EHRR 10;

[4] A recent and interesting example is provided to illustrate the power of the Court with respect to just satisfaction, thus enlivening what might otherwise be a very descriptive account.

[5] The essay displays a sound knowledge of recent developments and proposals for reform of the European Court, together with an appreciation of concerns over that machinery.

[6] The essay uses examples of how the Convention has enhanced the position of vulnerable groups to support the argument that the Convention has been a success. This is followed by less controversial evidence that the Convention and the court has established and maintained basic principles of justice.

Al-Saadoon and Mufhdi v United Kingdom (2010) 51 EHRR 9), ill-treatment of detainees (*Ireland v United Kingdom*), and freedom of the press (*Sunday Times v United Kingdom* (1979) 2 EHRR 245 and *Lingens v Austria* (1986) 8 EHRR 407). These principles continue to inform the content and application of domestic human rights law.

Further, the obligation imposed by **article 1** on each member state to secure human rights within their own jurisdiction has led to the incorporation of Convention rights and principles into each state's domestic law. The European Court has not insisted on incorporation for the state to offer effective remedies under **article 13** (*Silver v United Kingdom* (1983) 5 EHRR 347), but this represents one of the essential aims of the Convention and of the Council of Europe. Consequently, the passing of the **Human Rights Act 1998** has been welcomed as providing a more effective and immediate remedy for human rights violations; its threatened repeal causing concern among civil libertarians.[7]

Despite the prominence of the Court's role, the number and success rate of applications brought before the European Court should not be used as the sole measure of the Convention's success.[8] Such figures illustrate the ability of the Court to hear adjudications and make binding decisions, which should in turn inform and change domestic law. On the other hand, the fact that so many applications continue to be brought, particularly against established member states, might indicate that the central aim of the Convention—of providing effective domestic protection against the violation of human rights—is not being realised. It may further suggest that the Court is not respecting the subsidiarity principle. Further, the machinery provided under the Convention concentrates on judicial remedies to deal with established violations, to the exclusion of monitoring and investigative procedures that might prevent violations taking place.

In conclusion, the Convention's machinery for enforcement may be seen as a panacea of international legal protection against human rights abuses. However, it needs to exist alongside wider and different mechanisms of protection, including effective incorporation of its principles, which are intended to address and improve the human rights records of each state.

[7] A recent and topical area of debate has been introduced to illustrate the benefits of using the Convention in domestic law and of the danger of departing from that system.

[8] The author provides a measured and tempered view of the success of the Convention and the Court in achieving the aims of the Convention, accepting its successes but noting its limitations.

➕ LOOKING FOR EXTRA MARKS?

- Show a clear appreciation of the advantages of regional protection of human rights and the advantages of establishing this system in Europe after the Second World War.
- Appreciate the novelty and impact of the European Court of Human Rights in the context of international human rights law.
- Explain and analyse how that system has achieved the objectives of the Convention, assessing its success and limitations via case law and other relevant data and adopting a critical approach to the Court's initial purpose and recent jurisprudence.

QUESTION | 2

Critically assess the extent to which the European Court of Human Rights has struck a balance between on the one hand ensuring that member states comply with the standards laid down by the Convention, and on the other respecting the autonomy of each member state and its legal system. How have recent cases and political debates highlighted this dilemma?

CAUTION!

▨ This question requires a very sound knowledge and appreciation of the *recent controversies* surrounding the *role and power of the European Court of Human Rights* and the general relationship of the Convention with domestic law.

▨ The answer needs to include recent cases and other developments which have highlighted these controversies and use those examples to critically illustrate the original and changing role of the European Court.

▨ The question requires some knowledge of the process of the Court and of applications to it, but should not include too much descriptive information on that process, or on the substantive rights contained in the Convention.

DIAGRAM ANSWER PLANS

Explanation of the general conflict between state sovereignty and universal protection and examination of the ECHR machinery with respect to its relationship with the state's domestic law

▼

Critical examination of the doctrine of the margin of appreciation (and margin of error) and the setting of common European standards by the European Court of Human Rights

▼

Critical examination of recent cases and events surrounding the role and power of the Court

▼

Conclusions as to the balance between enforcing human rights standards and respecting state autonomy

SUGGESTED ANSWER

[1] The introduction provides a clear explanation of the aims of international human rights law, together with the inevitable controversy with respect to the conflict between national and international law.

Any international or regional human rights treaty requires the acceptance of universal standards and seeks to measure the legality of each state's laws and practices with those standards. This threatens the state's power to protect the human rights of those within its jurisdiction in a manner that is consistent with its community values.[1]

This conflict is particularly acute in the **European Convention on Human Rights 1950**, where each state's obligations are monitored by a Court that has the power to rule on the compatibility of state law. Such is the conflict that there are now proposals to reign in the Court's powers, discussed below.

The European Court has recognised this friction and has devised mechanisms by which it can show a level of respect to each member state, although many commentators, in particular Timothy Jones ('The Devaluation of Human Rights' [1995] PL 430), have criticised them as devaluing the rights in the Convention. Specifically, the European Court has shown a good deal of deference when interpreting and applying **article 15** of the Convention, which allows states to derogate from their Convention obligations in times of public emergency. The Court has insisted that these measures will need to correspond to a very pressing social need and meet a strict test of proportionality, However, it has also recognised that the state should have a good deal of discretion in such cases (*Lawless v Ireland (No. 3)* (1961) 1 EHRR 15, on detention without trial and **article 5**). However, the decision of the House of Lords in *A v Secretary of State for the Home Department* [2005] 2 AC 68 shows that there is a limit to judicial deference,[2] even in this sensitive area. Further, the decision of the domestic court was confirmed by the Grand Chamber of the European Court (*A v United Kingdom* (2009) 49 EHRR 29).

More generally, the Court offers some discretion to a member state when deciding whether a potential violation is justified for reasons of other individual or state interests. In particular, the conditional rights contained in **articles 8–11** of the Convention, require the Court to decide whether an interference is 'necessary in a democratic society' and proportionate. In *Handyside v United Kingdom* (1976) 1 EHRR 737 the Court stressed that the machinery of the Convention is subsidiary to the national systems safeguarding human rights. This leaves to each state the initial task of securing the rights and liberties in the Convention.[3] Thus, each state has a 'margin of appreciation' given both to the domestic legislature and to bodies called upon to interpret and apply the laws.

The doctrine exists for a number of reasons.[4] First, it recognises that the Court's role under the Convention is subsidiary to the system adopted and carried out by each member state, borne out by **article 1** of the Convention. Secondly, it allows the Court to apply an element of judicial respect to the law and decision-making of a particular state when determining whether something is necessary and proportionate. Thirdly, in certain cases, for example on public morals, it is difficult to establish a common European standard by which the necessity of a particular law or practice can be measured (*Handyside*).

---

[2] A clear example of the principle of legality is provided by explaining the need for non-arbitrary interference with liberty of the person.

[3] A case example is used to explain the relationship between the Court, the Convention, and domestic law; this will then put into context the next paragraph, where the reasons for the margin of appreciation are explored.

[4] The essay can now provide a brief, and neutral, list of reasons why the doctrine exists and is required for the Convention and Court to operate effectively.

[5] The essay can now examine the doctrine's controversial nature, followed by examples where the margin will, or should be, wide or narrow.

Nevertheless, the doctrine is a potential threat to the universal enforcement of human rights and has been applied with caution. Further, it does not apply equally in all contexts.[5] Thus, the Court has afforded a wide margin of appreciation in cases of public morality (*Handyside*, *Wingrove v United Kingdom* (1996) 24 EHRR 1 and *Otto-Preminger Institut v Austria* (1994) 19 EHRR 34). In contrast, it has applied a narrower margin where the restriction in question impinges on the enjoyment of the individual's right to private life (*Dudgeon v United Kingdom* (1982) 4 EHRR 149, *Smith and Grady v United Kingdom* (2000) 29 EHRR 493, and *Goodwin v United Kingdom* (2002) 35 EHRR 18).

The Court has also given a narrow margin in the area of press freedom. Thus, it has recognised that most laws which impinge on press freedom display a reasonably common European standard and accepted that press freedom is fundamental to democracy and thus requires the greatest degree of protection (*Sunday Times v United Kingdom* (1979) 2 EHRR 245). Whatever the level of margin, the Court will insist that the very essence of that right is not destroyed. For example, in *Hirst v United Kingdom (No. 2)* (2006) 42 EHRR 41 the Grand Chamber held that a blanket ban on convicted prisoners voting in elections was beyond the state's margin of discretion and thus in violation of the Convention.

The doctrine strictly applies only to the enforcement of conditional rights, but even in relation to absolute rights the Court has offered each state an area of discretion when interpreting such rights. For example, in *Pretty v United Kingdom* (2002) 35 EHRR 1 the Court noted that there was no general right to die under **article 2** of the Convention, and that even though some states practised controlled euthanasia there was no obligation on any state to introduce such a right. Further, in *Vo v France* (2005) 40 EHRR 12 the Court confirmed that the right to life did not on its proper interpretation cover the right of the unborn child. In this case it noted that there was still a considerable amount of difference of opinion among member states as to when 'life' begins. Equally, in *V and T v United Kingdom* (2000) 30 EHRR 121, when two young boys were given life sentences for murder, the Court recognised that there was no fixed or common agreement among European states on the minimum age for incarceration.

[6] The essay begins to debate recent issues and concerns, first providing examples where the Court has, controversially, disagreed with domestic law and practice.

Although the judgment in *Hirst* allowed the state a limited discretion as to which prisoners should receive the right to vote under domestic law,[6] the question is whether states should be provided with greater autonomy in such areas of criminal justice policy. Thus, in addition to the prisoner voting saga, the UK government has expressed concern over a number of judgments which questioned UK law and domestic judicial decisions. For example, in *Othman v United*

Kingdom (2012) 22 EHRR 1, the Grand Chamber decided that there was a flagrant violation of article 6, when the applicant was to be extradited to Jordan to face terrorist charges when there was a likelihood that his trial would include evidence obtained through torture. This was controversial as the domestic courts had decided that such evidence would not automatically be in breach of article 6 if the individual would have received a fair trial in the round (*R (Othman) v Secretary of State for the Home Department* [2010] 2 AC 110). Equally, in *Vinter v United Kingdom*, (2013) 38 BHRC 65, the Grand Chamber ruled that the imposition of whole life sentences was unlawful in the absence of a clearly formulated policy for review and possible release on grounds of rehabilitation. This judgment conflicted with domestic case law that validated such sentences provided they were proportionate to the crime (*R v Bamber* [2009] EWCA Crim 962) and this conflict was only resolved when the Court of Appeal interpreted the relevant legislation in a manner which was consistent with the decision in *Vinter* (*R v McLoughlin* [2014] 1 WLR 3964).

In other cases, however, the European Court has allowed a greater area of discretion, particularly where there is room for different national practices.[7] Thus, in *Al-Khawaja v United Kingdom* (2012) 54 EHRR 23 the Grand Chamber held that the use of decisive hearsay evidence in a criminal trial was not necessarily in breach of article 6 provided safeguards were in place to secure a fair trial. Importantly, it agreed with the House of Lords' decision in *R v Horncastle* [2010] 2 WLR 47 that the hearsay rules should not be applied in a blunt and indiscriminate way, *ignoring the specificities of the particular legal system concerned*. Further, in *Hutchinson v United Kingdom*, *The Times*, 17 January 2017, the Grand Chamber upheld UK law on whole life sentences despite the absence of clear legislative provisions allowing release on grounds of rehabilitation; the Court being satisfied that the existing law had been interpreted in a Convention-friendly manner by *McLoughlin*.

Despite such evidence there is constant debate surrounding the appropriate role of the Convention and the Court, and **Article 1 of the new Protocol No. 15** affirms that the High Contracting Parties, in accordance with the principle of subsidiarity, have the primary responsibility to secure the rights and freedoms in the Convention.[8] Thus, states enjoy a margin of appreciation, subject to the supervisory jurisdiction of the European Court. This move will be welcomed by the UK government, who have considered repealing the **Human Rights Act 1998** replacing it with a UK Bill of Rights. This would mean that domestic law would not be so dependent on Convention rights and principles, which would allow the domestic courts to ignore European Court rulings. This latter proposal reflects the unease that the government and the domestic courts feel about the duty of the domestic

[7] The author now provides case examples where the Court has taken a more subsidiary role and allowed state law to balance respective interests.

[8] The essay displays a knowledge and appreciation of recent reforms and of ongoing concerns on the issue of state sovereignty and subsidiarity, summarising them concisely.

courts to follow European jurisprudence, under **s.2 of the Human Rights Act 1998** (*Price v Leeds City Council* [2005] 1 WLR 1852 and *R v Horncastle*).

In conclusion, the doctrines of the margin of appreciation, and the margin of error, have been employed by the Court to balance its role in upholding Convention rights with ensuring the autonomy of each state's law. Such doctrines are essential in recognising the state's legal culture and are legitimate provided the margin is not extended unduly and is not inconsistent with the aims of the Convention. However, it is clear that many states, including the UK, are concerned with the present balance and wish to address the power of the Court and the issue of subsidiarity.[9]

[9] The conclusion neatly and concisely summarises the main issues, stressing the importance of the margin of appreciation and noting the states' desire to extend that discretion.

LOOKING FOR EXTRA MARKS?

- Show a clear and critical appreciation of both the role of the Court in upholding the values of the Convention and of the principles of subsidiarity.

- Ensure that you read any relevant cases, case comments, journal articles, and government and other papers in this area and include these, where necessary, in your answer.

- Use various examples of how the Court has used its powers and the reaction to those judgments (in areas such as prisoner voting rights, whole life sentences, deportation, and extradition).

QUESTION | 3

'The role of the European Court is to ensure that any interference with Convention rights is not arbitrary'

With respect to that role explain how the Court has employed the principles of legality and necessity when adjudicating human rights violations.

CAUTION!

- This question does not require a *detailed* knowledge of particular Convention rights or of the European Court's process and procedure.

- Rather, you should be aware of *how the Court resolves human rights disputes* when that right is in conflict with other rights or social interests.

- The student needs to appreciate the values underpinning the principles of legality and necessity in restricting arbitrary interference with Convention rights.

DIAGRAM ANSWER PLANS

General explanation of the role of the European Court, and in particular in challenging arbitrary interferences with Convention rights

▼

Critical analysis of the term 'prescribed by/in accordance with law' and critical analysis of relevant case law

▼

Critical analysis of the term 'necessary in a democratic society' as interpreted and applied by the European Court of Human Rights

▼

Critical analysis of the doctrine of proportionality and its impact on human rights adjudication, as applied by the European Court of Human Rights

▼

Conclusions regarding the Court's use of these concepts in controlling arbitrary interferences with Convention rights

 SUGGESTED ANSWER

[1] The introduction clearly explains the type of rights that are subject to restrictions, and then highlights the basic principles of legality that such restrictions must comply with.

Some rights contained in the European Convention can be interfered with provided the interference possesses certain characteristics of legality and reasonableness. For example, the rights contained in **articles 8–11** of the Convention, guaranteeing rights to private life, religion, freedom of expression, and the right to association and peaceful assembly,[1] state that everyone has the right to, for example, freedom of expression. However, in the next paragraph it is stressed that such rights are subject to such restrictions that are prescribed by law (or in the case of **article 8**—guaranteeing the right to private and family life—'in accordance with law') and necessary in a democratic society for the protection of a legitimate aim. Thus, although certain rights are not absolute, any qualifications must meet generally recognised standards of legality and fairness.

[2] The author uses an article other than the conditional rights highlighted in paragraph 1 to illustrate the basic principle of legality and its importance in halting arbitrary interference (with liberty).

With respect to the requirement that a restriction is 'prescribed by law' (or 'in accordance with law') any interference must first be justified by reference to some provision of domestic law. For example, **article 5** of the Convention allows interference with a person's liberty and security of the person, but only in accordance 'with a procedure prescribed by law'.[2] Here, the law not only must have a legitimate source, but comply with the rule of law in that it is sufficiently fair, impartial, and clear (***Steel v United Kingdom*** **(1999) 28 EHRR 603**).

[3] The well-known case of *Malone* is used to illustrate the requirements of legality and the dangers of them not being followed.

The phrase 'in accordance with the law' employed in **article 8** was considered by the Court in ***Malone v United Kingdom*** **(1984) 7 EHRR 14**.[3] Here it was held that a measure had to have a sufficiently established legal basis, be accessible to those affected by it, and be formulated with sufficient certainty to enable people to understand it and to regulate their conduct. Consequently, the rules relating to telephone tapping, being included in secret administrative guidance, were not in accordance with law.

In *Malone* the Court held that there must be a measure of legal protection against arbitrary interference by public authorities with the right in question. Thus, as telephone tapping was controlled by administrative regulation rather than formal law subject to judicial supervision, such measures were unlawful under **article 8**. Further, the requirement that the rule has to be accessible, insists that a person who is likely to be affected by the rule should have access to it. Thus, in ***Silver v United Kingdom*** **(1983) 5 EHRR 347**—a case involving the regulation of prisoners' correspondence via administrative guidance produced by the Secretary of State—restrictions on prisoners' correspondence authorised by non-legal and non-published Standing Orders were not in accordance with law.

In addition, law should be sufficiently certain and clear and in ***Sunday Times v United Kingdom*** **(1979) 2 EHRR 245** the Court held that law must be formulated with sufficient precision to enable the citizen to regulate his conduct. Thus, a person must be able to foresee, to a degree that is reasonable in the circumstances, the consequences which a given action may entail. Those consequences need not be foreseeable with absolute certainty, as most laws are inevitably vague, and the legal provisions do not have to be in statutory form, but could derive from common law. Thus, in ***Sunday Times***, the Court noted that the common law of contempt of court was inevitably uncertain and dependent on interpretation. Nevertheless, a person could, by examining its application via the case law, predict with a sufficient degree of certainty whether their publication would be caught by the law. Conversely, if a rule is so vague that its meaning and extent cannot be reasonably predicted, then the rule will not be regarded as law. Thus, in ***Hashman and Harrap v United Kingdom*** **(1999) 30 EHRR 241** the Court held that the power of the domestic courts to order a person to desist in conduct that was *contra bones mores* (conduct which is seen as wrong in the eyes of the majority of contemporary citizens), failed to give sufficient guidance to the applicants as to what conduct they were not allowed to partake in.[4]

[4] The author explains the difficulties of measuring certainty in the law, but then provides a clear example where those requirements were not met.

All restrictions on rights in **articles 8–11** must be 'necessary in a democratic society' for achieving one of the legitimate aims listed in the article. In ***Handyside v United Kingdom*** **(1976) 1 EHRR 737** the Court established that there must be a 'pressing social need' for the restriction. Further, that restriction must corresponds to that need, and must be a proportionate response, so that the reasons advanced by the authorities are relevant and sufficient. The Court has also stressed that it is not faced with a choice between two conflicting principles, but with a principle of (freedom of expression) subject to a number of exceptions, which must be narrowly interpreted (*Sunday Times v United Kingdom*).

In *Handyside* the Court held that the word 'necessary' did not mean 'absolutely necessary' or 'indispensable', but neither did it have the flexibility of terms such as 'useful' or 'convenient'. Instead, there must be a 'pressing social need' for the interference which must be proportionate to the protection of a legitimate aim (see below).[5] Thus, the Court will not accept a restriction merely because it provides a useful tool in achieving a social good. For example, in *Smith and Grady v United Kingdom* (2000) 29 EHRR 493 the Court was not satisfied that in practice the ban on homosexuals in the armed forces served any real purpose of maintaining national security via an effective national fighting force.

The Court insists that there is strong objective justification for the law and its application, and that the state can point to a real social harm and show that the law's application was necessary to achieve that aim. For example, in *Dudgeon v United Kingdom* (1982) 4 EHRR 149 it noted that, as opposed to the time when legislation prohibiting homosexual conduct was passed in Northern Ireland, there was evidence of a greater understanding and tolerance of such conduct. Accordingly, a blanket prohibition of such conduct, irrespective of the age of the participants, did not correspond to a pressing social need. The European Court's review, however, may be weakened when it recognises that the state should be provided with a wide margin of appreciation. For example, in *Handyside* it accepted that the prosecution of an obscene publication was justified even though the publication was freely available in most other European states.

In assessing the necessity of any restriction the doctrine of proportionality ensures that a fair balance is achieved between the realisation of a social goal, such as the protection of morals, and the protection of fundamental rights.[6] In *Handyside* the Court insisted that any restrictions should be strictly proportionate to the legitimate aim being pursued. Thus, the restriction in question must not go beyond what is strictly required to achieve that purpose. The extent of this inquiry may depend on the importance of the right that has been interfered with, the extent to which the right was violated, the urgency of the pressing social need, and the sanction imposed on the right user. For example, in *Mirror Group Newspapers v United Kingdom* (2011) 53 EHRR 5 the Court held that the award of over £1m fees in a libel action was disproportionate, as it would have a

[5] The essay begins to explore the meaning and scope of the concepts of necessity and proportionality, providing case examples to illustrate the extent of the Court's supervisory powers.

[6] The essay explores the balancing of rights and interests via the doctrine of proportionality, providing a clear and well-known example of a disproportionate interference with press freedom.

chilling effect on freedom of the press, and was not necessary to protect the claimant's legal or financial situation.

It is clear that the margin of appreciation plays a vital role in determining the extent of the Court's interference. Further, the Court has adopted a number of approaches in determining the necessity and proportionality of restrictions depending on the context.[7] Thus, where the Court feels that there is little evidence of a common European approach to the matter (such as public morality), and wishes to give the state a wide margin, it has simply asked whether the state has advanced relevant and sufficient reasons for the interference (*Handyside*). Conversely, where the Court is intent on thorough scrutiny, and where there is evidence of a common European standard, it asks whether the domestic authorities had available to them a less restrictive alternative. This approach is taken when the Court is faced with restrictions on press freedom (*Goodwin v United Kingdom* **(1996) 22 EHRR 123**) or the public right to know (*Sunday Times v United Kingdom*). The Court may also ask whether the restriction destroys the very essence of the Convention right (*Hamer v United Kingdom* **(1982) 4 EHRR 139**; *Hirst v United Kingdom (No. 2)* **(2006) 42 EHRR 41**).

The need to establish necessity and proportionality bestows a potentially wide power on the Court to judge the acceptability of state law and practice, arguably taking the European Court beyond a mere reviewing function.[8] In *R (Daly) v Secretary of State for the Home Department* **[2001] 2 AC 532**, Lord Steyn observed that proportionality requires the reviewing court to assess the balance that the decision-maker had struck and requires attention to be directed to the relevant weight accorded to the interests and considerations. Such powers may be restricted by the domestic principle of judicial deference and, with respect to the European Court's powers, similar deference might be shown by the Court employing the margin of appreciation. Thus, in *Scoppola v Italy (No. 3)* **(2013) 56 EHRR 13**, the Grand Chamber allowed a wide area of discretion to states in disenfranchising prisoners, and did not insist on judicial involvement in such decisions.

In conclusion, the fact that restrictions on Convention rights have to be prescribed by law and be necessary and proportionate ensures that fundamental rights are not violated unless there are legitimate and pressing reasons for doing so. The requirement that restrictions are prescribed by law upholds the rule of law, and necessity and proportionality recognises that rights should not be interfered with unless there is a pressing and urgent need to do so.[9] Although the Court's application of these principles is tempered by the margin of appreciation, such principles act as a safeguard against unlawful and unnecessary interference with basic rights.

[7] The author explains the importance of the doctrine of the margin of appreciation and its relationship with the doctrine of necessity.

[8] The author points out the danger of bestowing wide powers on the European Court to judge the reasonableness of state law, but provides an example where a dialogue exists between the Court and member states.

[9] The conclusion stresses the importance of the principles of legality and necessity in safeguarding human rights from arbitrary interference, adding a word of caution with respect to the application of the margin of appreciation.

LOOKING FOR EXTRA MARKS?

- Clearly explain the various concepts and the underlying values of each, with particular reference to adherence to the rule of law and the control of arbitrary government and law.
- Stress their importance in weighing the protection of rights with other rights and interests.
- Use various case examples of how the Court uses these concepts, adding academic comment and critical analysis where necessary.

QUESTION | 4

Critically examine the extent to which article 15 of the European Convention allows member states to derogate from their obligations under the Convention in times of war or other emergency.

CAUTION!

- This question requires a *detailed* knowledge of how Convention rights can be formally compromised in times of war and other emergencies via article 15.
- You also need to be aware of how emergencies may compromise the enjoyment of human rights beyond the formal derogation procedure.
- The answer should be approached critically, incorporating the arguments for both preserving and limiting human rights in the name of national security and democracy.

DIAGRAM ANSWER PLANS

Explanation of the rationale behind article 15 and how human rights might be compromised in times of war and emergency

Examination of the wording of article 15 and its restrictions and limitations

Critical examination of the monitoring of state derogation under article 15, together with relevant case law of the European Court and recent domestic decisions

Conclusions as to the scope of the power of derogation and its compatibility with the protection of fundamental human rights

Article 15 provides that member states can derogate from their obligations under the Convention during times of war or other public emergency threatening the life of the nation. This article reflects the fact that during emergencies individual liberty might need to be further compromised to maintain social order and national security. For example, a state threatened by war or terrorism may need to provide extra legal powers with respect to arrest and questioning and detention of individuals suspected of endangering society.[1] This power of formal derogation is in addition to the increased area of discretion given by the European Court to states in the control of serious crime, including acts of terrorism (*Fox, Campbell and Hartley v United Kingdom* **(1991) 13 EHRR 157** and *O'Hara v United Kingdom* **(2002) 34 EHRR 32**). Nevertheless, it has stressed that such circumstances should not destroy the very essence of the due process rights contained in the Convention.

> [1] An example of how rights are naturally restricted in times of emergency is provided by the author, before the specific issue of derogation is considered.

However, it is essential that any derogation measures are subject to limitations and judicial control. As Gearty states, fundamental rights can be under the greatest threat during such times and governments can often overreact and impose draconian measures. This in turn may threaten the very democratic values that such rights purport to uphold.[2] Accordingly, **article 15** is circumscribed by a number of rules that limit derogation and place it under the control of the Convention's supervisory organs.

> [2] The author uses academic opinion to explain the dilemma in balancing rights with the protection of national security and public safety, setting the context of all further discussion and analysis in the essay.

First, **article 15(3)** provides that any High Contracting Party using derogation must keep the Secretary-General of the Council of Europe informed of the measures which it has taken, along with the reasons for derogation. In addition, the state must inform the Secretary-General when such measures have ceased to operate. Secondly, if the derogation is challenged before the European Court, it must be satisfied not only that an emergency threatening the life of the nation exists, but that any measures taken are *strictly required* by the exigencies of the situation. Thus, the measures must correspond to a very pressing social need and meet a strict test of proportionality. Although the state will be afforded a wide margin of error in such situations, **article 15** gives the Convention organs the right to monitor the emergency situation and to provide some objective review of the emergency and the relevant measures.

Thirdly, the measures taken by the member state must not be inconsistent with its other obligations under international law. This ensures that any derogation must comply with other internationally accepted standards applying to war or other emergency situations, such as those under the Geneva Convention. Fourthly, no derogation is allowed in respect of certain Convention rights, such as **article 2** (the right to life), although an exception is made in respect to deaths resulting from lawful acts of war. Further, **article 3** (prohibition of torture and inhuman or degrading treatment or punishment), **article 4(1)** (prohibition of slavery or servitude), and **article 7** (prohibition of retrospective criminal law) are excluded. Thus, certain rights should never be transgressed, even in the defence of the state and of social justice. In addition, the European Court has stressed that there should be no devaluation of absolute rights, such as freedom from torture, in the context of the fight against terrorism[3] (*Chahal v United Kingdom* **(1996) 27 EHRR 413**). Further, in *Saadi v Italy* **(2009) 49 EHRR 30** it refused to alter the test of risk of torture when a state decides to remove a suspected terrorist to another state.

The above cases aside, the Court will offer states a wide degree of discretion in this area. In *Lawless v Ireland (No. 3)* **(1961) 1 EHRR 15**,[4] the applicants claimed that their internment without trial was in breach of their right to liberty of the person and not justified by the emergency situation existing in Ireland and the UK. The Court found that the detention of the applicant without trial for a period of five months was in violation of **article 5**. However, it held that the government was entitled to derogate by virtue of a public emergency. Although the Court stressed that derogation measures are strictly limited to what is required by the exigencies of the situation, it held that the respondent government should be afforded a certain margin of error or appreciation in deciding what measures were required by the situation. Further, it was not the Court's function to substitute for the government's assessment any other assessment of what might be the most prudent or most expedient policy to combat terrorism.

In that case, the Court also stressed that it must arrive at its decision as to the compatibility of the measures in the light of the conditions that existed at the time of the original derogation, rather than reviewing the matter retrospectively. This judicial reticence was evident in *Brannigan and McBride v United Kingdom* **(1993) 17 EHRR 539**, concerning the United Kingdom's derogation in relation to **article 5** following the European Court's decision in *Brogan v United Kingdom* **(1989) 11 EHRR 117**. In the latter case it had held that detention provisions contained in the **Prevention of Terrorism Act 1978** contravened **article 5(3)**. Following that decision, the government lodged a derogation because of the emergency position in Northern Ireland. Those measures and the derogation were challenged in *Brannigan and McBride*, but the Court held that they were justified despite the derogation only being lodged after the Court's decision in *Brogan*. The derogation was not invalid merely because the government had decided to keep open the possibility of finding a means in the future, other than employing **article 15**, of ensuring greater conformity with its Convention obligations. The Court also

[3] The answer clearly states the exceptions to article 15 and then provides case examples which support those exemptions in an area where there is a natural request from the states for a more flexible approach (deportation of suspected terrorists).

[4] The European Court's traditional and conservative stance is illustrated through the case of *Lawless* and is then supplemented by a further example of deference in the *Brannigan* case.

found that there were effective safeguards, such as the availability of *habeas corpus*, to safeguard against arbitrary action.

Thus, this margin of error will force the European Court to take a 'hands off' approach and allow the state wide latitude in compromising human rights for social order. However, the events surrounding the challenge of provisions allowing detention without trial in the UK have shown that the domestic judiciary will be unwilling to relinquish their role of safeguarding basic rights, even in times of emergency.[5] In *A v Secretary of State for the Home Department* **[2005] 2 AC 68** a challenge was made to provisions in the **Anti-terrorism, Crime and Security Act 2001**. These measures provided for an extended power to arrest and detain foreign nationals suspected of terrorism and whose removal was not possible because they would face ill-treatment in violation of **article 3** of the Convention if returned to that particular country. The government had consequently derogated from **article 5(1)** of the European Convention. A majority of the House of Lords held that the measures allowing indefinite detention without trial or charge were incompatible with Convention rights and could not be excused within **article 15**. The majority accepted that there existed a 'public emergency threatening the life of the nation' so as to allow derogation, adding that great weight should be given to the judgement of the Home Secretary and Parliament because they had to exercise a pre-eminently political judgement. Lord Hoffmann, dissenting, believed that the real threat to the life of the nation came not from terrorism but from laws such as those in issue.

However, the majority then held that the measures were not strictly required or proportionate. Lord Bingham conceded that during terrorism the decision of a representative democratic body demanded a degree of respect. However, he stressed that even in a terrorist situation neither the Convention organs nor the domestic courts were willing to relax their supervisory role.[6] The measures were disproportionate because they did not deal with the threat of terrorism from persons other than foreign nationals and permitted suspected foreign terrorists to carry on their activities in another country provided there was a safe country for them to go to. Lord Bingham concluded that, if the threat posed by UK nationals could be addressed without infringing the right to personal liberty, it had not been shown why similar measures could not adequately address the threat posed by foreign nationals.

Their Lordships also held that the measures were in violation of **article 14** of the European Convention, that Convention rights should be enjoyed without discrimination. This was because the provisions allowed foreign nationals to be deprived of their liberty but not UK nationals. Accordingly the appellants were treated differently because of their nationality or immigration status. Subsequently, the Grand Chamber of the European Court upheld those findings on **article 15**, refusing to interfere with the government's assessment of the

[5] The newer approach adopted by the judiciary is illustrated through the case of *A*, providing a clear account of the background facts and then moving to the decision.

[6] A clear summary of the decision in *A* is needed to illustrate on what grounds the courts will challenge derogation measures, then allowing the author to draw conclusions from the case and the overall position, below.

emergency or the House of Lords' findings on necessity (***A v United Kingdom* (2009) 49 EHRR 29**).

The decisions of the House of Lords and the Grand Chamber confirm that the courts' role in safeguarding human rights should not be diminished to the point that a government can compromise rights without strong and cogent evidence and justification. Although both courts accept that the question of whether an emergency exists is primarily political, the proportionality of such measures is for the courts to determine. This highlights that violation of basic rights can be as damaging to democratic principles as the initial threats to order.

[7] The author now starts to conclude by summarising the overall position with respect to how article 15 resolves the dilemma.

In conclusion, **article 15** has the potential to endanger fundamental rights and to undermine the central aims of the Convention if it is not effectively monitored. The case law of the Court suggests that it will offer a very wide margin of appreciation, leaving each state to decide how to deal with the situation.[7] However, the decision in ***A v Secretary of State for the Home Department***—and the subsequent decision of the Grand Chamber—clearly indicates that the state will not be left with an unlimited discretion in this area.

LOOKING FOR EXTRA MARKS?

- Show an appreciation of how emergencies, such as terrorism, pose a threat to democracy, as does the erosion of human rights during such times.
- Stress the importance of *maintaining a balance* in such a situation and identify how international provisions and relevant case law has achieved this balance.
- Use various case examples that illustrate the above dilemma and how the Convention has responded to pressure from states to relax control in these times.

TAKING THINGS FURTHER

- Bratza, N, 'Living Instrument or Dead Letter: The Future of the ECHR' [2014] 2 EHRLR 116
  Explores the future role of the ECHR in safeguarding rights in Europe
- Costa, JP, 'The Relationship between the European Court of Human Rights and the National Courts' [2012] 3 EHRLR 264
  Explores the effect of European Court decisions on the decisions of domestic courts
- Council of Europe, *Protocol No. 15 amending the Convention on the Protection of Human Rights and Fundamental Freedoms Strasbourg* (2013)
  The attempt by the Council of Europe to accommodate state sovereignty and subsidiarity in the Convention machinery
- Elliot, M, 'After Brighton: Between a Rock and a Hard Place' [2012] PL 619
  Examines recent proposals to reform the role and power of the ECHR and the Court

- Harris, DJ, O'Boyle, M, Warbrick, C, and Bates, E, *The Law of the European Convention on Human Rights*, 4th edn (OUP 2018)

  A thorough account of the Convention, its process, and its individual rights and case law

- Mowbray, A, *Cases and Materials on the European Convention on Human Rights*, 3rd edn (OUP 2012)

  A thorough coverage of ECHR case law under each right

Online Resources

www.oup.com/uk/qanda/

Go online for extra essay and problem questions, a glossary of key terms, online versions of all the answer plans and audio commentary on how selected ones were put together, and a range of podcasts which include advice on exam and coursework technique and advice for other assessment methods.

The Human Rights Act 1998

4

ARE YOU READY?

In order to attempt questions in this chapter, which covers the passing, operation, and possible repeal of the UK's Human Rights Act 1998, you will need to have acquired a sound knowledge of the areas listed below during the course and your revision programme:

- A range of questions have been included to reflect the fact that different courses concentrate on different aspects of the Act: such as the reason for its passing, the courts' success in achieving its aims and maintaining basic constitutional principles, and the reasons why the Act may be repealed and replaced with a 'British' Bill of Rights.

- The history of human rights protection in the UK, from the traditional common law system to the 'incorporation' of European human rights law and the passing of the 1998 Act.

- The key provisions of the 1998 Act, most notably those that give the domestic courts the power to interpret and apply domestic law in line with the European Convention and it case law.

- The manner in which the courts have employed those powers to resolve human rights disputes, together with the controversies caused by such cases.

- The constitutional and legal controversies that led to proposals to repeal the 1998 Act and replace it with a 'British' Bill of Rights.

KEY DEBATES

The Act, together with the reform of the European Convention on Human Rights dealt with in Chapter 3, is the subject of much political, constitutional, diplomatic, and legal debate, largely concerned with the relationship between the European Convention and domestic law and the possible repeal of the Human Rights Act 1998 and its replacement with a British Bill of Rights. Accordingly, the student should be aware of papers and journal articles on the controversies caused by the passing and opera-

$\blacktriangleright$

tion, and the possible repeal of the Human Rights Act 1998; and in particular the reasons why the government wish to repeal, and civil libertarians wish to retain, the present position. These changes need to be noted on a regular basis, as the legal and political landscape is constantly changing.

Debate: The Human Rights Act and the Constitution

This debate centres around the appropriate role of the courts in upholding human rights under the Act and what impact that has on parliamentary sovereignty and the separation of powers. The Act provided the courts with extra powers to interpret and apply the law in line with European Convention rights and to question the compatibility of domestic statutory law with the Convention and its case law. These powers question the position of parliamentary sovereignty and the proper constitutional role of the courts if, for example, anti-terrorism legislation were to be declared incompatible.

Debate: The Relationship between the ECHR and European Court and Domestic Law

There is an ongoing debate about how the Convention, and the case law of the Court, affects domestic law and whether the Convention and the Court should respect the sovereignty of domestic law to a greater extent. Decisions made by the Court on matters such as prisoner voting, whole life sentences and deportation question the legitimacy of the European Court's power to lay down guidance on the extent to which human rights should be enjoyed. Such decisions will need to be adhered to by member states, and followed by the domestic courts, and this will excite suggestions for the reigning in of the Court's powers.

Debate: The Repeal of the Human Rights Act and a British Bill of Rights and Responsibilities

There have been a number of proposals for reforming or repealing the 1998 Act and replacing it with a domestic Bill of Rights and Responsibilities in order to accommodate government proposals to reduce reliance on European human rights law. This proposal has at the time of writing been shelved, but there is an ongoing debate about the power of the European Court and the extent to which decisions of the European Court should be followed by the domestic courts. Thus, although the repeal of the Act is unlikely, at least until BREXIT is complete, there will be an ongoing debate as to whether our human rights law should be shaped by European law, or rather by British principles of justice.

Q QUESTION 1

With respect to the role of the courts in the protection of human rights, what constitutional difficulties have been highlighted by the passing and implementation of the Human Rights Act 1998? In your opinion, are the courts' powers under the Act 'unconstitutional'?

! CAUTION!

■ This question does *not* require an analysis of the *rights* contained in the Act; neither does it require a general explanation of the Act's provisions. A general knowledge of the rights and of the overall provisions of the Act can be cited where this allows you to address the question.

- Rather the question is asking you to address the *constitutional* issues surrounding the passing and implementation of the Act (using case examples to illustrate): the effect of such on the separation of powers, parliamentary sovereignty, and the rule of law *vis-à-vis* the constitutional role of the courts in safeguarding human rights.

- The question asks for your opinion, but you must appreciate the general arguments surrounding the courts' role in upholding human rights and the powers given to them under the Act. Thus, appreciate all arguments in this area before you give your views and conclusions on the issue of constitutionality: there is no right answer or conclusion provided the student incorporates the opposing arguments.

DIAGRAM ANSWER PLANS

> Very brief explanation of the traditional method of rights protection before the 1998 Act together with the reasons why the Act was passed

▼

> Overall examination of the various changes made to the powers of the courts under the Act: ss.2–4 HRA

▼

> Critical examination of case law under the Act which highlights any constitutional issues arising from such powers

▼

> Consideration of the constitutional legitimacy of the courts' powers under the Act, together with conclusions on the ultimate question

SUGGESTED ANSWER

[1] The author displays an awareness of recent proposals for reform of the Act, which although is not mentioned in the question is central to concerns about the constitutional integrity of court's powers under the 1998 Act.

[2] The author begins the examination of the constitutional issues by stressing the traditional view and by explaining the Act's effect on that approach.

[3] The author then provides case examples which illustrate the effect of this change in practice, offering examples of both a robust and conservative approach.

The passing of the **Human Rights Act 1998** raised a number of constitutional arguments from those who felt that the traditional system would be replaced by the employment of European human rights principles that would undermine parliamentary sovereignty and the general public good. Indeed, this concern has caused governments to consider repealing the Act and replacing it with a domestic bill of rights.[1]

A central argument concerns the powers of the courts to resolve human rights disputes by going beyond its traditional constitutional role of simply applying the law and allowing them to judge the merits of particular laws and practices.[2] This includes the power, under **s.2**, to consider the case law of the European Convention and to apply necessity and proportionality when judging the compatibility of legislative or other acts. In *R (Daly) v Secretary of State for the Home Department* **[2001] 2 AC 532,** Lord Steyn held that proportionality required the court to assess the balance that the decision-maker had struck, together with the relevant weight accorded to various interests, and to assess whether any restriction was necessary in a democratic society.[3] Despite this, Lord Steyn did not believe that there had been a shift to merits review and in certain cases the courts are prepared to offer decision-makers, including Parliament, a great degree of discretion. For example, in *R v Countryside Alliance v Attorney General* **[2007] 3 WLR 922**, the House of Lords held that the ban on hunting with hounds by the **Hunting Act 2004** was not incompatible with the hunters' Convention rights. This was because the provision had been passed by a democratically elected Parliament on moral grounds. Conversely, the House of Lords took a more robust approach in *A and others v Secretary of State for the Home Department* **[2005] 2 AC 68** in deciding that the detention of foreign nationals under the **Anti-terrorism, Crime and Security Act 2001** was a disproportionate response to the threat of terrorism. Lord Bingham held that the traditional *Wednesbury* approach was no longer appropriate and the domestic courts themselves had to form a judgment whether a Convention right was breached. Further, given the importance of **article 5**, judicial control of executive interference with liberty was essential and the courts were not precluded by deference from scrutinising such issues. Similar concerns have been raised regarding the requirement to take into account the case law of the European Court of Human Rights. This has led to the government proposals' that domestic courts follow European case law rather than decisions of our own Supreme Court.[4] In response, **s.2** does not require domestic courts to follow such decisions, and in *R (Nicklinson) v Ministry of Justice* **[2014] UKSC 38**, the Supreme Courts stressed that domestic courts were not precluded from departing from European decisions when applying the rights laid down in the 1998 Act.

There are also concerns regarding the courts' powers under **s.3** of the Act to interpret both primary and secondary legislation 'so far as is possible' in a way that is compatible with Convention rights. This gives the courts a greater power to interpret legislation. However, **s.3** does not affect the validity of any incompatible primary legislation, or the validity, continuing operation, or enforcement of any incompatible subordinate legislation if primary legislation prevents removal of the incompatibility. Consequently, whether parliamentary sovereignty is compromised will depend on the extent to which they use their interpretation powers under the Act.[5] A robust approach was taken by the House of Lords in *R v A (Complainant's Sexual History)* **[2002] 1 AC 45**. Here it was held that the interpretative obligation under **s.3** of the **Human Rights Act 1998** applied even where there was no ambiguity and placed a duty on the court to strive to find a possible interpretation compatible with Convention rights. Thus, **s.3** required the courts to proceed on the basis that the legislature would not, if alerted to the problem, have wished to deny the right of an accused to put forward a full and complete defence in his rape trial. However, **s.3** does not entitle the courts to legislate or to radically alter a statute

[4] The author deals with a highly controversial and topical concern—to follow domestic or European case law.

[5] The author makes a reasoned statement about the potential of increased powers of interpretation, then offers case examples to illustrate various judicial approaches.

in order to achieve compatibility. In *Re S and W* [2002] 2 AC 291, the House of Lords stressed that the 1998 Act maintained the constitutional boundary between the interpretation of statutes and the passing and repeal of legislation. Thus, a meaning that departed substantially from a fundamental feature of an Act of Parliament was likely to have crossed the boundary.

[6] The discussion continues with various examples where the constitutional concerns are explored and explained.

Nevertheless, there is still judicial argument regarding the scope of **s.3** and the extent to which the courts should interpret and rectify incompatible legislation, or whether they should declare such legislation as incompatible and leave any change to Parliament.[6] Thus, in *Bellinger v Bellinger* [2003] 2 AC 467 it was not possible to use **s.3** to interpret the words 'man and woman' to include a person who had undergone gender reassignment, so as to comply with the decision of the European Court in *Goodwin v United Kingdom* (2002) 35 EHRR 18. However, in *Mendoza v Ghaidan* [2004] 2 AC 557 the House of Lords held that the words 'as his wife or husband' could be interpreted to mean 'as if they were his wife or husband' so as to give a homosexual the right to inherit his partner's tenancy. Lord Millett dissented on the grounds that it was for Parliament to change a law that was quite clearly not intended to cover same-sex relationships. Further, in *Attorney-General's Reference (No. 4)* [2005] 1 AC 264 it was possible to read down a statutory provision so as to avoid incompatibility, even though Parliament had intended a consequence inconsistent with the Convention. Having regard to its intention in passing **s.3** of the **Human Rights Act 1998**, it was permissible to assume that other statutory provisions should not be incompatible with a person's Convention rights.

[7] The author now moves on to the next, critical, constitutional issue—providing the reader with the central concerns and then the relevant case law to illustrate the dilemma and to prove the thesis of the essay.

Issues concerning parliamentary sovereignty are raised with respect to the power under **s.4** to declare primary and secondary legislation incompatible.[7] This does not allow the courts to strike down or disallow primary legislation. However, they have the power to make a declaration of incompatibility, leaving Parliament with the choice to amend or repeal the relevant law, under the procedure laid down by **s.10** of the Act. This power has, thus far, been used with a good deal of caution, the courts showing some reluctance to question primary legislation passed by the democratically elected Parliament. For example, in *R v Shayler* [2002] 2 WLR 754 the House of Lords held that the **Official Secrets Act 1989** was compatible with **article 10** of the Convention despite the absence of a public interest defence. Further, in *Nicklinson*, the majority of the Supreme Court held that **s.2(1)** of the **Suicide Act 1961** was not incompatible with **article 8** because any legislative change in the controversial area of assisted suicide should be left to Parliament. In that case, some of the Court felt that it would be constitutionally improper for the courts to make a declaration whilst Parliament was considering legislative change. Again, in *Chester v*

Ministry of Justice **[2014] UKSC 63** it refused to declare electoral law in breach of the right to vote in **article 1** of the **First Protocol** to the Convention until Parliament had had an opportunity to change the law; otherwise the function of Parliament would be usurped.

Despite this general reticence, there have been occasions where the courts have been prepared to grant declarations of incompatibility. Thus in *Bellinger v Bellinger*, legislation which did not recognise the right of transsexuals to marry was declared incompatible with **article 8** and relevant case law of the European Court (*Goodwin v United Kingdom*). Again in *A and others v Secretary of State for the Home Department*, detention provisions under the **Anti-terrorism, Crime and Security Act 2001** were declared incompatible with **article 5** and not justified under **article 15**, which allows derogation in times of war or other emergency threatening the life of the nation. The decision arguably breaches the separation of powers by not offering the government and Parliament appropriate deference on matters of national security and public safety, but was confirmed by the European Court in *A v United Kingdom* **(2009) 49 EHRR 29**.

But are these powers unconstitutional?[8] First, the courts have always had the power to safeguard human rights against arbitrary interference, including the power to interpret legislation in line with human rights norms (*Waddington v Miah* **[1974] 1 WLR 683**; *Raymond v Honey* **[1983] AC 1**). Secondly, although the courts now have the power to apply Convention law and principles, and to declare legislation incompatible with Convention rights,. this power has been bestowed by Parliament with the intention that the court's constitutional powers be extended in this area. Thus, in *A v Secretary of State for the Home Department* Lord Bingham rejected any assertion of undemocratic powers, noting that the courts had been given a wholly democratic mandate by Parliament.

Thirdly, the Act has been carefully constructed so as to avoid any direct conflict with parliamentary sovereignty. The courts have no power to strike down incompatible primary legislation, or secondary legislation clearly authorised by primary legislation. Accordingly, the ultimate legislative power is still being vested in Parliament—including the power to pass new legislation, correcting the court's interpretation. Thus, the decision in *HM Treasury v Ahmed and others* **[2010] 2 AC 534**, was followed by the **Terrorist Asset Freezing (Temporary Provisions) Act 2010** retrospectively validating incompatible freezing orders. Fourthly, although the doctrines of necessity and proportionality no doubt depart from the more restrictive traditional grounds of review, there is evidence that the courts are willing to display a good deal of judicial deference where they feel that a matter is better resolved by a government official or by Parliament itself (*Chester* and *Nicklinson*).

[8] The student is now in a position to consider the central question, drawing on the information and the critical analysis that have been made throughout the essay.

[9] The student provides clear, crisp, concluding remarks which support his thesis and the evidence throughout the essay.

In conclusion, it should be stressed that in most jurisdictions the courts' constitutional role includes the power to question and, in many cases, strike down legislative and executive acts that conflict with fundamental constitutional rights.[9] Although the Act extended the power of the courts to protect human rights, given the scope of the Act—in particular its retention of parliamentary sovereignty—it would be wrong to allege that these powers are unconstitutional.

LOOKING FOR EXTRA MARKS?

- Show that you understand the 'constitutional' issues and dilemmas of courts questioning Parliament and the executive in human rights claims.

- Appreciate the extent to which the Act increased the domestic courts' powers in this respect and the dilemma caused by such. This can be done by reading leading academic and news articles in this area.

- Use leading, controversial, cases which illustrate the constitutional issues and dilemmas and which allow you to conclude on the central question; and display strong critical and reasoning skills in presenting such information as evidence.

QUESTION | 2

In August 2018, in response to the formation and activities of a number of right-wing extremist groups, Parliament passed the (imaginary) Public Order (Proscription of Associations) Act 2018. The Act made it an offence to belong to, to assist in the recruitment and organisation of, or to take part in the activities of any group that has been proscribed by the Secretary of State under the Act. Under s.2 of the Act, the Secretary of State may proscribe any group if he has reasonable grounds for believing that such a group advocates the use of violence for the purpose of expressing the views or agenda of such a group, or where the agenda or activities of such a group are such that they would cause gross offence to any racial or religious group, or to any members of such group. Acting under s.2 of the Act, the Secretary of State proscribed a group known as Freedom Against Religious Terror, which suggested banning all 'extremist' religious groups that advocated religious following above the enjoyment of individual liberty. The head of the group had recently been found guilty of arson after burning down an Islamic Centre, and several members of the group had been found guilty of assaults on a number of Muslims. In July 2019, Boris and Billy, both members of the group, were arrested for distributing leaflets produced by the group outside the local town hall. The leaflets attempted to recruit new members and invited people to a proposed rally to promote 'religious tolerance and the freedom of the individual'. They were both subsequently charged under the Act, for recruiting and taking part in the activities of a proscribed group, and at their trial they claimed that the Act, the group's proscription, and the proceeding were contrary to their Convention rights.

Advise Boris and Billy as to what Convention rights might be at issue and how those rights might be raised in the domestic courts by employing the relevant provisions of the Human Rights Act 1998. In particular, how might the Public Order (Proscription of Associations) Act 2018, the Secretary's proscription, and the prosecution be challenged under the Human Rights Act 1998, and what are their chances of success?

CAUTION!

- Although the scenario raises possible violations of the rights of association and assembly and freedom of expression, the student *does not* need an in-depth knowledge of those rights or the relevant case law of the European and domestic courts.

- The question is principally testing the student's knowledge of the machinery for the enforcement of human rights under the 1998 Act, the principles of legality and reasonableness that the courts will use in resolving the case, and of any remedies available to the victims of any violation.

- Ensure that you deal with each issue in order by applying your knowledge of the process followed under the Act—together with the wording of the legislative power—and consider the arguments of legality and compatibility from both sides.

- Note, such a question may alter if the Act is replaced by a British Bill of Rights; although any new provisions will have similar powers of interpretation regarding a new Bill of Rights.

DIAGRAM ANSWER PLANS

Identify the issues	▨ The legal issues, relevant Convention rights, and the claims made by the claimants ▨ Articles 10 and 11 ECHR; application for judicial review; ss.2–4, 6 HRA
Relevant law	▨ Outline the rules and relevant cases relating to the claims together with any remedies
Apply the law	▨ Application of the rules and cases to the facts
Conclude	▨ Conclude on whether the claims would be likely to succeed

SUGGESTED ANSWER

The Convention Rights at Issue

[1] The introduction identifies the Convention rights at issue, together with their values and conditional status.

The proscription of the group engages the right to freedom of association under **article 11**, a right regarded as a fundamental aspect of any democratic society (***United Communist Party v Turkey (1998) 26 EHRR 121***).[1] Further, as the Act makes it an offence to take part in the activities of a proscribed group, and Boris and Billy were charged for distributing leaflets publicising the agenda and forthcoming rally of the group, the right to peaceful assembly under **article 11** and the right to freedom of expression under **article 10** are also engaged (*Chorherr v Austria* **(1993) 17 EHRR 358**). These rights are conditional and can be interfered with provided the interference is prescribed by law, pursues a legitimate aim, and is necessary in a democratic society to achieve that aim.

The Mechanism for Challenge

[2] The author supplies a clear and concise explanation of the process of challenge under the Human Rights Act.

With respect to the Secretary's proscription, Boris and Billy are able to challenge the decision via judicial review. Further under **s.7(3)** of the **Human Rights Act 1998** they can rely on the Act in such proceedings provided they are 'victims' of any potential violation of their Convention rights, which they clearly are.[2] With respect to the prosecution, **s.7(1)** of the Act provides that a person can rely on their Convention rights 'in any legal proceedings'. Thus, Boris and Billy's prosecution could be challenged in the trial itself, when arguing that the conditions of liability under the Act have not been met in their case. Further, Boris and Billy could argue that the 2018 Act itself is incompatible with their Convention rights. The Crown Court cannot issue a declaration of incompatibility under **s.4** of the 1998 Act (such a right only applies to the High Court and above). However, the court can ask the High Court to decide the compatibility of the prosecution as a preliminary issue (*R v Shayler* **[2002] 2 WLR 754**).

The Home Secretary's Proscription

[3] The author begins to examine the legality of the Secretary's actions, by comparing those actions in line with the words and intention of the parent Act; thus, employing sound interpretation skills and legal reasoning.

As the Secretary's power is derived from the 2018 Act, they would argue that the proscription was *ultra vires*, using the **Human Rights Act** and the relevant Convention rights to argue that the Secretary has acted unlawfully.[3] Thus, it could be argued that Parliament did not intend to interfere with the rights of political groups, or groups with a genuine political agenda, and that **s.2** of the Act should be construed so as to exclude such groups (*Raymond v Honey* **[1983] AC 1**). **Section 3** of the **Human Rights Act** allows the courts to adopt a strained interpretation to ensure compatibility (*R v A* **[2002] 1 AC 45**). However, to interpret **s.2** so as to exclude political groups would be in conflict with the clear intention of the Act, which was to proscribe any group, political or otherwise, who used violence or whose agenda or activities caused gross offence. Such interpretation would amount to judicial legislation (*Re S and W* **[2002] 2 AC 291**).

[4] The author begins to offer an examination of possible further grounds of review.

If the Secretary's duty to identify the grounds of proscription was mandatory, then the proscription would be unlawful.[4] The Secretary does not appear to have identified which of the two grounds under **s.2** he has relied on in proscribing the group. Although the Secretary may have evidence of violence on behalf of the group, the group's existence would not be likely to cause gross offence, as opposed to mere annoyance and affront, to any religious group. Further, Boris and Billy could argue that the proscription in this case was unlawful and disproportionate since he did not have grounds for believing that the group met either of the relevant criteria. They can also rely on the doctrine of proportionality in challenging the decision (*R (Daly) v Secretary of State for the Home Department* **[2001] 2 AC 532**). However, there would appear to be ample grounds for believing that the group did advocate the use of violence for the purpose of expressing its views and its agenda. Thus, given the power vested in the Home Secretary, the decision would appear to be both a rational and proportionate use of such powers.

[5] The author now moves on to examine the possible compatibility of the parent Act with Convention rights, having dealt with the lawfulness and proportionality of the Secretary's actions.

If those challenges failed, they could challenge the 2018 Act itself, seeking a declaration under **s.4** that its provisions are incompatible with Convention rights.[5] The court, having established that there had been a *prima facie* breach, would consider first whether the relevant provisions of the Act are sufficiently clear to be 'prescribed by law' under **articles 10 and 11**. It may be argued that the wording of **s.2**—'cause gross offence to any racial or religious group, or to any member of such group'—is vague and subjective, and provides an individual with insufficient guidance as to what sort of group would come within the terms of the section (*Hashman and Harrap v United Kingdom* **(1999) 30 EHRR 241**). Although such phrases as 'gross offence' can be clarified by subsequent case law (*Müller v Switzerland* **(1991) 13 EHRR 212**), it might be argued that a prosecution under this provision at such an early stage of the Act's life, makes the provision too vague. On the other hand, the phrase 'gross offence' might be regarded as readily understandable by everyone. Thus, the court could apply a common-sense interpretation (as they did to the word 'insulting' in *Brutus v Cozens* **[1972] 2 All ER 1297**). Further, the Secretary's discretion in this statutory power is phrased objectively ('reasonable grounds for believing') and would be subject to intense judicial review.

Assuming the Act passes the above test, the court would then ask whether the Act and its provisions pursued any of the legitimate aims recognised in **paragraph 2 of articles 10 and 11** of the Convention. It would be argued that **ss.1 and 2** pursued aims such as the protection of the rights of others, public safety, the prevention of crime and disorder, and the protection of morals. Finally, it would need to be decided whether the Act and its application in this case was necessary in a democratic society. In other words, whether there was a pressing social need to pass and apply the Act and whether its application to them was truly proportionate to achieving those legitimate aims (*Handyside v United Kingdom*). The court would consider a number of matters, such as the level of judicial deference and institutional respect it should offer to the Secretary. Further, it would consider the importance and extent of the violation, the importance of the legitimate aim, and whether any other, less intrusive measures were available to the government and the police to deal with the activities of such groups (*R (Lord Carlile) v Secretary of State for the Home Department* **[2015] UKSC 60**).

The court would need convincing evidence that the draconian step of proscription was really necessary, and that the normal criminal law,[6] which would punish individuals for committing specific illegal acts other than mere association with a particular group, would be inadequate to deal with the threats from the groups. Although the European Court has accepted that a state may proscribe an organisation, such measures would be acceptable only when the groups pose a real threat to the security of the state or its citizens (*Refah Partisi Erbakan Kazan and Tekdal v Turkey* **(2002) 35 EHRR 3**). In addition, the Secretary could rely on **article 17** of the Convention—that the enjoyment of Convention rights does not extend to activities aimed at the destruction of the rights of others. Although the views of such groups are unlikely to be regarded as an activity for this purpose (*Lehideux and Irsoni v France* **(2000) 30 EHRR 665**), the violent activities of the group in our scenario might be sufficient to engage **article 17**.

It is suggested that the power of proscription and its application in this case is disproportionate.[7] First, there was some evidence of violence on behalf of a number of such groups, including the one in this scenario. However, there does not appear to be *sufficient* evidence to suggest that the normal criminal law and police powers are inadequate to deal with the danger. It is not clear why offences such as incitement to racial or religious hatred, and the variety of racially or religiously aggravated offences under public order legislation, cannot be used effectively against such groups as an alternative. Secondly, although there is evidence that several of its members have been acting violently and unlawfully, the group's mandate appears to be entirely peaceful and advocates a reasonable, although controversial, agenda. Finally, following proscription the Act has the ability to interfere with entirely peaceful and non-provocative behaviour such as distributing leaflets. Such effects might be the natural product of proscribing dangerous groups. However, such effects should only follow in the most exceptional circumstances, which it could be argued do not exist in our scenario.

The Prosecution under the Act

Boris and Billy could raise the same arguments of interpretation and compatibility as outlined above.[8] Further, it could be argued that **s.2** should be interpreted so that the word 'activities' meant unlawful and violent activities, so as to exclude entirely peaceful activities such as distributing leaflets. As Boris and Billy were clearly 'assisting in the recruitment' of the organisation, the argument appears redundant; unless the charge is solely for taking part in the activities of the group. Given the clarity of the provisions of the Act, the court would have no

[6] The author provides a clear explanation of the relevant test for judging compatibility, together with supporting case law.

[7] The author now provides the basis of the argument that the Act is incompatible; this is based on the evidence provided in the question and knowledge of the relevant principles.

[8] The author now considers the challenge to the prosecution, drawing on information provided in the earlier part of the answer.

option but to find that they have clearly committed an offence under the Act. Accordingly, Boris and Billy's remedy would be to seek a declaration of incompatibility under **s.4** of the 1998 Act.

Conclusions

[9] The conclusion is a brief summary of the author's various findings and views, suitable for exam answers.

It appears that both the proscription and the prosecution were within the Act and the Secretary's powers, and appear to have been exercised proportionally. However, it is suggested that the power of proscription is incompatible with **articles 10 and 11**, and that the provisions be declared incompatible with the Convention as far as their application to this case is concerned.[9] This would not affect the validity of the proscription, or of the legality of Boris and Bill's prosecution or subsequent conviction.

LOOKING FOR EXTRA MARKS?

- Show a clear appreciation of the process and order of the questions that the court would have to deal with when resolving disputes about conditional rights.
- Display clear and strong interpretation and analytical skills when interpreting the legislative provisions and actions of the Secretary and judging their legality and compatibility.
- Illustrate an awareness of the *constitutional* issues surrounding the court's role—deference to Parliament and the executive—and the likely impact of such on the court's decision.

QUESTION | 3

'A return to a pre-Human Rights Act method of protecting human rights would be damaging to both the protection of basic liberties in domestic law and the UK's relationship with the European Convention on Human Rights.'

Analyse that statement with respect to recent proposals to repeal the Human Rights Act 1998.

CAUTION!

- This question does *not* require an analysis of any specific *rights* contained in the Convention or the Act; cases concerning certain rights can be employed to illustrate the answer.
- You should explain the traditional method of rights protection and its limitations, before examining the purpose and provisions of the 1998 Act; note the proposals for a British Bill of Rights will not mean a *total* return to the pre-Act position.
- The question primarily asks for an analysis of the two methods, but be careful to address the quote and the question and examine the likely impact of repeal on both the protection of rights and the relationship with the European Convention.

DIAGRAM ANSWER PLANS

Introduction to the government's recent proposals to repeal the Act and replace it with a British Bill of Rights and Responsibilities; now shelved

▼

The position of residual civil liberties under the pre-Act method, together with the advantages and efficacy and drawbacks of that system

▼

Analysis of the Human Rights Act method and its attempt to make domestic law consistent with the European Convention

▼

Consideration of the efficacy of both methods and the advantages and disadvantages of repeal

SUGGESTED ANSWER

[1] The author provides a clear introduction, covering the recent proposals and the reasons for such.

In 2015, the then Conservative government promised to repeal the Human Rights Act 1998 and replace it with a British Bill of Rights and Responsibilities.[1] Although these plans have been shelved, pending BREXIT, they are worth considering to assess their potential impact on human rights enforcement in the UK. The main aim was to reduce the domestic law's reliance on European law and principles—most significantly the jurisprudence of the European Court of Human Rights. These proposals stemmed from concern over a number of decisions from the European Court which forced the government to initiate or consider changes to our law. Accordingly, it was suggested that the domestic courts should no longer have to rely on the case law of the European Court, as is currently required under **s.2** of the **Human Rights Act 1998**. This would break the formal link between British courts and the European Court and make our own Supreme Court (and perhaps other commonwealth courts) the ultimate arbiter of human rights matters in the UK.

In addition, the government wished to introduce a British Bill of Rights and Responsibilities, entrenching essential principles of British justice and tradition and encompassing corresponding duties on individual right holders. The 2015 Manifesto promised that the Bill would reverse the 'mission creep' that has meant human rights law being used for more and more purposes, and often with little regard for the rights of wider society. This refers to cases where the Act has been used by prisoners, sex offenders, suspected terrorists, and those seeking to stall deportation or extradition on the grounds that their human rights would be compromised.

[2]The author addresses the question of whether the proposals will involve a return to the traditional position, together with the disadvantages of such.

These proposals may to a certain extent have returned the UK to a pre-Human Rights Act position, where the 'traditional system' suffered from many disadvantages.[2] For example, parliamentary sovereignty allowed Parliament the theoretical, and often practical, power to interfere with human rights without restriction (*R v IRC, ex parte Rossminster* [1980] AC 852). Further, our courts lacked the express power to apply principles such as proportionality, which ensures a correct balance between rights and other interests, such as national security (*R v Secretary of State for the Home Department, ex parte Brind* [1991] 1 All ER 696, *R v Ministry of Defence, ex parte Smith* [1996] 1 All ER 257). Indeed, the latter case led to defeat in the European Court (*Smith and Grady v United Kingdom* (2000) 29 EHRR 493). It is unclear whether any new Bill of Rights would allow the courts to employ proportionality, despite the plans to reduce reliance on European Court case law. However, if such a doctrine were not available that would severely curtail the effectiveness of judicial review in this area. On the other hand, the failure of the pre-Act position to recognise specific rights, such as the right to privacy, which led to defeats in the European Court (*Malone v United Kingdom* (1984) 7 EHRR 14 and *Wainwright v United Kingdom* (2007) 44 EHRR 40), would no doubt be rectified by the inclusion of such rights in the new Bill of Rights.

[3]Specific reference is made to past failures and the danger that they may be repeated under the new proposals.

However, the failure to incorporate the Convention into domestic law allowed Parliament and the courts to ignore the rights of certain unpopular groups, and the European Court found violations of the rights of prisoners[3] (*Golder v United Kingdom* (1975) 1 EHRR 524 and *Thynne, Wilson and Gunnell v United Kingdom* (1990) 13 EHRR 666), and persons subject to deportation or extradition (*Chahal v United Kingdom* (1997) 23 EHRR 413 and *Soering v United Kingdom* (1989) 11 EHRR 439). In this respect, the repeal of the Human Rights Act might lead to reduced protection for such groups and a conflict between domestic law and the European Court.

[4]The author places the repeal of s.2 into historical context and then provides evidence of the extent of its impact and application.

The **Human Rights Act 1998** was indeed passed in the context of the government's unsatisfactory record under the Convention, and to give 'further effect' to Convention rights to make domestic law more Convention-compliant.[4] Under **s.2** domestic courts must *take into account* the case law of the European Court when adjudicating Convention rights. This means that a decision of the European Court should be followed where it was intended to be of general application in respect of that Convention right (*Manchester City Council v Pinnock* [2010] UKSC 45). This sparked arguments about the supremacy of the Convention and its case law. Although the courts are not bound to *follow* such case law, it is expected that they will do so and thus decide cases in a manner more akin to the European Court, thus avoiding, where possible, subsequent applications to Strasbourg

(*R (Anderson and Taylor) v Secretary of State for the Home Department* [2002] 2 WLR 1143). However, our courts have refused to follow the case law on occasions (*R v Horncastle* [2009] UKSC 14, approved by the European Court of Human Rights in *Horncastle v United Kingdom* (2015) 60 EHRR 1), to allow for the application of Convention rights in the context of domestic law and practice. Further, the domestic courts have made it clear that they have the power and duty to interpret and apply Convention rights, and their limitations, as domestic rights (*Nicklinson v Ministry of Justice and others* [2014] UKSC 38). Such decisions have rejected the 'mirror principle' advocated by the House of Lords in *R (Ullah) v Special Adjudicator* [2004] UKHL 26 and have led to the development of Convention and common law rights independent of the European Court's jurisprudence.

Despite the above, the government were adamant that domestic courts would be bound to follow the decisions of the Supreme Court, rather than the European Court. This would have created a possible, and largely unnecessary, conflict between the two courts and compromise the government's relationship with the European Convention and the European Court. The government hoped that the Supreme Court would offer due deference and respect to the executive and legislative bodies where in the past the European Court has refused to extend the margin of appreciation to those bodies.[5] This included examples concerning stop and search: *R (Gillan) v MPC* [2006] 2 AC 307—overturned by the European Court in *Gillan v United Kingdom* (2010) 52 EHRR 45; admissibility of torture evidence abroad: *Othman (Qatada) v United Kingdom, judgment 17 January 2013*; and prisoner voting: *Hirst v United Kingdom (No. 2)* (2006) 42 EHRR 41. However, many of the defeats have come from the British courts applying traditional principles to cases involving detention without trial (*A v Secretary of State for the Home Department* [2005] 2 AC 68), and admissibility of torture evidence in domestic proceedings (*A v Secretary of State for the Home Department (No. 2)* [2006] 2 AC 221). It is questionable, therefore, whether the Supreme Court would be more deferential to the government and Parliament.

Repeal of **s.2** of the **Human Rights Act** may not, therefore, result in a reduction of rights protection, although it may cause friction between domestic law and the case law of the European Court.[6] This would compromise the government's obligations under the European Convention to abide by the decisions of the European Court (**article 46**) and to provide an effective remedy for breach of Convention rights (**article 13**). What was unclear was whether the domestic courts would be able even to consider ECHR case law or employ the principles of legality and proportionality when

[5] The author provides information on cases that question the government's concerns over the power of the European Court.

[6] The author concludes on the likely impact of the repeal of s.2, stressing that much depends on the content of the new proposals.

balancing and interpreting rights. If this is not the case, this will lead to multiple applications to the European Court. This would be the case unless the government frees itself from European human rights law by leaving the Council of Europe; something that it currently does not wish to do.

[7] The author now considers the second leg of the proposals, providing a measured and balanced analysis of their impact and validity.

Turning to the idea of a British Bill of Rights and Responsibilities, such a Bill and the repeal of the HRA would not *necessarily* be in breach of the obligations owed under the Convention.[7] This is because **articles 1 and 13** require domestic law to give *effective* protection of ECHR rights, and incorporation of the ECHR is not essential to achieve that. Presumably, any Bill would include rights similar to the ECHR and include reference to other values such as the rule of law, and the right to judicial and administrative justice. However, the Manifesto, which talked of stripping rights from terrorists and those fighting deportation and extradition, suggested that the current protection of those groups would be limited beyond that which is accepted under the Convention.

[8] The author refers to recent reports from bodies set up to consider a British Bill of Rights, using those views to question the government's most recent proposals.

The Joint Committee on Human Rights has warned against a concept of a 'British' Bill of Rights as it risks alienating non-British residents and fails to comply with the international and universal nature of human rights[8] ('A Bill of Rights for the UK?', Report of the Joint Committee of Human Rights, 10 August 2008, HL Paper 165-1; HC 150-1). The Commission also argued against any specific reference to *responsibilities* with respect to qualified and conditional rights, ensuring that the enjoyment of these rights will be dependent on the right holder carrying out their responsibilities to society and other rights' holders ('Commission on Bill of Rights: A UK Bill of Rights— the Choice Before Us'). Any proposals will have to comply with Convention standards of rights' restriction, as the Convention does not expressly limit the enjoyment of any rights by insisting on compliance with responsibilities.

[9] The author provides a neat conclusion which refers clearly and specifically to the quote and the question.

In conclusion, any future repeal of the **Human Rights Act** will not necessarily be in breach of the UK's obligations under the Convention; provided any new Bill of Rights gives at least equal protection to human rights.[9] Indeed, repeal will not necessarily mean a return to the pre-Act position, as many of the rights and principles of the Convention and the case law of the European Court will be incorporated into the new Bill. However, the repeal of **s.2** may cause a further conflict between domestic and European case law, reducing rights protection and putting into jeopardy the UK's duties under the Convention. Similarly, if the Bill incorporates many of the ideas reflected in the Manifesto, certain rights and groups will inevitably be left unprotected, causing a similar gap and conflict with European human rights law.

LOOKING FOR EXTRA MARKS?

- Show a clear appreciation of the reasons why the present government wish to repeal the Human Rights Act and the context of the proposals, together with the benefits it feels would result from repeal.
- Show a clear appreciation of the relationship between the Human Rights Act and the European Convention and how that relationship would be affected by repeal; noting that a British Bill of Rights may achieve some harmony with the Convention.
- Use clear and relevant cases to explain and analyse how both the pre- and post-Act system protected rights and the various constitutional, legal, and political advantages and disadvantages of each system *vis-à-vis* repeal.

TAKING THINGS FURTHER

- Bates, E, 'British Sovereignty and the ECHR' (2012) 128 LQR 382
  Discusses how the Convention impacts on the sovereignty of the UK and the UK Parliament

- Bowen, P, 'Does the Renaissance of Common Law Rights Mean that the Human Rights Act 1998 is Now Unnecessary?' [2016] 4 EHRLR 361
  Considers the development of common law rights alongside the consideration of Convention rights under the HRA

- Costa, JP, 'The Relationship between the European Court of Human Rights and the National Courts' [2012] 3 EHRLR 264
  Examines the extent to which the case law of the European Court dictates the interpretation and application of domestic law

- Elliot, M, 'A Damp Squib in the Long Grass: The Report of the Commission on a Bill of Rights' [2013] 2 EHRLR 137
  Examines the limited recommendations of the Commission on human rights reform

- Fenwick, H, Phillipson, G, and Masterson, R, *Judicial Reasoning under the Human Rights Act* (Cambridge 2011), Part 1
  Discusses the impact of the Act on the constitutional role of the courts

- Fenwick, H and Masterman, R, 'The Conservative Project to "Break the Link between British Courts and Strasbourg"—Rhetoric or Reality?' (2017) 80(6) MLR 1111
  A criticism of the government's plans to allow British courts to ignore ECHR jurisprudence in favour of that of the UK Supreme Court

- Grieve, D, 'Can a Bill of Rights do Better than the Human Rights Act?' [2016] PL 223
  Considers whether the repeal of the HRA would enhance human rights' protection in the UK

- Slowe, R, 'The Conservatives' Proposals for a British Bill of Rights' [2015] 4 EHRLR 372
  Examines the proposals to scrap the Human Rights Act

■ Wadham, J, and Mountfield, H, *Blackstone's Guide to the Human Rights Act 1998*, 7th edn (OUP 2015), chs. 1, 3, and 4

A clear and comprehensive coverage of the Act and the relevant case law

Online Resources   www.oup.com/uk/qanda/

Go online for extra essay and problem questions, a glossary of key terms, online versions of all the answer plans and audio commentary on how selected ones were put together, and a range of podcasts which include advice on exam and coursework technique and advice for other assessment methods.

The Right to Life 5

ARE YOU READY?

In order to attempt questions in this chapter, which covers various aspects of the right to life, contained in article 2 of the European Convention on Human Rights, you will need to have acquired a sound knowledge of the areas listed below during the course and your revision programme:

- A range of questions have been included to reflect the fact that different courses concentrate on different aspects of the right to life: such as its scope and limitations; the state's positive obligation to protect and preserve life; the procedural duties under article 2; the question of assisted suicide and the right to die; and the relationship between article 2 (and 3) and the death penalty.

- The wording and scope of article 2, including whether it gives the right to die and the right to life to the unborn child.

- The permitted exceptions to the right to life contained in article 2(2) of the Convention.

- The relationship between the death penalty and articles 2 and 3 of the Convention.

KEY DEBATES

This area of substantive human rights law is the subject of much case law from both the domestic and European courts with respect to the interpretation of its wording and limitations and restrictions. In particular, there is much legal, political, and constitutional debate surrounding issues such as assisted suicide, abortion, and the rights of the unborn child, the use of lethal force by the state, the legality of the death penalty, and the extent of the state's positive obligation to protect life. These developments need to be noted on a regular basis, as the legal and political landscape is constantly changing.

Debate: The Right to Life and the Right to Die

There has been an ongoing debate about the right to die and UK law on assisted suicide. Domestic legislation outlaws assisted suicide and disabled individuals unable to end their own lives have petitioned the courts in order to challenge that legislation (Suicide Act 1961). Such challenges have failed, largely because of the respect shown to Parliament by the domestic courts, and the margin of appreciation shown by the Strasbourg Court to the domestic authorities. Follow the case law in the domestic courts and the European Court (*Pretty, Niklinson*, and *Conway*) and the failure of Parliament to change the law. Note, this area also impacts on the right to private life and article 8 ECHR, considered later in the text.

Debate: Investigations and the Right to Life

The state has an obligation to investigate deaths that may have been in violation of their duty to preserve life; for example if a death were to occur in police custody or other forms of detention. The shooting of Charles de Menezes by the police in 2005, believing him to be a terrorist, also gave rise to questions of state liability and the duty to investigate and prosecute such actions. The topic is particularly relevant given the recent case law which establishes liability under article 2 for deaths outside UK territory (in Iraq and Afghanistan), and the government have considered lodging a derogation from the Human Rights Act 1998 with respect to such liability.

Debate: Use of Lethal Force and Article 2

The circumstances in which it is permissible to use lethal force against an individual is especially topical given the recent decision of the European Court of Human Rights in the Charles de Menezes case. That decision has resulted in a great number of academic articles and public debate concerning the correct balance between the prevention of crime and defence of national security, and the liability towards individuals for the negligent actions of state officials, and the planning of such operations. These cases have raised the question of whether the domestic law on self-defence is compatible with article 2 ECHR.

QUESTION | 1

By the use of the case law of the European Court of Human Rights, critically examine how article 2 of the European Convention on Human Rights has protected various aspects of the individual's right to life.

CAUTION!

- This question requires a general knowledge of the right to life as protected by article 2, but the answer should concentrate on controversial and topical areas of discussion once the overall scope of the article has been examined.

- The question is asking you to *critically examine* how the article protects the right to life, so choose areas and cases which have excited legal and other argument and which allow you to display your understanding and your critical skills.

- Although the question refers to cases from the *European Court*, it is acceptable to include complimentary case law from the domestic courts in order to illustrate how European jurisprudence has influenced jurisprudence in this area.

- The answer should, where relevant, include reference to other articles of the Convention, such as article 3 (freedom from torture).

DIAGRAM ANSWER PLANS

General explanation of the importance of the right to life, to democracy, and protection of human rights

▼

Examination of the wording and scope of article 2

▼

Critical examination of the case law of the European Court of Human Rights with respect to the interpretation and application of article 2 with respect to the right to die, permitted exceptions, the death penalty and positive obligations

▼

Conclusions with respect to the extent of protection of the right to life under article 2 by the European Court

SUGGESTED ANSWER

Article 2 of the European Convention on Human Rights provides that 'everyone's right to life shall be protected by law and that no one shall be deprived of his life intentionally'. **Article 2** protects the most fundamental of all human rights, as the enjoyment of all other rights depends on the preservation of the individual's life.[1] Thus, in **McCann v United Kingdom (1995) 21 EHRR 97**, the Court noted that together with **article 3** (the prohibition of torture) it enshrines one of the basic values of all democratic societies. The right is regarded as absolute in the sense that under **article 15(3)** it cannot be derogated from even in times of war and other public emergency (except in respect of deaths resulting from lawful acts of war).

Nevertheless, the scope of the article is subject to judicial interpretation and application. For example,[2] in **Vo v France (2005) 40 EHRR 12** the Grand Chamber of the European Court decided that on the proper interpretation of **article 2** an unborn child was not 'a person'. This was because there was no European consensus on the nature and status of the embryo/foetus, and this was confirmed in **Evans v United Kingdom (2008) 46 EHRR 34**. Similarly, in **Pretty v United Kingdom (2002) 35 EHRR 1** the Court held that the right to life did not include the right to die, the principal thrust of **article 2** being the state's obligation to preserve life. The Court thus refused to recognise a general human right of self-determination; although issues of euthanasia do engage the right to private and family life under **article 8**. Further, the Court is prepared to offer individual states a margin of appreciation in deciding issues regarding the termination of life

[1] The author provides a clear and basic introduction to article 2 and its scope and value.

[2] The author begins to highlight the complexities of article 2 and its interpretation by the European Court.

(*Lambert v France*, Application No. 46043/14 Decision of the Grand Chamber, 5 June 2015).

[3] The author introduces the concept of positive obligations and the right to life, which has resulted in a great deal of interesting case law.

Article 2 covers deaths caused by the deliberate, or negligent acts, or omissions, of the state (*McCann v United Kingdom*). Thus, in cases where the state or state actors have allegedly been involved in the victim's death, the Court will place a burden of proof on it to explain the circumstances of the death (*Jordan v United Kingdom* (2003) 37 EHRR 2).[3] A positive duty to protect individuals from unreasonable environmental hazards was also accepted in *LCB v United Kingdom* (1999) 27 EHRR 212. Specifically, in cases where it has been shown that the individual entered state custody in good health, the Court has stressed that the state has a strong duty to provide a satisfactory account of the events (*Salaman v Turkey* (2002) 34 EHRR 17). This obligation is supported by the state's procedural obligations, examined below, and reflects the necessity of imposing strict duties on the state to protect the lives of those within its jurisdiction.

Article 2 not only imposes a negative duty on the state not to interfere with a person's right to life, but also a positive duty to ensure that an individual's life is not taken unnecessarily. This includes having in place appropriate criminal laws and proper procedures to ensure that persons are deterred from committing such acts, and are appropriately sanctioned. This duty is not absolute and an applicant would need to show that there was a real risk of a violation of **article 2**. Thus, in *Osman v United Kingdom* (2000) 29 EHRR 245, it was held that although the state had a positive obligation to take preventive operational measures to protect an individual from the criminal acts of another, that obligation should not impose an impossible and disproportionate burden on the state (see also *Van Colle v United Kingdom* (2013) 56 EHRR 23).

[4] The debate about the extent of state liability is continued, using a successful application and then a case on liability for suicides in detention.

However, although the Court is cautious in this area, it will find liability in clearer cases. Thus, in *Edwards v United Kingdom* (2002) 35 EHRR 19, the Court found a violation of **article 2** when the applicant's son had been stamped and kicked to death by his violent cell mate.[4] In this case, the Court found that the cell mate posed a real and serious risk to the applicant's son and that the prison authorities had not been properly informed of the cell mate's medical history and perceived dangerousness. In addition, **article 2** can be engaged where the individual has taken his or her own life, although the Court requires a specific and real risk of self-harm. Thus, in *Keenan v United Kingdom* (2001) 33 EHRR 38, in finding that there had been no violation of **article 2** when the applicants' son committed suicide in prison, the Court noted that he had not been formally diagnosed as schizophrenic and was, therefore, not considered an immediate risk while in detention.

The Court has also developed the state's duty to carry out a proper investigation into any deaths that have occurred within their jurisdiction. In *Jordan v United Kingdom*, it held that **article 2** required there to be some form of effective official investigation when individuals had been killed as a result of the use of force.[5] This ensures state accountability for deaths in their jurisdiction. Further, any investigation had to be capable of leading to a determination of whether the force used in such circumstances was justified, and to the identification and punishment of those responsible. In addition, the investigation would need to be undertaken with reasonable expedition. The Court has also stressed the importance of independence, and in *McShane v United Kingdom* **(2002) 35 EHRR 23** held that an inquiry into the lawfulness of a civilian's death during a disturbance in Londonderry was in violation of **article 2** because the police officers investigating the incident were not independent of the officers implicated in the incident. The Court has also stressed the need for the availability of civil remedies in the case of established liability. Thus, in *Finucane v United Kingdom* **(2003) 37 EHRR 29** it noted the need for publicity of the proceedings and the need for the DPP to give reasons for his decision not to prosecute those suspected. This procedural aspect of **article 2** is supported by **article 13**—guaranteeing an effective remedy—*Bubbins v United Kingdom* **(2005) 41 EHRR 24**.

In contrast, the Court has offered member states a wide area of discretion in deciding whether the state has violated the substantive duty to protect life. This has been noted in cases such as *Osman* when the Court is judging the legitimacy of state action under the exceptions permitted under **article 2(2)**. This provides that the deprivation of life will not be in contravention of **article 2** when it results from the use of force which is no more than absolutely necessary in cases such as the defence of any person from unlawful violence, or in order to effect a lawful arrest or to prevent the escape of a person from lawful detention. In *McCann*, the Court noted that **article 2** included a strict and compelling test of necessity, so that the Court must subject deprivations of life to the most careful scrutiny. Nevertheless, it drew a distinction between the actual shooting of the terrorist suspects and the planning of the operation leading to the shootings. It thus found that although the SAS members had used no more force than was necessary in the circumstances, there had been a violation of the right to life through the careless planning of the operation by the administrative authorities. This suggests that the Court is more likely to find a breach of **article 2** when there has been a breach of procedure, or an error in the overall decision-making process. However, in *Bubbins*, where the police had shot dead the applicant's brother mistakenly believing that he was a burglar, the Court granted the authorities a margin of discretion and found that it had not been established that there had been a failure to plan and organise the operation in such a way as to minimise to the greatest extent possible any risk to the right of life. Despite this general reluctance to gainsay the judgement of state actors who have used fatal force for the protection of the safety of others, the Court has insisted that life is not taken away arbitrarily[6] (*Demir and others v Turkey* (2001) 33 EHRR 43). Further, in *Armani Da Silva v United Kingdom* (2016) 63 EHRR 12, regarding the shooting of a mistakenly suspected terrorist in London in 2005, the Grand Chamber held that the domestic law of self-defence was compliant with the test of absolute necessity in article 2, and that the DPP's decision not to prosecute was subject to adequate review so as to ensure that the law provided adequate accountability.

Finally, although **article 2** expressly provides for the death penalty, most member states have ratified **Protocols 6 or 13** prohibiting such. The death penalty may violate other provisions of the Convention (*Soering v United Kingdom* (1989) 11 EHRR 439), and in *Al-Saadoon and Mufhdi v United Kingdom* (2010) 51 EHRR 9, the Court accepted that the death penalty was contrary to article 3 per se as it had by that stage been accepted by member states as constituting inhuman suffering.[7] Thus, the Court has continued to interpret **article 2** so as to impose the most stringent duties on the state to preserve life. In addition, the Court has imposed strict duties on states to investigate deaths in their jurisdiction. In contrast, the Court has shown a greater reluctance to interfere with the decisions of state actors when life has been taken for the purpose of achieving public security, and is also prepared to leave individual states an area of discretion in areas such as assisted suicide.

[6] The author examines the difficult and controversial area of the use of fatal force by state authorities, examining the relevant case law—including the very topical case of *De Menezes*.

[7] The author combines the conclusion with coverage of a final point on the issue of the compatibility of the death penalty with article 2 and the Convention.

LOOKING FOR EXTRA MARKS?

- Show that you understand the scope of article 2 and its general purpose—to protect an individual's right to life by law and to safeguard it from arbitrary interference.
- Appreciate the dilemma facing the Court in interpreting the article's wording and extending the scope of the article to new areas, such as the right to die.
- Use leading, controversial, cases which illustrate those dilemmas and which allow you to conclude on the central question.

QUESTION | 2

How has the European Convention on Human Rights and the European Court of Human Rights tackled the question of whether the death penalty is consistent with the absolute character of the right to life under article 2 and of the rights and values contained in the Convention?

CAUTION!

■ This question requires a specific examination of whether the death penalty is consistent with article 2 and other rights contained in the European Convention, but a general knowledge of the scope and content of article 2 will be helpful in examining that question.

■ The question is asking you how the *European Court* has addressed this question: you should deal with the cases both chronologically and in a way which examines the death penalty's legality from various aspects.

■ The question requires both a knowledge of various other Convention articles and the overall situation in international human rights law; remembering that the question is related to the European Convention and Europe, but that the jurisprudence in this area might affect international norms.

DIAGRAM ANSWER PLANS

Brief explanation of the wording and scope of article 2 of the European Convention, together with consideration of the absoluteness of the general right to life

▼

Examination of the legality of the death penalty within article 2 and relevant protocols abolishing the death penalty

▼

Consideration of the case law of the European Convention with respect to the compatibility of the death penalty with various articles of the Convention

▼

Conclusions, including the impact of the position in Europe on the international position

SUGGESTED ANSWER

[1] The author begins the essay with a general discussion on the importance and absolute character of the right to life and article 2.

Although it has been accepted by the European Court that **article 2** of the Convention, which provides that everyone's right to life shall be protected by law, protects the most fundamental of human rights (*McCann v United Kingdom* (1995) 21 EHRR 97), the right to life is not absolute in every sense.[1] First, although the right is absolute in the sense that it cannot be derogated from even in times of war or other public emergency, **article 15(2)** excludes deaths arising from lawful acts of war. That makes it clear that there may be circumstances where it is permissible to take life and thus interfere with this most fundamental of all human rights.

Further, the Convention recognises that the right to life may be compromised in peacetime, providing in **article 2(2)** a number of circumstances that provide justification for the taking of a person's life. Thus, in addition to the exception provided for by the death penalty in **article 2(1)**, **article 2(2)** provides that the deprivation of life shall not be regarded as inflicted in contravention of **article 2** when it results from the use of force which is no more than absolutely necessary in certain circumstances. This includes: in defence of any person from unlawful violence; in order to effect a lawful arrest or to prevent the escape of a person lawfully detained; or in action lawfully taken for the purpose of quelling a riot or insurrection. However, the exceptions must be strictly and narrowly construed so that the use of fatal force should be regarded as absolutely necessary (*McCann v United Kingdom*).

The right to life is, of course, compromised by the existence of the death penalty in any domestic legal system. However, although such a sentence clearly falls within the state's duty to protect a person's life within the law, **article 2** appears to legitimise it as the second sentence of **article 2(1)** provides that no one shall be deprived of his life intentionally *save in the execution of a sentence of a court* following his conviction of a crime for which this penalty is prescribed by law.[2] This would appear to reflect the position of the death penalty in international law, in that, although there may exist a universal movement for its abolition, it is not automatically in violation of international human rights law. Thus, **article 6 of the International Covenant on Civil and Political Rights 1966** appears to accommodate the death penalty by providing that in countries where the death penalty has not been abolished, a sentence of death can only be imposed for the most serious crimes and pursuant to a final judgment by a competent court. **Article 6** also presses for its abolition by providing (in **article 6(6)**) that nothing shall delay or prevent the abolition of the death penalty. Thus, although there is a movement to abolish capital punishment, and an opportunity for states to abolish it within their own jurisdictions, international human rights law does not make it unlawful.

However, despite **article 2** appearing to accept the legitimacy of the death penalty, such a sentence may still be in violation of the European Convention, or other international human rights treaties. First, the death penalty may constitute a violation of an individual's Convention rights other than the right to life.[3] In *Soering v United Kingdom* **(1989) 11 EHRR 439**, the European Court held that, the *manner of its execution and the circumstances surrounding the death penalty* may be inconsistent with **article 3**, which prohibits torture and inhuman and degrading punishment. Thus, it held that the subjection of a young man of limited mental ability to the death row phenomenon constituted inhuman and degrading treatment within **article 3**. Similarly, there would be a violation of **article 3** if the death sentence prisoner had been or was to be kept in intolerable prison conditions awaiting his death sentence (*Kalashnikov v Russia* **(2003) 36 EHRR 34**). This possibility is highlighted in **article 6(2)** of the International

[2] The author now approaches the issue of the death penalty and its position *vis-à-vis* article 2, starting with the traditional position when the Convention was formulated.

[3] The author now considers the position despite the wording of article 2, examining the potential of other Convention rights.

Covenant, which provides that the sentence should not be inconsistent with other provisions of the Covenant. Further, **article 6(5)** of the Covenant provides that pregnant women and persons under 18 shall not be sentenced to death, and it is probable that the European Court would always have regarded such sentences as in violation of **article 3**. As we shall see, these specific cases may form part of a more general rule that the death penalty is inconsistent with **article 3**.

Secondly, the exception to the right to life provided in **article 2** only applies where a death sentence has been passed by a court of law, and after the individual has been convicted of a prescribed criminal offence. Accordingly, if the death penalty occurred without due process then there would be a potential violation of **article 6**, guaranteeing the right to a fair trial. Further, there would be a violation of **article 2**, which guarantees protection against the arbitrary taking of life by insisting that the law and the criminal process comply with principles of legitimacy and natural justice. This is stressed in **article 6** of the International Covenant so that a death sentence in violation of a right to a fair trial under **article 14** of the Covenant would breach the right to life.

[4]The content of the optional protocols are examined, together with their practical effect on the question of legality.

Thirdly, optional **Protocol No. 6 of the European Convention** provides for member states to abolish the death penalty so that no one shall be condemned to such penalty or be executed.[4] Once a member state signs this Protocol then the exemption contained in **article 2** ceases to operate and the death penalty would be contrary to the member state's Convention obligations. In addition, the deportation or extradition of a person to face the death penalty in another country would be in violation of their Convention responsibilities, assuming that on the facts there is a real risk that the applicant would be executed. Such is the desire in the Council of Europe to eliminate the death penalty in domestic law that all states have now ratified **Protocol No. 6**, and most have ratified **Protocol No. 13**, which extends the abolition of the death penalty in wartime.

Despite the above, until recently the death penalty had not automatically been held to be in violation of either the Convention or more general international human rights norms.

[5]The author begins a more specific discussion about the legality of the death penalty *vis-à-vis* human dignity and the values of the ECHR.

The decision of the European Court in *Ocalan v Turkey* (2005) 41 EHRR 45, provided some grounds for arguing that the death penalty was inevitably in violation of **article 3**[5] and thus incompatible with the Convention, whether the state has signed **Protocol No. 6 (and 13)** or not. In that case, the Grand Chamber observed that in the light of recent developments in this area it could be argued that the member states had agreed, through their practice, to modify the second sentence of **article 2(1)** in so far as it permitted capital punishment in peacetime. Consequently, the death penalty would be regarded as inhuman and degrading punishment within **article 3** whatever the circumstances, with the express words of **article 2** being read against the total prohibition of torture and other ill-treatment by **article 3**. However, the Grand Chamber held that until **Protocol No. 13** was ratified by all states, **article 3** did not prohibit the death penalty outright.

The traditional stance—that the death penalty is not per se in violation of international law—was reaffirmed in *R (Al-Saadoon and Mufhdi) v Secretary of State for Defence* **[2008] EWHC 3098**, where the High Court held that it was not unlawful for British troops to hand over two Iraqis to the Iraqi authorities to face the death penalty. The decision was upheld on appeal to the Court of Appeal: *The Times*, 3 February 2009, where the court stated that there was insufficient evidence that international law prohibited executions by hanging because it was in violation of the prohibition of inhuman treatment. However, in *Al-Saadoon and Mufhdi v United Kingdom* **(2010) 51 EHRR 9** the European Court of Human Rights reviewed its decision in *Ocalan* and was now satisfied that there was a common consensus among member states that the death penalty constituted inhuman suffering and was thus in breach of the Convention.[6] Accordingly, the death penalty exception was to be read in the light of **article 3**, and, at least as far as the Convention was concerned, the death penalty was unlawful. This illustrates the dynamic nature of the Convention and the Court's willingness to interpret its provisions in the light of changing values (*Selmouni v France* **(1999) 29 EHRR 403**)—the member states feeling that the death penalty is no longer consistent with its values.[7]

In conclusion, although the right to life under **article 2** is clearly fundamental, and is absolute in the sense of not allowing derogation under **article 15**, there are circumstances where it is acceptable to intentionally take life.[8] More specifically, although the death penalty is not in violation of international law per se, the accommodation of the death penalty in international treaties has been compromised by a number of exceptions and by state practice. Further, following the recent judgment in *Al-Saadoon*, it is now clear that the death penalty is incompatible with the right to life under article 2 and the European Convention in general.

[6] The author displays knowledge of the most recent position, which concludes the discussion on legality.

[7] The author makes reference to a wider issue about the Convention and its values and evolution and applies it to the question.

[8] The author provides a neat conclusion, summarising the main issues and reminding the reader that this is the position in Europe and not globally.

✚ LOOKING FOR EXTRA MARKS?

- Show that you understand the scope, purpose, and value of article 2 and the extent to which a state can be responsible for protecting and preserving life.
- Appreciate the extent to which the death penalty poses a dilemma to states with respect to the absolute nature of the right to life contained in the article.
- Use various provisions and protocols of the Convention to question the legality or otherwise of the death penalty, and deal with the points chronologically so as to display the Convention's dynamic approach in this area.

QUESTION | 3

Fred was a serving prisoner at Greentree Prison. In January 2013, Fred came into possession of a handgun and took three fellow prisoners and a prison officer hostage in the prison kitchen. Fred remained in the kitchen for three days and when his demands for release were refused, he shot and killed Peter, one of the prisoners. On hearing the gunshot, prison officers and police moved into the kitchen and found Peter dead on the floor, with Fred hovering over him with the gun in his hand. Two policemen immediately fired shots and killed Fred. It subsequently transpired that several prison officers suspected that Fred had a gun in his possession, but felt that there was insufficient evidence to search his cell. The Prison Service held an internal inquiry into the incident but attached no blame to the Prison Service for either death. A request for a public legal inquiry was made by both Fred's and Peter's families, but was refused by the Secretary of State.

Advise both families of any claim they may have with respect to article 2 of the European Convention on Human Rights.

CAUTION!

- This question requires a knowledge of both the *substantive and procedural obligations* placed on public authorities under article 2 of the Convention and the student needs to appreciate those obligations and their scope as well as the process by which the issues would be raised under the Human Rights Act 1998.

- The question needs to be dealt with under three headings: the liability owed by the state for acts of private individuals; the extent of the state's liability for the use of lethal force; and the procedural obligation to conduct an effective investigation into the deaths.

- To answer the question the student needs to be aware of relevant case law and to be able to apply it to the facts of the scenario so as to provide credible and clear advice.

DIAGRAM ANSWER PLANS

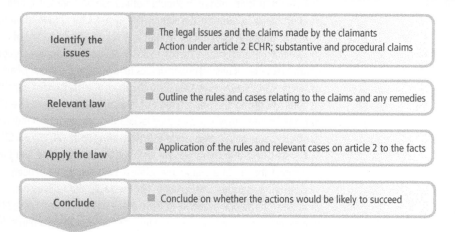

Identify the issues	The legal issues and the claims made by the claimants Action under article 2 ECHR; substantive and procedural claims
Relevant law	Outline the rules and cases relating to the claims and any remedies
Apply the law	Application of the rules and relevant cases on article 2 to the facts
Conclude	Conclude on whether the actions would be likely to succeed

The scenario raises the question of the state's liability for the deaths of Peter and Fred under **article 2 of the European Convention on Human Rights.** Because the events took place after the **Human Rights Act 1998**, a claim under **article 2** can be made under the Act in the domestic courts. The proceedings may be brought under the Act by the families of Peter and Fred, because they will be regarded as 'victims' of a violation of the Convention.[1] **Article 2** of the Convention provides that everyone's right to life shall be protected by law, and this imposes an obligation on the state not to take life arbitrarily or unnecessarily (*McCann v United Kingdom* (1995) 21 EHRR 97). It also protects a person's life from acts and threats of other individuals (*Osman v United Kingdom* (2000) 29 EHRR 245). In addition, it places a procedural obligation on the state to carry out an effective investigation into any death that may engage the state's obligations under **article 2**. This is bolstered by **article 13** of the Convention, which guarantees the right to an effective domestic remedy.

Peter's Death

Article 2 places a positive duty on the state to ensure that an individual's life is not taken unnecessarily, whether the act in question is one of a state actor or a private citizen (*Osman v United Kingdom*). This involves the duty to take measures to ensure that foreseeable and real risks to the life of an individual do not materialise.[2] In such a case it would have to be established that the authorities had failed to take the appropriate standard of care in ensuring that Peter's life was adequately protected against Fred's actions.

In *Osman* the European Court held that **article 2** imposed on the state a duty to take preventative operational measures to protect an individual whose life is at risk from the criminal acts of another. However, it noted that that obligation should not impose an impossible and disproportionate burden on the authorities. It must be shown, therefore, that the authorities did not do all that was reasonably expected of them to avoid a real and immediate risk to life. In *Osman*, the applicants could point to a series of missed opportunities to neutralise the threat of attack by an individual. However, the police could not be criticised for attaching greater weight to the presumption of innocence or failing to use their powers because they felt that they lacked the appropriate standard of suspicion. Similarly, in *Van Colle v United Kingdom* (2013) 56 EHRR 23, it was held that there was no violation when the police had failed to protect the life of a vulnerable witness who should have been on a secure witness protection scheme. On the facts, the police could not, from the information available to them at the time, have anticipated that the assailant constituted a real and imminent risk to the claimants' life.

[1] An overall account of the relevant law and how the case would be dealt with in judicial proceedings is supplied by the author.

[2] The author explains, simply, the principle of positive obligations and then illustrates the extent of the obligation via case law.

[3] The author outlines the arguments that would be put forward by both parties.

The authorities in our case would argue that although prisons by their nature impose a serious risk of harm, even fatal harm, to their inmates, they should not be held responsible for the unlawful and unforeseeable act of an inmate.[3] In addition, the courts usually give some discretion to the authorities with respect to the manner in which they carry out their operations (***Andronicou v Greece* (1998) 25 EHRR 491**), and this might defeat the claim that the police and the prison authorities acted negligently in not securing Peter's release within the three days of his incarceration at the hands of Fred. However, *Osman* might be distinguished because the incident took place in a state-controlled institution (***Edwards v United Kingdom* (2002) 25 EHRR 19**), and because prison officers suspected that Fred was armed and thus a specific danger to other inmates. In *Edwards*, the applicant's son had been killed by his cell mate, who had a history of violent outbursts and assaults and who had been diagnosed as schizophrenic. The European Court found that the cell mate posed a real and serious risk to the applicant's son and that the prison authorities had not been properly informed of the cell mate's medical history and perceived dangerousness.

[4] The author examines the facts in the scenario and can now provide advice on the likely outcome of that claim.

Thus, Peter's death could reasonably have been avoided and it is submitted that he was killed in violation of **article 2**. In particular, the prison authorities had failed to take action when they suspected Fred of being in possession of a gun and as a result Fred was a known danger to his fellow prisoners.[4] The question then would be whether the prison authorities acted reasonably in not searching Fred's cell and giving precedence to his presumption of innocence and his residual privacy as a prisoner. In the present case, the possession of a gun by a prisoner in a prison would pose a specific and direct threat, and the authorities have wide powers to search cells under the Prison Rules. It is likely therefore that the European Court would find that the authorities had failed in their duty under **article 2**.

Fred's Death

[5] The author deals with the issue on the use of fatal force, outlining the essential principles and cases.

Article 2(2) provides that the deprivation of life shall not be regarded as inflicted in contravention of **article 2** when it results from the use of force that is no more than *absolutely necessary* in the defence of any person from unlawful violence or in order to effect a lawful arrest.[5] The government will argue that shooting Fred in these circumstances was absolutely necessary to arrest Fred and to prevent him from causing further fatal harm, whilst the families will argue that more careful planning of the operation, and a less hasty reaction by the two police officers, would have avoided Fred's death.

In *McCann*, three IRA terrorists were shot dead by SAS officers when it was suspected that they were to detonate a bomb in Gibraltar. The Court held that it must subject deprivations of life to the most careful scrutiny and that the term 'absolutely necessary' meant that a strict and compelling test of necessity should be used. On the facts, although the soldiers could not be faulted for using fatal force, the intelligence authorities had been negligent in the planning of the operation and had fed misinformation to the soldiers. *McCann* suggests that the Court is more likely to find a breach of **article 2** when it has found an error in the overall decision-making process, rather than where there is an alleged error of judgement on behalf of a state official. Thus, in the present case, if it was alleged that Fred's death was caused by the, perhaps, over-zealous acts of the police officers, rather than incompetence of the overall planning of the operation, the court may be reluctant to find the state liable. Equally, in *Armani Da Silva v United Kingdom* (2016) 63 EHRR 12)—regarding the shooting of a mistakenly suspected terrorist in London in 2005—the Grand Chamber provided the state with a high level of discretion. The Grand Chamber also held that the domestic law of self-defence was compatible with article 2, and that was accepted by the domestic courts in *Davis v Commissioner of Police for the Metropolis* **[2016] 36 EWHC (QB)**, which confirmed that the law must accommodate a certain respect for individual judgement in such cases.

If the Court was satisfied that the whole operation had been handled without proper care then it may find the authorities in breach, although *Andronicou* suggests that a reasonable amount of discretion will be given to the authorities. Here, although there had been a number of areas of concern with respect to a rescue operation, there had been no violation of **article 2** because it had not been shown that the operation had not been planned in a way that minimised to the greatest extent possible any risk to the victims' lives.[6] Despite the discretion given to the authorities when carrying out an operation to defend the lives of others, the killing of Fred when he did not appear to be a danger to the officers or anyone else could be described as reckless, perhaps suggesting inexperience or a lack of care on behalf of the officers. Thus, we might conclude that the use of fatal force was not absolutely necessary.

The Investigation into the Deaths

Article 2 imposes a duty to carry out a proper investigation into any deaths that have occurred within a state's jurisdiction and which may be in violation of its general duty to protect life. In *Jordan v United Kingdom* (2003) 37 EHRR 2, the Court held that where the events lay within the knowledge of the authorities, the burden of proof would be on the state to provide a satisfactory and convincing explanation of the death.[7] **Article 2**, thus, requires some form of effective official investigation when individuals had been killed as a result of the use of force.

The Court laid down some essential requirements of effectiveness: it should be carried out by persons independent of those implicated in the events; be capable of leading to a determination of whether the force used in such circumstances was justified, and to the identification and punishment of those responsible; the authorities must take

[6] The author now applies those principles to the facts, identifying the relevant evidence and concluding on liability.

[7] The author now deals with the issue of procedure and investigation, providing an overall account of the principles and cases, before applying them to the facts in the summary at the end.

reasonable steps to secure the evidence concerning the incident, including eyewitness testimony; and it should be carried out with sufficient promptness and reasonable expedition. Further, in *Edwards*, the Court stressed the need for openness and for relatives to be allowed to participate in any inquiry, including the ability to attend and to be represented at it. These principles were upheld in *Amin v Secretary of State for the Home Department* **[2004] 1 AC 653**, where the House of Lords quashed the decision of the Home Secretary not to order a public inquiry into the death of a prisoner at the hands of a racist and violent cell mate, the court noting that the Prison Service's investigation did not enjoy independence, had been conducted in private, and had not been published.

Conclusions

[8]A clear and very brief conclusion of all issues is provided.

It is suggested that following *Edwards* the domestic court would find a violation of **article 2** in respect of Peter's death and that despite the area of discretion given to the authorities there had been a similar violation with regards to Fred's death.[8] In addition, applying *Jordan*, there would appear to be a clear violation of the procedural duties under **article 2** in respect of both deaths.

LOOKING FOR EXTRA MARKS?

▨ Show that you understand the distinction between the procedural and substantive obligations and the likelihood of the courts imposing liability on the authorities for breach of such.

▨ Appreciate the jurisprudence of the European Court of Human Rights in this area and then provide advice as to the likely success of the actions on the basis of your understanding of the relevant case law and principles.

▨ Display clear and strong interpretation and reasoning skills in applying the principles and cases to the factual scenario, and clear problem-solving skills in dealing with each issue in turn.

QUESTION | 4

In May 2013, John, a 20-year-old citizen of the United Islands of Montrovia (a small group of islands in the South Pacific), landed illegally in the UK, having escaped from a remand prison in his home country whilst awaiting trial for murder. The UK has an extradition agreement with the United Islands and has agreed to extradite any person, provided that person would not be subjected to the death penalty upon extradition. John claimed that he would be subject to the death penalty if convicted, although the authorities in the United Islands assured the British authorities that no person under the age of 21 had ever been sentenced to death (even though the death sentence was, theoretically, applicable to anyone over the age of 18 where the circumstances of the murder were sufficiently serious to warrant the death penalty). The Home Secretary decided to extradite John and his application for judicial review of that decision, and his claim under the Human Rights Act 1998 was refused on the basis that the Home Secretary was entitled to believe that the death penalty would not be imposed. He now makes a claim under the European Convention, claiming that his extradition would constitute a violation of articles 2, 3, and 13 of the Convention.

Advise John as to the process involved in that application and as to the likely success of his claim.

CAUTION!

- This question requires a knowledge of article 2 of the Convention, together with Protocols 6 and 13 relating to the death penalty and the application of article 3 (prohibition of inhuman and degrading treatment).

- The question also requires a specific knowledge of article 13 (effective remedies) and the principles established by the relevant cases.

- To provide advice the student needs to examine the facts of the case very carefully and employ sound reasoning skills in coming to any conclusions. Note: the events have taken place after the Human Rights Act 1998 had come into force and thus the Act has been applied directly to the events. This may be important with respect to the European Court's willingness to interfere with the domestic authorities' decisions and the effectiveness of the review proceedings *vis-à-vis* article 13 of the Convention.

DIAGRAM ANSWER PLANS

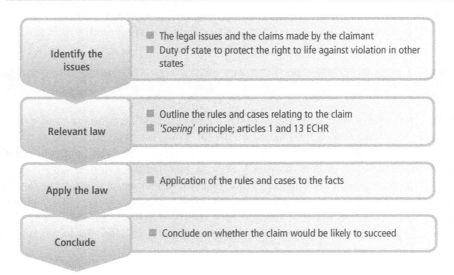

Introduction

[1] The introduction provides a clear overview of the main issues raised by the question and the scenario.

John's possible extradition to the United Islands of Montrovia raises the question whether such a measure would engage the UK's liability under **article 2** of the Convention, which provides that everyone's right to life shall be protected by law, and **article 3**,[1] which provides that no one shall be subject to torture or inhuman or degrading treatment or punishment. In *Soering v United Kingdom* **(1989) 11 EHRR 439**, the European Court established that a member state could be liable for the breach of an individual's Convention rights in another territory. For such liability there must exist a real risk that if that individual was removed from the member state he or she would face treatment in violation of the Convention. Thus, as John is presently within the UK's jurisdiction, the government is responsible for securing the enjoyment of his Convention rights and must not expose him to an unnecessary risk of a violation of **articles 2 and 3**.

In addition, John's failure to succeed in the domestic judicial review proceedings raises the question of whether there has been a violation of **article 13**, which guarantees an effective remedy for any violation of a person's Convention rights.

The Death Penalty

[2] The author outlines the potential basis for the UK's liability in this case.

John's claim in respect of the death penalty would succeed if the Court was satisfied that there was a real risk of the death penalty being carried out in this case, and that the death penalty or the manner of its execution was incompatible with the Convention.[2] In *Soering*, there had to be a *real risk* that the applicant would face, in that case, ill-treatment in violation of the Convention, as opposed to a mere possibility (*Vilvarajah v United Kingdom* **(1992) 14 EHRR 248**). In John's case it could be argued by the government that John's execution was a mere or remote possibility. Thus, given the fact that it had been told by the Montrovian authorities of the policy regarding the execution of persons under the age of 21, the government would argue that it was entitled to conclude that there was no realistic possibility of John facing the death penalty if convicted. Further, there is still uncertainty as to whether John will be convicted of murder, and more importantly, whether the circumstances of this alleged murder were sufficiently serious to warrant the death penalty. John would argue that the fact that the death penalty remains on the domestic statute books, and thus available in theory, amounts to a sufficient risk.

[3] The author then supplements the previous information by examining the scenario and considering the factual issues and possible interpretations of the facts.

The fact that the death penalty could in theory be granted, would be insufficient for the Court to establish a real risk, although it will not take the promises of the government or the Montrovian authorities at face value, and will search for further evidence in order to assess the risk.[3]

For example, in *Chahal v United Kingdom* **(1997) 23 EHRR 413** there was a real risk of the applicant being subjected to torture, despite assurances to the contrary from the relevant Indian authorities. The Court took into account the recent human rights record of that country and the troubles which still existed in a particular region of the country. In our case the Court would investigate the human rights record of Montrovia and the feasibility of relying on the assurance given to the government. Further, the Court would need to clarify this assurance; for example, by asking whether anyone under the age of 21 had ever been convicted of murder, and whether, if they had, there had existed mitigating circumstances that had spared the convicted prisoner the death penalty. It would also want to be satisfied that the age exemption applies to not only those who were under 21 at the time of the offence, but also to those who were under that age after being found guilty and at the time of any execution.

[4]The author then examines the *legal* issues surrounding the death penalty, assuming that there was a real risk of it being carried out.

If it was satisfied that there existed a real risk of John being executed it would then examine whether any execution would be in violation of the Convention.[4] **Article 2** provides that no one shall be deprived of his life intentionally *save in the execution of a sentence of a court following his conviction of a crime for which the penalty is provided by law*. Despite this, John might still claim that his execution would be in breach of his Convention rights.

First, whether the death penalty itself is in violation of the European Convention (*Al-Saadoon and Mufhdi v United Kingdom* **(2010) 51 EHRR 9**), the manner of its execution and the circumstances surrounding the death penalty may be inconsistent with **article 3**, which prohibits inhuman and degrading punishment. Thus, in *Soering* the Court held that the subjection of a young man of limited mental ability to the death row phenomenon constituted inhuman and degrading treatment within **article 3**. A similar claim could also be made if the prison conditions under which the prisoner is kept are inhuman or degrading (*Kalashnikov v Russia* **(2003) 36 EHRR 34**). Secondly, the exception provided in **article 2** only applies where the death sentence has been passed by a court after the individual has been convicted of a criminal offence. Accordingly, if it can be shown that John will receive the death penalty without due process then there will be a violation of **article 2**. Thirdly, **Protocol No. 6** of the European Convention provides for member states to abolish the death penalty so that no one shall be *condemned to* such penalty or be executed. As the UK has signed this Protocol, any death penalty carried out in the UK would certainly be contrary to that Protocol, and states that deport or extradite a person to face the death penalty in another country would be in violation of their Convention responsibilities.

Finally, in *Al-Saadoon and Mufhdi*, it was accepted that the death penalty constitutes suffering in breach of **article 3** of the Convention and that given modern state practice the death penalty exception in **article 2** was now displaced by **article 3**.[5] As the UK is a party to that protocol, the extradition would be in breach of its obligations, provided the Court finds that there was a real risk of John facing the death penalty. On the facts, therefore, it appears that John's extradition would be in breach of the UK's obligations under the Convention.

[6] The author begins to discuss the article 13 issue and then outlines the claimant's arguments.

The Claim under Article 13

Article 13 provides that everyone whose Convention rights are violated shall have an effective remedy before a national authority.[6] Thus, where an individual has an arguable claim under the Convention, he should have a remedy before a national authority in order both to have his claim decided, and, if appropriate, to obtain redress (*Silver v United Kingdom* **(1983) 5 EHRR 347**).

John's main argument, therefore, is that the judicial review proceedings did not allow him to raise his claims under **articles 2 and 3** of the Convention and that the courts gave insufficient weight to those arguments. Although the European Court does not insist that a domestic court has the power to substitute its opinion for that of the original decision-maker, the reviewing court should have adequate powers to question the original decision (*Thynne, Wilson and Gunnell v United Kingdom* **(1990) 13 EHRR 666**). Further, an individual should be able to argue his or her case in accordance with Convention principles, including whether the restriction was unnecessary or disproportionate (*Smith and Grady v United Kingdom* **(2000) 29 EHRR 493**). With particular relevance to John's case, the domestic court must not be precluded from examining the facts of the case, or of looking behind the reasons given by the decision-maker. Accordingly, in *Chahal*, there was a clear violation of **article 13** when a decision to deport the applicant was not reviewed solely with reference to the question of the risk to the applicant of ill-treatment in breach of **article 3**. In that case, the domestic court was limited to asking whether the Home Secretary had balanced the risk with issues of national security. Similarly, in John's case if the domestic courts had not reviewed the evidence of the Home Secretary in assessing the risk of John's Convention rights being violated, and had instead relied on the Home Secretary's assessment of the fact and the risk, then there would be a clear violation of **article 13**.

On the other hand, if the proceedings were full and complied with **article 13** and the decision of the Home Secretary was consistent with the evidence, then the European Court might defer to him and the domestic courts (*Launder v United Kingdom* **[1998] EHRLR 337**).

[7] The author then provides the likely outcome given the impact of the Human Rights Act.

As the domestic decision was made after the **Human Rights Act 1998** came into force, provided the court subjected the decision to a suitably stringent test, it is unlikely that there would be a violation of **article 13**.[7]

Conclusions

[8] The author provides a neat conclusion on both the factual and legal issues before giving final advice.

Whether there has been a violation of **articles 2 and 3** of the Convention depends principally on whether the European Court is satisfied there was a real risk of John being subjected to the death penalty.[8] If that is the case, the death penalty and its circumstances appear to be clearly in violation of John's Convention rights. The question is then whether the judicial review proceedings allowed the domestic courts to assess those risks in line with the principles and case law of the European Convention. In other words, whether they were an effective remedy under **article 13** of the Convention.

LOOKING FOR EXTRA MARKS?

- Show a clear and thorough understanding of the issues surrounding the death penalty and its legality under the Convention, together with its potential relationship with other articles.
- Show an appreciation of both the human rights issues and of the diplomatic problem of the European Convention interfering with the decisions of national authorities in this area.
- Display clear and strong interpretation and reasoning skills in applying the principles and cases to the factual scenario.

TAKING THINGS FURTHER

- Amos, M, *Human Rights Law*, 2nd edn (Hart 2014), ch. 7
  Contains a comprehensive coverage of the right to life under the ECHR and the HRA 1998
- Ferreira, N, 'The Supreme Court in a Final Push to Go Beyond Strasbourg' [2015]; 1; PL 367
  Critically examines the judicial challenges to assisted suicide law, in both the domestic court and the European Court
- Foster, S and Leigh, G, 'Self-Defence and the Right to Life: The Use of Lethal or Potentially Lethal Force, UK Domestic Law and Article 2 ECHR' [2016] 4 EHRLR 398
  Examines recent High Court decisions on the compatibility of domestic law with article 2 ECHR.
- Leverick, F, 'Is English Self-defence Law Incompatible with Article 2 of the ECHR?' [2002] Crim LR 347
  Examines UK Law on self-defence and its compatibility with article 2 ECHR; very relevant in respect of the de Menezes case

Mowbray, A, 'Duties of Investigation under the European Convention on Human Rights' [2002] 51 (2) ICLQ 437

Examines the procedural obligation under article 2; essential reading so as to make sense of the recent case law in this area

Yorke, J, 'The Right to Life and Abolition of the Death Penalty in the Council of Europe' [2009] 34 (2) ELR 205

Discusses the gradual outlawing of the death penalty under the ECHR

Online Resources
www.oup.com/uk/qanda/

Go online for extra essay and problem questions, a glossary of key terms, online versions of all the answer plans and audio commentary on how selected ones were put together, and a range of podcasts which include advice on exam and coursework technique and advice for other assessment methods.

6 Freedom from Torture and Inhuman and Degrading Treatment

ARE YOU READY?

In order to attempt questions in this chapter, which covers various aspects of freedom from torture and other ill treatment, contained in article 3 of the European Convention on Human Rights, you will need to have acquired a sound knowledge of the areas listed below during the course and your revision programme:

● A range of questions have been included to reflect the fact that different courses concentrate on different aspects of this article: such as its values and its scope; the state's positive obligation to protect individuals from such treatment; and the procedural duties under article 3.

● The absolute nature of article 3, and whether that nature can ever be compromised, particularly in the context of the fight against terrorism.

● Article 3's application to issues such as prison conditions and deportation and extradition.

● The relationship between article 3 and other rights contained in the Convention.

 ## KEY DEBATES

This area of substantive human rights law is the subject of much case law from both the domestic and European courts with respect to the interpretation of its wording and limitations and restrictions. In particular there is much legal, political, and constitutional debate surrounding the absolute nature of the article and whether its scope should be compromised in the interests of national security and public safety. This is especially so in cases where the state is fighting the threat of terrorism; should there be a right to torture terrorists? There is also discussion on the thresholds necessary to find a breach, particularly in areas such as conditions of detention and deportation and extradition cases.

Debate: Absolute Nature of Article 3

There is a good deal of political and legal debate as to whether article 3 has, or should, retain its absolute status, or whether its protection should be compromised for the public good or the rights of others. As it stands, there can be no justification for an act which constitutes torture etc., but there is an argument that in the context of public emergencies and the fight against terrorism such a principle should be compromised, if not for torture, at least for the purposes of defining inhuman and degrading treatment or punishment. There is, therefore, a clash between those who cling on to the traditional values of human rights law, and those who wish to apply a more pragmatic approach.

Debate: Article 3 and Prison Conditions and Sentences

The application of article 3 to prison conditions has caused some controversy in terms of the extent to which the courts can regulate inhuman and degrading conditions and treatment, including measures to maintain good order and discipline. Should the strict standards of article 3 be applied to those lawfully in detention, and how do the courts apply those standards in deciding whether the conditions reach the necessary threshold? Further controversy has been created by the challenge to the imposition and review of whole life sentences; is such a sentence, without review or possible release, inhuman and degrading, and should the European Court impose definite rules on each individual state?

Debate: Torture and the Prevention of Terrorism

Whether the absolute nature of article 3 applies where there is a state of emergency and in the control of terrorism has created case law and political and academic debate with respect to matters such as deportation of terrorist suspects, the admission of torture evidence, and the dilemma of whether we can torture terrorists—the 'ticking bomb' scenario. Thus far, the European Court has refused to compromise the absolute nature of article 3 in relation to state practices of interrogation and the treatment of terrorist suspects. However, there is a political and public call for compromise, which gives rise to concerns over the democratic legitimacy of human rights treaties and judicial interpretation.

QUESTION | 1

By the use of case examples, critically examine how the European Court of Human Rights has interpreted and applied article 3 of the European Convention, and how it has attempted to maintain its absolute character.

CAUTION!

- This question requires a general knowledge of article 3, but the answer should concentrate on the *values and absolute nature of the article* and how the European Court has dealt with the inherent difficulties of interpreting and applying the article.

- The question is asking you to *critically examine* how the Court has carried out this task, so choose areas and cases which are controversial and which have excited legal and other argument, and which allow you to display your critical skills.

- Although the question refers to cases from the *European Court*, it is acceptable to include complementary case law from the domestic courts in order to illustrate the scope and nature of the article.

- The answer should, where relevant, include reference to other articles of the Convention, such as article 2 (right to life) and article 8 (right to private life).

DIAGRAM ANSWER PLANS

Explanation of the wording, scope, and rationale of article 3

▼

Explanation, via relevant case law, of the process by which the European Court decides cases under this provision and an overview of the problems it faces

▼

Consideration of the various specific legal, jurisdictional, and moral difficulties facing the Court in resolving claims, using various cases and examples in illustration

▼

Consideration of cases where the absolute nature of article 3 has been questioned and conclusions as to the success of the European Court in maintaining the absolute character of article 3

SUGGESTED ANSWER

[1] The author provides a simple and incisive account of the article and its nature and scope.

Article 3 of the European Convention on Human Rights provides that no one shall be subject to torture or inhuman or degrading treatment or punishment. The prohibition is absolute and the state's obligations cannot be derogated from even in times of war or other emergencies (**article 15(2)**).[1] The Court has also strengthened the status of **article 3** by implying a procedural obligation to investigate suspected acts of ill-treatment taking place in its jurisdiction (*Askoy v Turkey* **(1996) 23 EHRR 553**).

In *Chahal v United Kingdom* **(1997) 23 EHRR 413**, the Court stated that the article enshrined one of the most fundamental values of a democratic society. Thus, although it recognised the immense difficulties faced by states in protecting their territory from acts of terrorism, it prohibited torture and other ill-treatment irrespective of the applicant's conduct. Consequently, there can be no justification for any violation, whatever the benefits arising from the relevant act or practice. For example, in *Tyrer v United Kingdom* **(1978) 2 EHRR 1** it was held that judicial corporal punishment was contrary to **article 3**, despite claims that birching had a deterrent effect on juvenile crime.

[2] The author moves on to the issue of interpretation of the article and employs relevant case law for definitions.

The absolute nature of this article thus gives rise to a number of dilemmas. Most significantly, the Court must define the terms 'torture' and 'inhuman or degrading treatment or punishment', and then determine whether the act or practice in question meets the necessary threshold.[2] In the *Greek Case* **(1969) 12 YB 170**, torture was defined as an aggravated and deliberate form of inhuman treatment causing very serious and cruel suffering, whereas inhuman treatment covered treatment that deliberately caused severe mental or physical suffering. The Commission then defined degrading treatment or punishment as that which grossly humiliates a person before others, or drives him to act against his will or conscience. This was applied in *Ireland v United Kingdom* **(1978) 2 EHRR 25**, where the Court found that interrogation techniques constituted inhuman treatment within **article 3** because they caused intense physical and mental suffering and acute psychiatric disturbances. They also aroused in their victims feelings of fear, anguish, and inferiority capable of humiliating the individuals, and were thus degrading. On the other hand, the Court held that the techniques did not constitute torture because they did not amount to deliberate treatment causing very serious and cruel suffering. Thus, torture is the most aggravated and deliberate form of inhuman treatment or punishment, the distinction lying in the intensity of the acts and the intention of the perpetrators.

The Court must then determine a violation by considering both the level of harm suffered by the victim and the acceptability of such treatment. For example, in *Selmouni v France* **(2000) 29 EHRR 403** the Court made a finding of torture when the applicant had been subjected to repeated physical and verbal assaults, had been urinated on by an officer, and had been threatened with a blow lamp. In this case it held that the Convention must be interpreted in the light of present-day conditions and that the increasingly high standard being required in the area of human rights required a greater firmness in assessing breaches of the fundamental values of democratic societies. Thus, certain acts which in the past were classified as inhuman and degrading treatment as opposed to torture could now be classified differently in the future.[3] It is arguable, therefore, that the treatment in **Ireland** might now be regarded as torture, and a renewed application is being made to the Court on the basis of new evidence (rejected by the Court on 20 March 2018). Further, in *Al-Saadoon and Mufhdi v United Kingdom* **(2010) 51 EHRR 9** the Court took into account the current views of member states with respect to capital punishment in finding that the death penalty was in violation of **article 3**.

For an act to be 'inhuman' there must have been a sufficiently serious attack on the victim's physical, mental, or psychological well-being. In *Tomasi v France* **(1993) 15 EHRR 1**, the applicant had been hit in the stomach, slapped, and kicked, had his head knocked against the wall, and been left naked in front of a window for several hours. On those facts the Court found that having regard to the number of blows and their intensity, such treatment was both inhuman and degrading. For treatment or punishment to be 'degrading' the humiliation or debasement must reach a particular level, such an assessment being relative and dependent on all the circumstances of the case, including the age of the victim (*Tyrer v United Kingdom*). Not all forms of ill-treatment that have a humiliating effect on the applicant will be in violation. For example, although arrest, detention, and imprisonment may degrade a person, they are regarded as perfectly acceptable under the Convention provided there are no aggravating circumstances. Accordingly, in *A v United Kingdom* **(2009) 49 EHRR 29** it was held that detention

[3] The author provides clear interesting examples of the Court's dynamic and robust approach in defining the values of article 3.

without trial did not breach **article 3** because there were procedural safeguards allowing the applicants to challenge the legality of the detention and its conditions. On the other hand, in *Tyrer* the Court labelled judicial corporal punishment as institutionalised violence, involving an unjustifiable assault on a person's dignity and, in *Vinter v United Kingdom* **(2014) 34 BHRC 605**, it was held that a whole life sentence without the possibility of review was inhuman and degrading and thus in breach of **article 3**. Generally, the Court will inquire into the extent of the ill-treatment, its duration, and the suffering of the individual applicant (*Costello-Roberts v United Kingdom* **(1993) 19 EHRR 112**). For example, in the context of prison conditions, the conditions must go beyond the normal harsh conditions associated with incarceration (*Valasinas v Lithuania* **(2001) 12 BHRC 266**). This has led to arguments by Smet (2013) that the absolute character of **article 3** has been diluted by the Court's employment of proportionality.[4]

The Court may face particular problems in identifying the scope and application of the article; for example, whether a member state can be held responsible for an act of ill-treatment committed outside its jurisdiction. In *Soering v United Kingdom* **(1989) 11 EHRR 439**, it held that a decision of a member state to extradite a person might engage the responsibility of that state where there were substantial grounds for believing that such a person would be faced with a real risk of being subjected to a breach of **article 3**. Thus, in that case, the Court held that there was a real risk that the applicant would be subjected to the death row phenomenon if extradited to the United States, and accordingly found a violation. In *Chahal*, the Court stressed that **article 3** remained absolute despite any threat to national security. It has re-affirmed this by stating that there can be no compromise of the *Soering* principle in order to accommodate the state's fight against terrorism (*Saadi v Italy* **(2009) 49 EHRR 30**). However, in *Babar Ahmed and others v United Kingdom*, **(2013) 56 EHRR 1**, it held that the extradition of a number of individuals to the United States to serve whole life sentences in high security prisons would not violate **article 3** as the sentences were proportionately handed down.[5] In any case, the Court has to make a distinction between a real risk and a mere possibility of ill treatment (*Vilvarajah v United Kingdom* **(1992) 14 EHRR 248**).

The Court has extended *Soering* to cases where the receiving state would not necessarily be in violation, but nevertheless the applicant would suffer inhuman or degrading treatment.[6] In *D v United Kingdom* **(1997) 24 EHRR 423**, D had entered the UK illegally and had contracted AIDS in prison. On his release he claimed that his deportation would constitute a violation of **article 3** because his home country lacked the facilities to provide him with adequate medical care. It was held that given the applicant's current condition and the inadequate medical facilities in that country, his removal by the UK to a country where he would face the risk of dying in the most distressing circumstances amounted to

[4] The author provides a number of case examples where the Court has found difficulty in defending the scope and absolute character of the article and has referred to academic authority to criticise.

[5] The case of *Ahmed* is used to highlight the Court's more practical approach in this area.

[6] The author discusses the highly controversial case of *D* with respect to state liability, together with its limitations.

a violation of **article 3**. However, in **N v United Kingdom (2008) 47 EHRR 39**, it was held that **article 3** does not require member states to afford medical treatment to *all* suffering from life-threatening diseases and that the decision in **D** was exceptional.

[7] The author discusses the state's positive obligations under article 3, explaining its scope and its limits.

The Court has also imposed a positive obligation on the state to ensure that a person does not suffer ill-treatment at the hands of others, including private individuals (**A v United Kingdom (1999) 27 EHRR 611** [7]—UK liable for the ill-treatment of the applicant at the hands of his stepfather because the domestic law provided the boy with inadequate protection against such treatment). Similarly, in **Z v United Kingdom (2002) 34 EHRR 3** the failure of social services to provide adequate protection against physical and other abuse at the hands of the applicants' family was in breach. However, the Court will only engage the state's liability when there is clear evidence that the authorities should have been aware of the abuse (**DP and JC v United Kingdom (2003) 36 EHRR 14**).

[8] The Conclusion summarises the overall position *vis-à-vis* the Court's approach, pointing to both positive and negative aspects.

In conclusion, the article's interpretation and application have given rise to a number of legal, jurisdictional, and moral dilemmas. The Court recognises that **article 3** is fundamental and absolute (**Chahal**), and that its meaning and application can adapt to new and enhanced ideals of human rights protection. On the other hand, it has insisted that the suffering of the applicant must reach a particular level, and that any suffering must exceed that which normally ensues from acceptable punishments and practices. [8] This has led to the argument that the Court has compromised human rights for the sake of pragmatism (as in **Baber Ahmed**).

LOOKING FOR EXTRA MARKS?

- Show that you understand the scope and character of article 3 and its general purpose—to protect an individual from unacceptable treatment and to impose an absolute prohibition on such treatment.

- Appreciate the dilemma facing the Court in interpreting the article's wording and maintaining its absolute character, especially where national security and public safety are at issue.

- Use leading cases (and academic arguments) which illustrate those dilemmas and which allow you to employ your critical skills and conclude on the central question.

Q) QUESTION | 2

In February 2015, Harry and Barry were taken into police custody following their arrest for theft and assault involving three old-age pensioners. Both were clearly under the influence of drugs at the time of their arrests and both were placed in police cells. After three hours, a police officer entered the cell and was attacked by Barry. Four officers then entered the cell and administered severe beatings to both Harry and Barry. Both were then taken to another cell, which was full of vomit and excrement and told that they could stay there for the night. They were refused permission to go to the toilet and were forced to urinate in the cell on three occasions before they were released. They were both subsequently charged with assault and Harry received a prison sentence of six months. Whilst in prison, the prison warders told Harry's cell mate that he had beaten up three old ladies and the same evening Harry was stripped and beaten up by three inmates at the prison. He also complained that when he had asked for medication to help him deal with his drug addiction he had been refused on the grounds that 'you can just bloody well suffer'. The following day, Harry told the prison doctor that he could stand no more of this place and that he felt suicidal. The prison decided not to put him in the medical centre, but placed him in a single cell and that night he committed suicide.

Advise Barry and Harry's family as to any action they might have under the Human Rights Act 1998 and what would be the likely success of any claim.

CAUTION!

- This question requires a general knowledge of article 3, but also the relationship between article 3 and article 2 (the right to life).

- Do not spend too much time explaining the basic principles or providing academic criticism of the law and cases—the answer should concentrate on its application to the treatment of detainees and giving advice to the parties in the scenario.

- The answer should display sound interpretation and analytical skills: ensure you read the facts very carefully and apply the relevant principles and cases; clearly this is a problem question so concentrate on providing clear and full advice.

DIAGRAM ANSWER PLANS

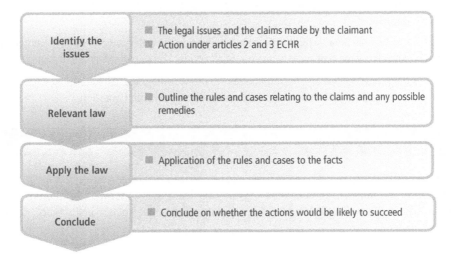

Identify the issues
- The legal issues and the claims made by the claimant
- Action under articles 2 and 3 ECHR

Relevant law
- Outline the rules and cases relating to the claims and any possible remedies

Apply the law
- Application of the rules and cases to the facts

Conclude
- Conclude on whether the actions would be likely to succeed

Introduction

The scenario raises issues under **articles 2 and 3 of the European Convention on Human Rights.** After the passing of the **Human Rights Act 1998**, both prisoners may bring proceedings claiming a breach of their Convention rights directly, as victims, under **s.6** of the Act. Alternatively, indirectly they may bring a private action, using any relevant Convention law in claiming that the prison authorities had broken common law duties.[1] In either case the domestic courts must, under **s.2** of the 1998 Act, consider the case law of the European Court of Human Rights in determining that claim.

[1] The brief introduction lays out the legal framework of the claim and the issues raised in the scenario.

Harry and Barry's treatment in police custody

Harry and Barry's arrest and detention raise issues under **article 3**, which prohibits inhuman and degrading treatment and punishment. For treatment to be inhuman there has to be a sufficiently serious attack on the victim's physical, mental, or psychological well-being. Thus, in *Ireland v United Kingdom* **(1978) 2 EHRR 25** the Court held that such treatment had to cause at least intense physical and mental suffering or acute psychiatric disturbance. To amount to degrading treatment it must arouse feelings of fear, anguish, and inferiority capable of humiliating and possibly taking away physical or moral resistance. (The facts do not require consideration of whether any of the treatment amounted to torture, which the European Court has defined as deliberate inhuman treatment causing very serious and cruel suffering).

The fact that the arrests were made when they were under the influence of drugs imposes a specific duty on the police authorities to make proper provision for the prisoner's health and well-being in the form of requisite medical assistance (*McGlinchey v United Kingdom* **(2003) 37 EHRR 41**).[2] Thus, Harry and Barry's subsequent treatment in the prison cell may well be exacerbated by the fact that both have drug problems and are under the influence of drugs at the relevant time. Further, both prisoners appear to have been left in the cell for three hours, without enquiry into their mental and physical health. However, in the absence of evidence that the influence of drugs had a substantial impact on their mental or physical health, it is difficult to find a violation of **article 3** solely on this ground.

[2] Having outlined the basic duty of care owed to prisoners, the author now examines their application with respect to the prisoners' situation and their treatment in the cell.

The attacks on Harry and Barry by the police officers after Barry had attacked an officer raises issues of assault and **article 3**.[3] At common law an officer commits an assault if he uses force on a prisoner without authority, or where he has authority but uses excessive force (*Rodrigues v Home Office* **[1989] Legal Action 14**). Although Barry had used force on an officer, the beatings appear

[3] The author deals with the attacks on the prisoners by examining both the common law and ECHR actions, using relevant case law to support the analysis and conclusions.

to be a punishment and not related to self-defence, and are too excessive to be related to the maintenance of order. Thus, in *Russell, McNamee and McCotter v Home Office, Daily Telegraph, 13 March 2001*, it was held that prisoners had been unlawfully assaulted by prison authorities after they had been captured after escape. This follows the decision in *Tomasi v France* **(1993) 15 EHRR 1**, where it was held that any wrongful and unnecessary use of force by state authorities on those in detention would constitute at least degrading treatment. Further, depending on the extent of the injuries, the court might find that Harry and Barry were subjected to inhuman treatment. In *Tomasi* the detainee had been hit in the stomach, slapped and kicked, had his head knocked against the wall, and been left naked in front of a window for several hours. In those circumstances such treatment was both inhuman and degrading. Because the prisoners in our case are under the influence of drugs, such beating might amount to inhuman treatment, thus affecting the measure of damages, and any just satisfaction under **s.8** of the 1998 Act.

With respect to the condition of the cell, for a claim to succeed under **article 3** the conditions of detention must go beyond the level that is inevitable from the fact of incarceration (*Valasinas v Lithuania* **(2001) 12 BHRC 266**). However, unacceptable conditions of detention can amount to a breach of **article 3** if the conditions denote a lack of respect for the applicant, capable of humiliating and debasing him (*Peers v Greece* **(2001) 33 EHRR 51**).[4] Although Harry and Barry were only required to occupy the cell overnight, the fact that human beings were placed in a cell that was full of vomit and excrement, particularly as it appears to have been done as some form of punishment or for administrative convenience, suggests that the necessary threshold was met. The situation was exacerbated by the fact that the authorities refused to allow them to go to the toilet, which meant that they had to urinate in front of each other on three occasions. In *Peers*, the Court found that it was unacceptable that each cell mate had to relieve themselves in an open toilet in front of each other. So too in *Napier v Scottish Ministers, The Times*, 13 May 2004, the Scottish courts held that prison conditions, including the lack of adequate sanitary conditions amounted to a violation of **article 3**.

Harry's treatment in prison

The prison authorities owe Harry a duty of care in the law of negligence to take care for his safety and to protect him from foreseeable harm caused by fellow inmates (*Ellis v Home Office* **[1953] 2 QB 135**).[5] By informing other prisoners of the nature of Harry's offence, it was reasonably foreseeable that he might be attacked

[4] The rules and case law regarding prison conditions are briefly but clearly laid out, followed by a careful application of those principles to the facts.

[5] The author provides a clear and referenced account of the duty of care owed to the prisoner, employing relevant case law.

and the authorities appear to have failed in their duty towards Harry in this respect. Also under **article 3** member states owe a positive obligation to protect individuals from an unacceptable risk of ill-treatment at the hands of others (*A v United Kingdom* **(1999) 27 EHRR 611**). Although this duty should not place an unreasonable burden on the state, the prison officers appear to have subjected Harry to an unacceptable and avoidable risk of ill-treatment. Further, the attack by the prisoners appears to clearly cross the threshold under **article 3**, and given the fact that he was stripped, it could be argued that the treatment amounted to inhuman treatment (*Tomasi v France*).

With respect to the failure to provide Harry with medication to deal with his drug addiction, there is no right under the Convention to be released from prison simply because one is ill (*Papon v France* **(2004) 39 EHRR 10**). However, the authorities owe a duty under the Convention to provide adequate medical and other assistance to those in detention and who have special needs (*Keenan v United Kingdom* **(2001) 33 EHRR 38** and *Price v United Kingdom* **(2002) 34 EHRR 53**).[6] More specifically, in *McGlinchey*, the Court held that there had been a violation of **article 3** when the inmate had died in prison after receiving inadequate medical care to deal with her withdrawal symptoms. In our case, the authorities have deliberately refused to offer assistance, and the remarks of the officer suggest that there may have been a definite intention to humiliate Harry. Accordingly, there appears to be a clear violation of **article 3**.

Harry's suicide

Harry's suicide raises issues under **articles 2 and 3** of the European Convention. The common law imposes a duty on the authorities to safeguard a prisoner's life from acts of self-harm[7] (*Kirkham v Chief Constable of Greater Manchester Police* **[1990] 2 QB 283**). This extends to prisoners who are not suffering from mental illness at the time of the suicide (*Reeves v Commissioner for the Police of the Metropolis* **[2000] AC 283**). This duty is also relevant to the state's obligation to protect the right to life under **article 2**, although in *Orange v Chief Constable of West Yorkshire Police* **[2001] 3 WLR 736** the Court of Appeal held that such a duty only applied where the prisoner was a clear suicide risk and the authorities have failed to take all reasonable steps to avoid the act of self-harm. Similarly, in *Keenan v United Kingdom*, where a prisoner with mental problems had committed suicide in prison after being placed in a segregation block for breach of the prison rules, the Court found that the prisoner was not considered an immediate risk while in detention. Thus, the authorities had made a reasonable response to his conduct,

[6] The author deals with the issue relating to the prisoner's drug addiction and treatment, employing both general and specific case law, and then giving advice on the facts.

[7] The author provides a neat summary of the law and cases on liability for suicides—both at common law and under the ECHR.

placing him in hospital care and under watch when he showed suicidal tendencies.

[8] The author analyses the facts of the case to draw a distinction between this scenario and previous case law.

In our case, however, the authorities do not appear to have conducted any professional inquiry into the risk of suicide, and thus the state's liability under **article 2** might be satisfied in the circumstances.[8] In any case, the authorities appear to have violated **article 3** by refusing to refer him to the medical centre and by placing him in a single cell. Thus, in *Keenan*, although the Court did not find a violation of **article 2**, it nevertheless found a violation of **article 3** with respect to the prisoner's treatment and lack of proper medical and psychiatric care.

Conclusion

Harry and Barry's treatment appears to amount to a number of violations of both domestic law and of **article 3** of the European Convention.

[9] The Conclusion neatly summarises the issues raised in the answer and adds some commentary as to the likely remedies available to the parties and relatives.

Given the attacks on their dignity and the threats to their health, they would expect to get substantial compensation for non-pecuniary loss under the principles of just satisfaction now contained in **s.8** of the **Human Rights Act 1998**. Further, the prison authorities appear to have clearly breached their duty of care with respect to the attack by fellow prisoners and the suicide.[9] In **Keenan** the Court stressed that family representatives should be able to claim such loss if the state was to fulfil its duty under **article 13** of the Convention to provide an effective remedy for breach of the victim's Convention rights. Thus, Harry's family would expect to receive substantial just satisfaction.

LOOKING FOR EXTRA MARKS?

- Show that you understand the application of article 3 (and article 2) in respect to the legal treatment of detainees.
- Explain the principles raised by the case law and use strong problem-solving skills to apply them clearly to the facts.
- Deal with each issue in turn (using sub-headings).
- Show an appreciation of the mechanism used in the domestic law in resolving this case: employment of the HRA (and common law principles) and the use of Convention rights and principles.

QUESTION | 3

Critically examine the case law of the European Court of Human Rights with respect to claims made by those facing deportation or extradition to countries where they face the risk of ill-treatment.

CAUTION!

- This question requires a general knowledge of the principles in article 3 ECHR, but the answer must concentrate on their application *to cases of deportation and extradition*.

- The question is asking you to *critically* examine how the European Court has dealt with cases involving deportation and extradition, so you need to be aware of the political, diplomatic, and human rights issues raised by these cases.

- Although the question refers to cases from the *European Court*, it is acceptable to include complementary case law from the domestic courts in order to illustrate if and how European jurisprudence has been followed.

- The answer should, where relevant, include reference to other articles of the Convention, such as article 2 (right to life) and article 6 (the right to a fair trial).

DIAGRAM ANSWER PLANS

Introduction to the possible human rights violations in cases of deportation and extradition

Consideration of the jurisdictional and legal difficulties raised in such cases

Critical examination of the relevant case law of the European Court in this area, including the effect of terrorist-related cases

Conclusions with respect to the level of protection afforded under the European Convention to such victims

SUGGESTED ANSWER

¹ The introduction provides a succinct overview of the rights which are at issue in cases of expulsion, displaying a sound overall knowledge of the Convention and its application in these cases.

The removal of individuals from a state engages the right to private and family life under **article 8** of the European Convention, liberty and security of the person (under **article 5**) via detention pending removal (*Chahal v United Kingdom* **(1997) 23 EHRR 413**), and **article 6** where the individual is likely to receive an unfair trial on their return (*Othman v United Kingdom* **(2012) 55 EHRR 1**).¹ In addition, deportation or extradition can often subject individuals to a real risk of torture or other ill treatment (**article 3**) and to their life (**article 2**).

Article 1 of the European Convention provides that every member state shall secure the rights and freedoms defined in **Part One** of the Convention to everyone within their jurisdiction.

[2] The author provides a clear explanation of the principles of liability, using relevant case law to illustrate the importance of protection in these cases.

This raises the question of whether an individual who is facing expulsion can bring proceedings against the expelling state in respect of violations which are to take place at the hands of the receiving state. In *Soering v United Kingdom* (1989) 11 EHRR 439,[2] the European Court held that a decision of a member state to expel might engage responsibility where there were substantial grounds for believing that if extradited such a person would be faced with a real risk of being subjected to a breach of **article 3**. In *Soering*, the United States had sought extradition of a young German national, who was wanted to stand trial for the murder of his girlfriend's parents. The UK government was given an assurance that the prosecutors would forward the views of the British government that he should not face the death penalty and the government agreed to his extradition. The Court held that exposure of the applicant to the Death Row phenomenon constituted a violation of **article 3** so that extradition in this case would constitute a violation of **article 3**.

In *Soering,* the European Court accepted that there were good human rights grounds for engaging the responsibility of a state where that person faces a real risk of being subjected to a violation of **article 3**. Thus, although it was not normal to pronounce on potential future violations of the Convention, it was necessary to depart from that rule in order to ensure the effectiveness of the safeguard provided by **article 3**. The principle was affirmed in *HLR v France* (1998) 26 EHRR 29, where the Court held that given the absolute character of **article 3** it could not rule out the possibility that a state may be responsible for the acts of private individuals in the other jurisdiction.

The European Court must address two fundamental and related questions: whether there is a real risk that the applicant will in fact be subjected to the alleged treatment; and whether such treatment is in violation of **article 3**. In these cases the Court must decide whether the applicant faced a *real risk* that they would be subject to conditions or treatment in violation of his Convention rights.[3] The prohibition under **article 3** is absolute, and once substantial grounds have been shown for believing that an individual would face such a risk, the activities of the person, however undesirable, cannot be a material consideration (*Chahal v United Kingdom*). In that case the Court concluded that the evidence, including continued international allegations of continued abuse and the fact that the applicant's high profile would make him a target for such mistreatment, meant that his deportation would lead to a violation of **article 3**. This was despite assurances given by the Indian government to the British government that the applicant would have no reason to expect to suffer mistreatment at the hands of the Indian authorities.

[3] The author begins to explain the basis of liability in such cases, highlighting the absolute nature of such liability once the test of risk is satisfied.

[4] The author provides a clear account of the principles and case law relating to the question of the level of risk required under the principle.

Although the obligations under **article 3** cannot be qualified by the behaviour of the applicant, or the pressing need to enforce relevant immigration and deportation policies, the Court insists that there is evidence of a real risk of ill-treatment (*HLR v France*).[4] Thus, the applicant must be subjected to both a direct and specific risk, allowing the Court to display deference to the domestic authorities in balancing Convention rights with the general interests of the community and in accepting diplomatic assurances with respect to such risks. In *Vilvarajah v United Kingdom* (1991) 14 EHRR 248, the applicants, Sri Lankan Tamils, had entered the UK and unsuccessfully claimed political asylum because of the civil war in that country. The Court held that the general unsettled situation in Sri Lanka at the time of the applicants' deportation did not establish that they were at greater risk than any other young Tamils who were returning there. Rather, the applicants had established only a *possibility* rather than a clear risk of ill-treatment. Although the Court held that it had a duty to rigorously examine the existence of the risk in view of the absolute character of **article 3**, there were no distinguishing factors to enable the Home Secretary to foresee that they would be ill-treated on their return.

[5] The author continues with this issue, illustrating the Court's approach by using examples of deference together with its restatement of the absolute nature of article 3.

The Court will offer states some discretion in deciding whether it is able to rely on diplomatic assurances made by the receiving state.[5] Thus, in *Othman v United Kingdom*, the Court agreed with the UK's decision to accept assurances from Jordan that Abu Qatada would not be subjected to ill-treatment in breach of **article 3**. However, the Court will make a thorough investigation into the potential risk and rule on the acceptability of that risk. Thus, in *Chahal* the Court rejected the government's pleas that it was not unreasonable for the Home Secretary to rely on the assurances given by the Indian authorities with respect to the risk of Chahal facing further torture. Further, the European Court has rejected the argument that in cases concerning the fight against terrorism, it was acceptable to apply a more flexible test under **article 3** (*Saadi v Italy* (2009) 49 EHRR 30).

[6] The area of expulsion and medical treatment and expulsion is covered carefully and critically, highlighting the compromise of interests in this area.

The Court has extended the *Soering* principle to the subjection of individuals to intolerable and unlawful prison conditions (*Hilal v United Kingdom* (2001) 33 EHRR 2), and in *D v United Kingdom* (1997) 24 EHRR 423 it applied it to cases where the receiving state would not necessarily be in violation of the Convention.[6] In this case, the applicant, a citizen of St Kitts, had entered the UK illegally and had been charged with the importation of drugs. He was sentenced to six years' imprisonment and during his sentence he contracted AIDS. On his release, he was ordered by the Home Secretary to be returned to his home country, and he claimed that the lack of medical and other care facilities in that country would subject him to intolerable conditions. The Court held that on the facts his removal to a country where he would face the risk of dying in the most distressing circumstances amounted to the subjection of the applicant to inhuman treatment.

Following *D v United Kingdom* the Court has attempted to place the enjoyment of the individual's rights under **article 3** alongside the member state's right to execute its lawful and necessary immigration policies. Thus, in *N v United Kingdom* **(2008) 47 EHRR 39**, the European Court held that the deportation of an asylum-seeking Ugandan citizen suffering from AIDS/HIV to Uganda was not in breach of **article 3**, even though access to medical treatment and facilities was problematic. The Court confirmed that exceptional circumstances were required to apply the decision in *D*. The test was whether the applicant's medical condition had reached such a critical state that there were compelling humanitarian grounds for not removing him to a place which lacked the medical and social services which he would need to prevent acute suffering. Further, **article 3** could not be interpreted so as to require contracting states to admit and treat AIDS sufferers from all over the world for the rest of their lives. The Court has also distilled the absoluteness of **article 3** in respect of expelling individuals to face whole life sentences (*Babar Ahmed v United Kingdom* **(2013) 56 EHRR 1**).

[7] The author moves on to the highly topical and controversial area of terrorism and rendition, highlighting the Court's continued robust approach.

The *Soering* principle is criticised by states, who argue that it should be relaxed in the context of terrorism (*A v The Netherlands* **Application No. 25424/05**).[7] In *Saadi v Italy*, the Court confirmed that it was not possible to weigh the risk of ill-treatment against the reasons put forward for expulsion in order to determine whether the state's obligation was engaged under **article 3**. Further, the considerable difficulties facing states with respect to terrorist violence did not call into question the absolute nature of **article 3**. Thus, the argument that the risk had to be established by solid evidence where the individual was a threat to national security was not consistent with **article 3**'s absolute nature. The test was whether there were substantial grounds for believing that there was a real risk that those found guilty of terrorist offences had been subjected to torture. In this case the authorities had failed to investigate relevant allegations of such.

[8] The Conclusion contains the author's informed views on the extent to which the Court has safeguarded individuals from ill-treatment, highlighting areas where the Court has been robust and deferential.

In conclusion, the *Soering* principle has allowed the Court to enhance its supervisory role with respect to **article 3**. This has expanded the state's duty to uphold the fundamental human rights of those within its jurisdiction, even where the threat emanates from another state or its citizens.[8] The Court has insisted that the risk of ill-treatment is real and specific, as opposed to fanciful or general. This has resulted in the Court compromising the full impact of the principle, whilst allowing it to interfere in cases where there is a real risk of the applicant being subjected to a violation of their absolute human rights. However, the decisions in *A v Netherlands* and *Saadi* are particularly significant in safeguarding the principles in **article 3**, showing that even in the face of the threat of terrorism, the obligation of the state is absolute.

LOOKING FOR EXTRA MARKS?

- Show that you understand the general purpose and scope of article 3 and its relationship to other complementary rights, together with the importance of protecting individuals in these cases.

- Appreciate the dilemma facing the European Court in applying human rights principles to these cases where there are strong public interest arguments for deporting or extraditing individuals (particularly in the context of the fight against terrorism).

- Use leading, controversial, cases which illustrate those dilemmas and which allow you to display your critical skills and to conclude on the central question.

TAKING THINGS FURTHER

- Clayton, G, *Textbook on Immigration and Asylum Law*, 5th edn (OUP 2014)
  A comprehensive and critical account of how this area is impacted by human rights law

- Harris, D, O'Boyle, K, Warbrick, C, and Bates, E, *The Law of the European Convention on Human Rights*, 4th edn (OUP 2018), ch. 6
  A comprehensive account of the principles and case law relating to article 3 and its application to various areas

- Foster, S, 'The Effective Supervision of European Prison Conditions' in F Ippolito and S Iglesias Sanchez (eds.), *Protecting Vulnerable Groups: The European Human Rights Framework* (Hart 2015), ch. 18
  An examination of the limited effectiveness of the European Court's case law in this area, together with other methods of protection

- Greer, S, 'Is the Prohibition against Torture, Cruel, Inhuman and Degrading Treatment Really "Absolute" in International Human Rights Law?' (2015) 15 (1) HRL Rev 101
  A critical examination of the absolute nature of article 3 and how that status has been upheld or compromised

Online Resources   www.oup.com/uk/qanda/

Go online for extra essay and problem questions, a glossary of key terms, online versions of all the answer plans and audio commentary on how selected ones were put together, and a range of podcasts which include advice on exam and coursework technique and advice for other assessment methods.

7 Due Process, Liberty and Security of the Person, and the Right to a Fair Trial

ARE YOU READY?

In order to attempt questions in this chapter, which covers various aspects of due process rights such as the right to liberty of the person and the right to a fair trial, you will need to have acquired a sound knowledge of the areas listed below during the course and your revision programme:

- A range of questions have been included to reflect the fact that different courses concentrate on different aspects of due process and articles 5–7 of the Convention: such as the values and scope of each article.
- The express and implied exceptions to the articles' application and how those rights can be compromised for the purposes of maintaining an effective justice system.
- The application of due process rights to specific groups such as prisoners and those suspected of involvement in terrorism.
- The relationship between due process rights and other rights contained in the Convention.

 ## KEY DEBATES

Due process rights are the subject of much case law from both the domestic and European courts with respect to the interpretation of their wording and limitations and restrictions; it is probably the most prolific area of the European Court's jurisprudence. This covers disputes concerning police powers of arrest and detention; the presumption of innocence; and the right of access to lawyers and legal aid.

Debate: Scope of Liberty

There is much legal and political debate surrounding the scope of the right to liberty—as opposed to freedom from movement—and its application to the control of demonstrations and the protection of those detained on mental health grounds. Case law over the last decade has attempted to reconcile the difference between the two with respect to police powers to hold sections of the

○

public ('kettling') when attempting to avoid a serious breach of the peace and this has often led to a conflict between domestic law and European jurisprudence (see *Hinks*).

Debate: Fair Trials, Legal Aid, and Use of Evidence

There is an ongoing and heated discussion surrounding the restriction on the availability of legal aid and its effect on justice as well as the use of secret and other evidence in criminal trials. Recent domestic decisions have successfully challenged government legislation which restricts legal aid and access to justice. This raises issues of Convention compatibility as well as wider constitutional issues of the separation of powers. In particular, you should be aware of the decision of the Supreme Court in *R (UNISON) v Lord Chancellor* [2017] UKSC 51 with respect to fees at employment tribunal hearings.

The use of secret and other (hearsay) evidence also concerns a conflict between the successful prosecution of crime and the preservation of the defendant's fair trial rights.

Debate: Fair Trials, Liberty, and Terrorism

The application of due process rights in the context of the fight against terrorism is another legal and political dilemma, with both politicians and the courts attempting to achieve a balance between liberty and justice and the fight against terrorism. Anti-terrorism measures often involve a compromise of due process rights and the rule of law in order to strengthen national security and public safety; and this encourages both academic criticism and strong public opinion.

QUESTION 1

What values and human rights principles does article 5 of the European Convention seek to uphold? How are those values reflected in the content of article 5 and the manner in which the courts have interpreted those rights and the various lawful interferences with liberty of the person?

CAUTION!

- This question requires a very sound overall knowledge of article 5, but the answer should concentrate on the *inherent values and human rights principles in article* 5 and how the courts have upheld those values when examining the legality of any interference with personal liberty.

- The question does not employ the phrase *critically examine*, but you should take a critical approach, particularly in the second part of the question, having understood the importance of the article in terms of due process, personal liberty, and the control of arbitrary state powers.

- The question refers to 'courts' so it is permissible to use cases from the European Court as well as domestic decisions; try to show the relationship between both sets of case law in examining whether the values have been upheld.

- Use cases which highlight controversial areas and which examine the dilemma faced by the courts in upholding the values of liberty.

- The answer should, where relevant, include reference to other articles of the Convention, such as article 6 (right to a fair trial) and article 8 (right to private life).

DIAGRAM ANSWER PLANS

> Analysis of the right to liberty and the aim of article 5, including the human rights values and principles evident from its wording

> Examination and explanation of the wording of article 5, its scope and application as applied by the judiciary

> Examination of the specific rights bestowed by article 5, together with relevant case law

> Examination of the restrictions imposed on liberty of the individual, together with the interpretation of such from the domestic and European courts

> Conclusions on how the courts have upheld the values of liberty and article 5

A **SUGGESTED ANSWER**

[1] The author immediately identifies the purpose and values of article 5, stressing the need for lawful interference.

Article 5 of the European Convention provides that everyone has the right to liberty and security of the person, providing freedom from arbitrary arrest and detention. Thus, although individuals may lose their liberty in prescribed circumstances, **article 5** will ensure that state power will be controlled by clear rules which will control unlawful and unreasonable intrusion into basic liberty (*Al-Jedda v United Kingdom* **(2011) 52 EHRR 23**).[1] **Article 5** thus gives precedence to liberty; placing the burden of proof on the state to justify any deprivation. Accordingly, in *Kurt v Turkey* **(1999) 27 EHRR 373** the European Court held that a state, having assumed control over an individual by taking him into detention, must account for the whereabouts of that person. Further, they must adopt effective measures to safeguard against the risk of disappearance and conduct a prompt and effective investigation into any claim of illegality. **Article 5** is complemented by other rights that are based on individual liberty and which control the power to intrude, such as the right to private life (*Gillan v United Kingdom* **(2010) 50 EHRR 45**).

[2] The author neatly illustrates the relationship between article 5 and other rights and distinguishes liberty from freedom of movement.

The right to liberty must be distinguished from freedom of movement (**article 2 of the Fourth Protocol:** *Guzzardi v Italy* **(1981) 3 EHRR 333**), although certain restrictions placed on an individual's movement can constitute a deprivation of liberty if they hamper the enjoyment of a normal life (*JJ v Secretary of State for the Home Department* **[2007] 3 WLR 642**).[2] In contrast the Court took a more pragmatic approach in *Austin v United Kingdom* **(2012) 55 EHRR 13** in finding that the temporary and necessary detention of bystanders during a violent protest was not a deprivation of liberty (see also *R (Hicks) v Commissioner of the Police of the Metropolis* **[2017] UKSC 9**). Conditions of detention do not normally engage **article 5** (*Ashindane v United Kingdom* **(1985) 7 EHRR 528**). However, in *Cheshire West and Chester Council v P* **[2014] UKSC 19** the Supreme Court held that it was appropriate for the courts to examine those conditions to see whether they involved a deprivation of liberty and whether any restraint on liberty was in the best interests of that person.[3]

[3] The author uses the recent dilemma about detention of the mentally unsound to illustrate the courts' role in defending liberty.

Under **article 5** all deprivations of liberty must be in accordance with a procedure prescribed by law and comply with the essential characteristics of the rule of law and principles of fairness and justice. For example, **article 5(1)(a)** provides for the lawful detention of a person after conviction by a competent court. By insisting that any detention is 'lawful' and that any detention be approved by a 'competent' court, the article ensures that the individual is protected by due process. Any conviction must have a sufficient basis in domestic law, and the relevant court must not interpret and apply the law in an arbitrary fashion (*Tsirlis and Koulompas v Greece* **(1998) 25 EHRR 198**). Further, there must be a sufficient connection between a court's finding of guilt and subsequent detention. This ensures that an individual is only in detention as a result of a judicial ruling, rather than at the discretion of the executive, although the executive may have a supervised role in detaining individuals (*Van Droogenbroek v Belgium* **(1982) 4 EHRR 443**).[4] Further, although **article 5** allows detention after the expiry of a fixed period of imprisonment within an indeterminate term (*Weeks v United Kingdom* **(1998) 10 EHRR 293**), there must be a causal connection between the sentence and the subsequent detention (*Stafford v United Kingdom* **(2002) 35 EHRR 32**).

[4] The author stresses the need for judicial involvement in detention cases, highlighting the illegality of certain executive involvement.

Article 5(1)(b) permits the arrest or detention of a person who has not complied with a court order when such arrest or detention is required for the fulfilment of an obligation that is prescribed by law. The European Court has ensured that the domestic court's decision to detain is not taken in an arbitrary fashion, and in *Beet and others v United Kingdom* **(2005) 41 EHRR 23** it was held that there had been a violation of **article 5** when poll tax defaulters were imprisoned after the magistrates had not properly considered whether the applicants were wilful defaulters.

Controlling the power of arrest is central to the values of individual liberty and although **article 5(1)(c)** allows for lawful arrest or detention, it must be for the purpose of bringing a person before a competent legal authority, either on *reasonable suspicion* of them having committed an offence or when it is necessary to prevent them committing one.[5] Any arrest must be for the purpose of enforcing the criminal law against that individual (*Ciulla v Italy* **(1991) 13 EHRR 346**), and the suspicion must be based on legitimate and objective grounds (*Fox, Campbell and Hartley v United Kingdom* **(1991)**

[5] The author deals with the vital area of police powers of arrest, including the interpretation of those powers in the context of terrorist crime.

13 EHRR 157). Reasonable suspicion presupposes the existence of facts that would satisfy an objective observer that the person might have committed the offence. However, a margin of discretion may be offered to the authorities, particularly in cases of suspected terrorism (*Ocalan v Turkey* **(2005) 41 EHRR 45**), although it has been held this should not undermine the essential safeguards provided by **article 5** (*O'Hara v United Kingdom* **(2002) 34 EHRR 32**). Further, in *Hicks*, the Supreme Court compromised this safeguard by allowing the police to use its holding powers to detain innocent individuals for the purpose of preserving the peace.

Article 5 allows the detention of those seeking to enter the country unlawfully. With respect to the detention of unlawful entrants, or those who are to be deported (**article 5(1)(f)**), an arrest or detention will be unlawful if the state authorities have acted in bad faith or have employed illegal means (*Boznao v Italy* **(1986) 9 EHRR 297**), the detention has been ordered for arbitrary reasons, or is excessive in length (*Quinn v France* **(1996) 21 EHRR 529**). However, the Court is prepared to take a flexible approach provided it is satisfied that a lengthy detention was necessary in the circumstances (*Chahal v United Kingdom* **(1997) 23 EHRR 413**).

Article 5 also provides specific rights to those who have been lawfully arrested or detained. For example, under **article 5(2)** everyone shall be informed properly of the reasons for an arrest and of any charge against him.[6] In *Fox, Campbell and Hartley v United Kingdom*, it was held that the full reasons for arrest need not be given immediately on or after arrest. In that case it was sufficient that they were arrested 'on suspicion of being terrorists' and then questioned about specific acts and allegations. Thus, the European Court is prepared to adopt a flexible approach in the context of terrorist offences, provided the essential values of **article 5** are adhered to. Further, **article 5(3)** provides that everyone arrested or detained shall be brought *promptly* before a judge or other officer authorised by law to exercise judicial power. That individual is then entitled either to a trial within a reasonable time, or to release pending trial. This does not prohibit pre-trial detention, provided there are sufficient safeguards against arbitrary or unnecessary loss of liberty. However, in *Caballero v United Kingdom* **(2000) 30 EHRR 643** it was held that automatic denial of bail pending trial was in violation of this right. This right has been robustly protected by both the domestic and European courts, even in the context of terrorism (*A v Secretary of State for the Home Department* **[2005] 2 AC 68**; *A v United Kingdom* **(2009)** *49 EHRR 29*).[7] Accordingly, in *Brogan v United Kingdom* **(1989) 11 EHRR 117** the Court held that the detention of suspected terrorists for periods between four-and-a-half and six days violated the notion of promptness laid down in **article 5(3)**. This ruling is, however, subject to a government's right

[6] The author uses article 5(2) to illustrate both the necessity of upholding the right to be informed of reasons for arrest and the flexible approach taken by the courts in this area.

[7] The author makes mention of the status of article 5 in the context of terrorism, critically examining the courts' role in that context.

of lawful derogation under **article 15** (*Brannigan and McBride v United Kingdom* **(1993) 17 EHRR 539**).

Article 5(4) provides that everyone deprived of their liberty by arrest or detention shall be entitled to take proceedings to test the lawfulness of that detention. This should be done speedily and a court should be able to order that person's release if it is found to be unlawful. This allows an individual to judicially review any detention to ensure that it is consistent with principles of due process. Although **article 5(4)** does not confer a right of appeal where the original detention is imposed by the court, it allows the individual to question the evidence upon which that individual has lost his liberty (*Chahal v United Kingdom* and *A v United Kingdom*).

In *Winterwerp v Netherlands* **(1979) 2 EHRR 387**, the Court stressed that a review must not be limited to the bare legality of the detention and, in *X v United Kingdom* **(1982) 4 EHRR 188**, it held that a review should be wide enough to bear on those conditions that are essential for the lawful detention of the individual. For example, a court must be allowed to ask whether the detention of a patient was still necessary in the interest of public safety. Full and meaningful judicial review has to be available and with respect to mandatory life-sentence prisoners the Court has held that the Home Secretary's role in setting the sentence was inconsistent with notions of the rule of law and the separation of powers (*Stafford v United Kingdom* **(2002) 35 EHRR 32**).

[8] The author merges the final point (about compensation) with the concluding remarks about article 5 and the courts' role in protecting its values.

Finally, **article 5(5)** provides that everyone who has been arrested or detained in breach of **article 5** shall have an enforceable right to compensation. This encapsulates the principle that where there is a right there should be a remedy,[8] and is of particular importance where the arrest or detention is lawful in domestic law, precluding the domestic courts from granting a remedy (*A v United Kingdom*). In conclusion, **article 5** enshrines fundamental values of liberty and the control of arbitrary state power. Any arrest or detention has to be prescribed by law, ensuring that a person only loses his liberty within laws that possess the essential qualities of law and of the rule of law. These principles have been robustly applied by the European Court, although it has been prepared to offer some flexibility in sensitive cases, such as the prevention of terrorism and the maintenance of public order.

LOOKING FOR EXTRA MARKS?

- Show that you understand the scope and values of article 5 and its general purpose—to protect an individual from *arbitrary* arrest and detention.

- Appreciate the dilemma facing the courts in interpreting the article's wording and maintaining its values when considering lawful interferences with liberty of the person; highlight where the courts have upheld or compromised the basic values of liberty and the control of arbitrary power.

- Use leading cases which illustrate those dilemmas and which allow you to employ your critical skills and conclude on the central question.

QUESTION | 2

To what extent have the courts allowed freedom from arbitrary arrest and detention to be lawfully compromised in the context of the fight against terrorism?

! CAUTION!

- This question requires a general knowledge of article 5 as it impacts on arrest and detention, but the answer should concentrate on the application of those rules and principles in the context of terrorist crime.

- The question does not use the phrase *critically examine*, but you should nevertheless take a critical approach to any relevant international and domestic law and case law.

- To offer that opinion you have to display an awareness of the importance of upholding these rights, together with an acceptance that those rights will need to be adjusted and compromised in this context: be careful to take an objective and reasoned view, considering all arguments.

- The answer should, where relevant, refer to relevant case law (domestic and European) to back up your arguments.

O DIAGRAM ANSWER PLANS

Definition of arbitrary arrest and detention and explanation of how article 5 of the European Convention safeguards against them

▼

Examination of relevant case law where article 5 rights can be compromised in cases of terrorism

▼

Specific examination of article 15 of the Convention allowing derogation in times of national emergency

▼

Explanation and critical examination of relevant domestic anti-terrorism provisions and case law

▼

Analysis of the above principles and any case law and legal reform so as to examine the extent to which terrorist threats can compromise such rights

[1] The answer begins by outlining the values of liberty and article 5 and then posing the question whether those values apply (to the same extent) in the terrorist context.

[2] The author deals first with the balance of liberty and safety in the non-emergency situation (before examining derogations later in the essay).

[3] The author examines how general powers of arrest and detention are interpreted in the terrorist context, examining the principles from the relevant case law.

The right to be free from arbitrary arrest and detention is at the heart of notions of liberty and the control of excessive government.[1] **Article 5** of the European Convention provides that everyone has the right to liberty and security of the person, and although this right can be compromised in a number of situations, that article ensures that any *prima facie* violation conforms to standards of procedural justice. However, does such a right and the restrictions on its interference apply (less stringently) in the context of the fight against terrorism; and should individual liberty take second place to national security and safety?

Outside formal derogations, the European Court has held that the state might be provided with a greater area of discretion when using its arrest and detention laws in the context of terrorism, provided the basic values of liberty are maintained.[2] **Article 5(1)(c)** allows for lawful arrest or detention on reasonable suspicion of having committed an offence, or when it is reasonably considered necessary to prevent the commission of such. This power must be exercised in good faith and for the purpose of bringing a person before the courts (*Ciulla v Italy* **(1991) 13 EHRR 346**).

These safeguards are particularly important in times of emergency, where the state may be tempted to abuse the power of arrest and detention for strategic purposes (*Ocalan v Turkey* **(2005) 41 EHRR 45**). Accordingly, the Court has insisted that suspicion for arrest is capable of being justified on legitimate and objective grounds.[3] Thus, in *Fox, Campbell and Hartley v United Kingdom* **(1990) 13 EHRR 157**, it held that in general the phrase 'reasonable suspicion' presupposes the existence of facts that would satisfy an objective observer that the person might have committed the offence. However, it added that what was reasonable would depend on all the circumstances of the case, and in respect of terrorist offences the test would differ from conventional crime. Nonetheless, the context of terrorism could not impair the essence of reasonableness; the state would need to furnish at least some information which could satisfy the Court that the arrested person was reasonably suspected of having committed the offence.

This 'compromise' was evident in *Murray v United Kingdom* **(1994) 19 EHRR 193**, where the Court accepted that due to the difficulties inherent in the investigation of terrorism the reasonableness of the suspicion could not always be judged according to the same standards that were applied in cases of conventional crime. Further, in *O'Hara v United Kingdom* **(2002) 34 EHRR 32** it noted that such a context gives the authorities a wide, *but not unlimited*, discretion and that the investigation of terrorist crime could not stretch the notion of reasonableness. Nevertheless, it approved the decision of the House of Lords in *O'Hara v Chief Constable of the RUC* **[1997] 1 All ER 129**, where it was accepted that a police constable could have a reasonable suspicion for arrest despite not being aware of all possible information.

Article **5(2)** provides that everyone arrested shall be informed properly of the reasons for his arrest, and of any charge against him. However, an individual need not be supplied with full information of the reasons for arrest at the actual time of that arrest, particularly in the terrorist context. Thus, in *Fox, Campbell and Hartley*, an interval of a few hours between the arrest and the provision of reasons did not violate **article 5(2)**. Further, the Court has accepted that merely telling the applicants that they were being arrested on suspicion of being terrorists was not sufficient to comply with **article 5**. However, the fact that they were questioned in relation to specific acts and allegations complied with the requirement that people should be informed promptly.

[4] The author deals with the important and controversial area of detention and *habeas corpus*, illustrating the Court's robust approach in this area.

The Court has shown less deference with respect to the requirement under **article 5(3)**—that everyone arrested or detained be brought promptly before a judge to exercise judicial power and to be entitled to trial within a reasonable time or to release.[4] In *Brogan*, the applicants had been arrested on suspicion of involvement in acts of terrorism and had been detained for periods between four-and-a-half and six days, eventually being released without charge. The Court concluded that even the shortest of the periods involved in this case was inconsistent with the notion of promptness laid down in **article 5(3)**. Such detention involved a serious weakening of the essence of the right. A similar breach was found in *O'Hara*, where the applicant had been held for six days and 13 hours before his eventual release. The right under **article 5(3)** is buttressed by the right under **article 5(5)** to be compensated for unlawful deprivation of liberty. This right is inevitably denied to the individual who has been subject to lawful, but excessive detention under domestic terrorism laws (*A v United Kingdom* **(2009) 49 EHRR 29**).

A state may also rely on **article 15** of the Convention, which allows it to derogate from its Convention obligations during times of war or other public emergency threatening the life of the nation.

[5] The author now moves on to formal derogations, outlining the scope of article 15 and the Court's initial approach in this area.

Although **article 15** only allows derogation measures that are strictly required by the exigencies of the situation, the European Court has been prepared to offer the state a certain margin of error in deciding what measures were required.[5] Thus, the Court's function was not to substitute the government's assessment of what might be the most prudent or most expedient policy to combat terrorism (*Lawless v Ireland* **(1961) 1 EHRR 15**).

A similar 'hands-off' approach was adopted in *Brannigan and McBride v United Kingdom* (1993) 17 EHRR 539, which challenged the UK's derogation in relation to **article 5(3)** following the European Court's decision in *Brogan v United Kingdom*. In *Brannigan,* the Court accepted the government's contention that there was an emergency situation. Accordingly, the derogation was not invalid merely because the government had decided to keep open the possibility of finding alternative means of complying with its Convention obligations. The Court was also satisfied that effective safeguards such as the availability of *habeas corpus* were available to the applicants.

[6] The author now assesses the very important case of A with respect to the Court's role in balancing human rights and the fight against terrorism.

However, a more dynamic approach has been adopted by the domestic courts. In *A v Secretary of State for the Home Department* [2005] 2 AC 68 the House of Lords held that the government's derogation of **article 5** of the Convention with respect to the power under the **Anti-terrorism, Crime and Security Act 2001**[6] were unlawful and incompatible with the UK's obligations under the European Convention. These powers allowed the detention of foreign terrorist suspects who could not be removed from the country because of the risk of ill-treatment at the receiving country and thus were *prima facie* in breach of article 5.

The majority accepted that there existed a public emergency threatening the life of the nation. They stressed that great weight should be attached to the judgement of the Home Secretary and Parliament because they had to exercise a pre-eminently political judgement (Lord Hoffmann dissented, believing that there was merely a threat of serious physical damage and loss of life). However, their Lordships held that the measures taken were not proportionate and strictly required by the exigencies of the situation. Lord Bingham noted that even in a terrorist situation the domestic courts were not precluded from scrutinising the relevant issues and deciding on the proportionality and necessity of emergency measures. These measures were disproportionate because they did not deal with the threat of terrorism from persons other than foreign nationals and permitted suspected foreign terrorists to carry on their activities in another country provided there was a safe country for them to go to. Further, in their Lordships' view, if the threat posed by UK nationals could be addressed without infringing the right to personal liberty, it had not been shown why similar measures could not adequately address the threat posed by foreign nationals. In the subsequent proceedings in Strasbourg (*A v United Kingdom*), the European Court refused to interfere with the House of Lords' assessment and also found that the provisions denied the applicants an effective remedy in challenging their detentions. This was because of the reliance on 'closed' evidence not made available to the detainees' lawyers. This decision was relied on by the House of Lords in *AF v Secretary of State for the Home Department* [2009] 3 WLR 74, in holding that controlees should be provided with a minimum amount of evidence in such proceedings.

The decisions in *A* suggest that the courts will be reluctant to interfere with political decisions of the government, such as whether to declare an emergency situation and put into place emergency provisions. However, it appears that they will not abandon its review role and will staunchly defend the fundamental values of individual liberty and the control of arbitrary detention.

[7] The author assesses the preceding case law and notes the impact it has had on government policy and legislation.

This approach has been continued by the domestic courts with respect to the legality of non-derogable control orders, introduced by the **Terrorism Act 2005** after the government's defeat in the House of Lords (*JJ v Secretary of State for the Home Department* [2007] 3 WLR 642[7] and *AP v Secretary of State for the Home Department*). This challenge resulted in the introduction into Parliament of the **Terrorism Prevention and Investigation Measures Act 2011**, which was supposedly compatible with articles 5 and 8.

In conclusion, both the European and domestic courts have insisted that the minimum standards laid down in **article 5** should not be unduly abandoned in the context of terrorism. Although the European Court has been prepared to compromise those standards in such a context, both in the interpretation of **article 5**, and under **article 15**, the decisions in *A* suggest that the courts will not offer an unlimited margin of error to the government and will stoutly defend liberty against any arbitrary interference.[8] Government has responded fairly swiftly to such decisions in an effort to ensure that legislation is compatible with **article 5**, although this may alter if the government were to repeal the **Human Rights Act** and replace it with a British Bill of Rights.

[8] The author concludes by offering a balanced view of the level of protection offered by the courts in this area, providing examples of that approach, and offering a pertinent and topical view of the future role of human rights law in this area.

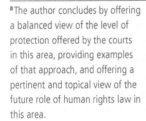

➕ LOOKING FOR EXTRA MARKS?

- Show that you understand the scope and character of article 5 and its underlying values and the importance of judicial protection of that right.

- Appreciate the dilemma facing the courts in maintaining article 5 and its values in the context of terrorist crime and threats, as well as the government's concerns and duties where national security and public safety are at issue.

- Use leading cases (and academic arguments) which illustrate those dilemmas and which allow you to employ your critical skills to conclude on the central question.

Q | **QUESTION** | **3**

'In the determination of his civil rights and obligations or of any criminal charge against him, everyone is entitled to a fair and public hearing within a reasonable time by an independent and impartial tribunal established by law'

(Article 6 of the European Convention).

What values does that article seek to uphold and in particular how has the European Court of Human Rights maintained those values in the interpretation of the following phrases:

'Criminal charge' and 'civil rights and obligations'

'Independent and impartial tribunal'

! CAUTION!

- This question requires a general knowledge of article 6 and its content, but the answer should concentrate on the *values* of article 6 (due process) and how the European Court has upheld those values with specific regard to the scope of article 6 and the concept of independence.

- The question does not employ the phrase *critically examine*, but to assess how the Court has upheld the values of article 6 you will need to take a critical approach.

- Choose cases which are controversial and which raise controversial issues about the scope of article 6 and the extent to which the courts have maintained its values.

- Although the question refers to cases from the *European Court*, it is acceptable to include complementary case law from the domestic courts in order to illustrate the scope and nature of the article.

DIAGRAM ANSWER PLANS

> Consideration of the general wording and scope of article 6, together with the values and principles embodied in it

⬇

> Consideration of the values and principles embodied in article 6, along with a brief overview of various procedural safeguards guaranteed by the article

⬇

> Analysis of the case law of the European Court on the respective terms, together with an assessment of those decisions *vis-à-vis* the values in article 6

⬇

> Critical conclusion as to the scope of article 6 and the interpretation of those respective terms

Introduction

Article 6 of the European Convention guarantees the right to a fair trial, ensuring what is commonly referred to as 'due process'. This article guarantees that legal rights are resolved within the law, and is regarded as fundamental to the values of a democratic society and to the principles inherent in the Convention.[1] **Article 6** mirrors the rules of natural justice, which have been applied in English domestic law (*Ridge v Baldwin* [1964] AC 40). These demand minimum standards of procedural fairness, such as the right to a hearing before an impartial and unbiased court or tribunal (*R v Bow Street Stipendiary Magistrate, ex parte Pinochet Ugarte (No. 2)* [2000] 1 AC 119), and access to the courts (*Chester v Bateson* [1920] KB 829).

Specifically, **article 6** guarantees the general right to a fair and public hearing within a reasonable time by an *independent and impartial tribunal* established by law. This ensures independence and objectivity and guarantees openness and public confidence in the justice system.[2] This right to speedy and effective justice requires the state to take measures to ensure that the courts provide reasonably prompt remedial action (*Robins v United Kingdom* (1997) 26 EHRR 527). **Article 6(2)** also upholds the presumption of innocence and liberty by providing that a person charged with a criminal offence shall be presumed innocent until proved guilty according to law (*Minelli v Switzerland* (1983) 5 EHRR 554). The Court has also recognised the right against self-incrimination (*Funke v France* (1993) 16 EHRR 297), stating that the right lies at the heart of the notion of a fair trial, having close links with the presumption of innocence contained in **article 6(2)** (*Saunders v United Kingdom* (1996) 23 EHRR 313). It has also accepted the qualified right of an accused to remain silent (*Condron v United Kingdom* (2001) 31 EHRR 1).

Article 6 allows the parties to participate effectively in the proceedings. Thus, in *V and T v United Kingdom* (2000) 30 EHRR 121, there had been a violation when two 11-year-old boys charged with murder had been subjected to an adult-like trial that made it almost impossible for them to comprehend the proceedings or to consult effectively with counsel. Equally, both parties have the right to access and to present relevant evidence to the court, enjoying this right equally with the opposing party (*Rowe and Davis v United Kingdom* (2000) 30 EHRR 1). The Court has also accepted the right to equality of arms, supplemented by the right to legal representation, guaranteed by **article 6(3) (c)** (*Steel and Morris v United Kingdom* (2005) 41 EHRR 22), and the right to examine witnesses, conferred under **article 6(3)(d)**.

Article 6(3) provides a number of specific due process rights which complement and strengthen the general right to a fair trial.

[1] The author provides a simple introduction to the purpose of article 6 and relates it to domestic rules on natural justice.

[2] The author highlights the requirement of an independent and impartial tribunal, before outlining the basic requirements of article 6 and due process.

For example, **article 6(3)(a)** provides that every person has the right to be informed promptly, in detail, and in a language which he understands, of the nature and cause of any accusation made against him (***Broziek v Italy* (1989) 12 EHRR 371**). Further, **article 6(3)(b)** provides the right to have adequate time and facilities for the preparation of one's defence, the extent of such a right depending on all the circumstances of the case, including the complexity of the charge (***Luedicke, Belkacem and Koc v Germany* (1978) 2 EHRR 149**). More specifically, **article 6(3)(c)** guarantees the right to defend oneself in person or through legal assistance of one's own choosing, and, in appropriate cases, confers the right to free legal assistance for the purpose of presenting legal arguments.[3] This provision upholds access to justice, although the Court has stressed that the right to legal representation is not absolute and depends on factors such as the seriousness of the charge (***Campbell and Fell v United Kingdom* (1984) *7 EHRR 165***). This provision also guarantees the right to have unimpeded legal assistance during detention and interrogation (***Brennan v United Kingdom* (2002) *34 EHRR 18***); although this was circumscribed recently in ***Ibrahim v United Kingdom* (Application No. 50541/08), European Court of Human Rights, 13 September 2016**, where it was held that the **Terrorism Act 2000** struck an appropriate balance between the importance of a suspect's right to legal advice and the need in exceptional cases to enable the police to obtain information necessary to protect the public.

Further, **article 6(3)(c)** provides that if a person has not sufficient means to pay for legal assistance he should be given it free if the interests of justice so require. **Article 6(1) and (3)(c)** are read together and there will be a violation of both provisions if a fair trial could not be conducted without free legal assistance (***Granger v United Kingdom* (1990) 12 EHRR 496**). Such rights allow the individual to effectively participate in the proceedings and **article 6(3)(e)** guarantees the right to have the free legal assistance of an interpreter if the individual cannot understand or speak the language used in court (***Cuscani v United Kingdom* (2003) 36 EHRR 1**).

Article 6 has been interpreted in a manner consistent with fundamental principles of access to, and the achievement of, justice. For example, the European Court has held that **article 6** contains an implied right of access to the courts and to legal advice (***Golder v United Kingdom* (1975) 1 EHRR 524**) and has held that the right to a fair trial includes the right to a fair sentence (***V and T v United Kingdom***).

'Criminal Charge' and 'Civil Rights and Obligations'

Article 6 applies only to proceedings where the applicant is either facing 'a criminal charge', or where 'civil rights and obligations' are subject to determination. The Court has taken a liberal approach in interpreting 'civil rights and obligations',[4] and in ***Ringeisen v Austria* (1991) 1**

[3] The author now deals with more specific provisions relating to access to justice and legal advice, stressing the importance of such to the general notion of a fair trial.

[4] The author now starts to examine the first specific aspect raised by the question—what is meant by civil obligations—employing clear case law to address that question.

EHRR 445 it held that it was not necessary that both parties to the proceedings were private individuals, provided the proceedings were to determine the private rights and obligations of the parties. Consequently, civil actions brought against public authorities would fall within the scope of **article 6**, provided the applicant's civil rights were at issue. Similarly, the fact that what is at issue is the determination of the applicant's statutory rights (to be free from discrimination), will not deny the claim the characteristic of a civil claim (*Tinnelly v United Kingdom* **(1998) 27 EHRR 249**). Proceedings are only excluded where they fail to impinge on the applicant's civil rights, for example where they are purely administrative (*Al-Fayed v United Kingdom* **(1994) 18 EHRR 393**).

The Court has adopted a similarly flexible approach in interpreting the phrase 'criminal charge'. In *Engel v Netherlands* **(1976) 1 EHRR 647** [5] it held that in determining whether a charge fell within **article 6**, it should address the following questions: whether the offence in question had been *classified* as criminal within the domestic legal system; the *nature* of the offence; and the *severity of the punishment*. The classification of the offence is not the decisive factor and the Court is more concerned with whether the charge itself, and the accompanying penalty, have the *characteristics* of a criminal offence.

The principles have been applied in the context of prison disciplinary proceedings, which are formally classified as disciplinary proceedings. For example, in *Campbell and Fell*, it held that prison disciplinary proceedings would amount to a criminal charge if the offence and the penalty were consistent with criminal proceedings. In that case, the applicants had been charged with very serious offences of mutiny and gross personal violence to a prison officer and had received over 500 days of loss of remission as a penalty. This protection was extended to less grave offences in *Ezeh and Connors v United Kingdom* **(2004) 39 EHRR 1**, and a similar rationale has been applied with respect to army discipline (*Findlay v United Kingdom* **(1997) 24 EHRR 221**).

'An Impartial Court or Tribunal'

A fundamental aspect of the right to a fair trial is the existence (and appearance) of an impartial court or tribunal. The Court has insisted that the judge or court is free from bias, or any reasonable appearance or fear of bias, irrespective of considerations of national security or convenience (*Ocalan v Turkey* **(2005) 41 EHRR 45**).[6] Thus, in *Findlay*, it was held that the body must present an appearance of independence and thus must be subjectively free of personal prejudice or bias and offer sufficient safeguards to exclude any legitimate doubt in this respect. In this case, the Court held that the close link between the convening officer and the members of the court and his sentencing powers amounted to a clear violation of **article 6**. Despite a number of legislative changes, the Court has found various violations of **article 6**, highlighting in particular the inadequate training of court officers (*Morris v United Kingdom* **(2002) 34 EHRR 52**) and the appointment of insufficiently independent personnel (*Grieves v United Kingdom* **(2004) 39 EHRR 2**). The Court has taken a similarly robust approach with respect to prison disciplinary proceedings that engage **article 6** (*Whitfield and others v United Kingdom* **(2005) 41 EHRR 44**). However, in *R (King) v Secretary of State for Justice* **[2010] EWHC 2522 (Admin)** the domestic courts held that prison disciplinary proceedings by the prison governor satisfied **article 6** because of the availability of judicial review.

[7]The author deals with the issue of constitutional bias and article 6 and relates the case law to a change in domestic law with respect to the role of the Lord Chancellor.

The principles of impartiality and independence have also been applied to judicial decisions taken by officers who have an interest or position in government.[7] For example, in *McGonnell v United Kingdom* **(2000) 30 EHRR 289** the Deputy Bailiff of Guernsey (a senior judge in the Royal Court, but also the President of the States of Election, of the States of Deliberation, and of the state legislative committees) had acted as the sole judge in the applicant's planning permission application. The Court held that there had been a clear violation of **article 6**. Specifically, it noted that any direct involvement in the passage of legislation or of executive rules was likely to be sufficient to question the judicial impartiality of someone who subsequently determined a dispute that raised matters of policy. This concern was reflected in the **Constitutional Reform Act 2005**, which reconsidered the constitutional role of the Lord Chancellor in the British constitution. However, the Convention does not prohibit all executive decision-making (*Pabla Ky v Finland* **(2006) 42 EHRR 34**). Thus, in *Bryan v United Kingdom* **(1996) 21 EHRR 342** it was held that, if the decision is sufficiently policy-based and was subject to appropriate judicial review of administrative action, the safeguards of **article 6** would be satisfied.

Despite the compromise allowed in cases such as *Bryan*, the Court has taken a consistently strict approach with respect to the requirements of impartiality and independence. Such an approach helps to uphold the central feature of the rule of law and general notions of justice. Equally, although the Court must only apply **article 6** to situations envisaged in the Convention it has avoided a dogmatic approach in this respect and extended **article 6** where justice requires it.[8]

[8]The author provides a neat summary of the points raised in the answer, highlighting the Court's robust but flexible approach to interpreting article 6.

LOOKING FOR EXTRA MARKS?

■ Show that you understand the scope and character of article 6 and its general values—to provide criminal and civil justice to individuals, to uphold the independence of the judiciary.

■ Appreciate the dilemma facing the Court in interpreting the article's scope and deciding whether particular proceedings are protected by it.

■ Use leading cases which illustrate those specific dilemmas and which allow you to employ your critical skills and conclude on the central question of whether the Court has upheld those values.

QUESTION | 4

With respect to cases brought against the UK under the European Convention on Human Rights, what conclusions can be drawn with regard to the compatibility of domestic law with the right to a fair trial under article 6 ECHR?

CAUTION!

- This question requires a general knowledge of article 6, but the answer should concentrate on cases brought against the UK before the European Court so as to draw conclusions regarding the compatibility of UK law with article 6.
- The question does not employ the phrase *critically examine*, but you should adopt a critical approach to the UK's approach to complying with article 6 and the European Court's examination of that law in line with Convention values.
- Although the question refers to cases from the *European Court*, it is acceptable to include complementary case law from the domestic courts in order to illustrate the compatibility of UK law in this area.
- The answer should highlight cases which have caused a conflict between UK law and ECHR law in the context of ongoing debates about the role and power of the European Court.

DIAGRAM ANSWER PLANS

Brief explanation of the purpose and content of article 6

⬇

Identification of central values within article 6 of the Convention and a critical examination of Convention case law with respect to alleged violations of article 6 brought against the United Kingdom

⬇

Analysis of the above cases to test the general compatibility of domestic law and practice with article 6 together with conflicts between UK and ECHR law

⬇

Conclusions on compatibility of UK law and conflicts between domestic and ECHR law

SUGGESTED ANSWER

[1] The author makes it clear that due process is protected both under the ECHR and in domestic law, which will then lead on to discussions of any conflict between the two.

Article 6 of the European Convention guarantees the right to a fair and public hearing before an independent and impartial tribunal, encapsulating notions of justice and equality underpinning both the Convention and domestic law.[1] Such a right has long been accepted in English law (since **Magna Carta 1215**) and is reflected specifically in the rules of natural justice (*Ridge v Baldwin* **[1964] AC 40** and *R v Bow Street Stipendiary Magistrate, ex parte Pinochet Ugarte (No. 2)* **[2000] 1 AC 119**).

Despite judicial recognition of this right as a constitutional fundamental, there have been many successful applications brought against the UK government alleging violations of the right to a fair trial. These cases have highlighted the friction between domestic and Convention law as to how to ensure compliance of **article 6** within a state's legal system and have concerned a number of specific areas of due process including the basic right of access to justice.[2] Thus, in *Golder v United Kingdom* **(1975) 1 EHRR 524**, the Court confirmed that **article 6(1)** contained an implied right of access to the courts and legal advice. In that case it held that there had been a violation of **article 6** when a prisoner had been refused permission to consult a solicitor with a view to bringing civil proceedings. The Court has also provided procedural protection to prisoners with respect to fairness at prison disciplinary proceedings (*Ezeh and Connors v United Kingdom* **(2004) 39 EHRR 1**). There the domestic courts had classified such proceedings as disciplinary and thus falling outside **article 6** (*R v Secretary of State for the Home Department, ex parte Greenfield* **[2002] 1 WLR 545**). The Court has also questioned domestic laws that preclude a party from bringing proceedings against public authorities. In *Osman v United Kingdom* **(2000) 29 EHRR 245** it held that the application of a blanket ban prohibiting civil actions against the police in negligence (*Hill v Chief Constable of West Yorkshire* **[1990] 1 WLR 946**) constituted a disproportionate restriction on the applicant's right to a fair trial under **article 6**. However, similar immunities have been upheld by the Court as part of the legitimate substantive law (*Z v United Kingdom* **(2002) 34 EHRR 3**).

Similarly, although the domestic rules of natural justice have protected the right to a fair trial free from bias and the *appearance* of bias (*R v Bow Street Stipendiary Magistrate, ex parte Pinochet Ugarte (No. 2)*), the government was found in violation of those principles in *McGonnell v United Kingdom* **(2000) 30 EHRR 289**.[3] In that case the Deputy Bailiff of Guernsey, who carried out roles in all three organs of government, acted as the sole judge in relation to a planning permission application and this was held in breach of **article 6**. The Court has taken a similarly robust approach in respect of the impartiality of courts martial (*Findlay v United Kingdom* **(1997) 24 EHRR 221**). These principles do not, however, preclude an executive officer from making a judicial decision, provided that such a decision is subject to sufficient judicial review (*Bryan v United Kingdom* **(1996) 21 EHRR 342**). This would appear to legalise many quasi-legal decision-making processes, and in *MB v Secretary of State for the Home Department* **[2006] 2 WLR 839** the Court of Appeal held that

[2] The author uses the issue of access to the courts to highlight the difference of approach in domestic law to due process that has led to applications to the European Court.

[3] The author adopts a similar approach with respect to due process and bias, highlighting the domestic law's inconsistency with the Convention's values.

control orders effected by the Home Secretary were not in breach of **article 6**. However, the European Court has made it clear that such procedures are subject to appropriate review by the courts and their ability to question the evidence (*A v United Kingdom* **(2009) 49 EHRR 29**).

[4] The author now provides a brief overview of cases on effective participation, highlighting the principles laid down by the European Court and cases where domestic law failed to comply.

Article 6 guarantees the right of effective participation, and in *V and T v United Kingdom* **(2000) 30 EHRR 121** it was held that there had been a violation when two 11-year-old boys, charged with murder, had been subjected to an adult-like trial.[4] Similarly, the Court has insisted that the parties to a dispute have the right to present and have access to all relevant evidence. For example, in *Rowe and Davis v United Kingdom* **(2000) 30 EHRR 1 article 6** had been violated when the domestic court had refused, on the grounds of public interest immunity, to order the disclosure of a document at the applicants' trial for murder. Exclusion of evidence on such grounds has been approved of in appropriate cases, provided its application does not interfere with the fundamental right to a fair trial (*Jasper and Fitt v United Kingdom* **(2000) 30 EHRR 411**).

[5] The author continues to examine cases where domestic law has failed to achieve a correct balance, but then includes cases where domestic law satisfied the European Court.

Such cases suggest that domestic law often fails to strike an appropriate balance between the individual's right to a fair trial and the successful prosecution of crime.[5] For example, **article 6(2)** states that everyone charged with a criminal offence shall be presumed innocent until proved guilty according to law (*Minelli v Switzerland* **(1983) 5 EHRR 554**) and that the accused should be protected from self-incrimination. However, in *Saunders v United Kingdom* **(1996) 23 EHRR 313** it held that the use by the prosecution at the applicant's trial of statements given under legal compulsion during a statutory investigation violated **article 6**. The Court has also examined cases concerning the domestic law's erosion of the right to silence. Thus, in *Condron v United Kingdom* **(2001) 31 EHRR 1** the Court found a violation of **article 6** when the trial judge had given a direction to the jury that might have left them at liberty to draw an adverse inference from the applicant's silence. However, in *Murray v United Kingdom* **(1996) 22 EHRR 29** the Court held that **article 6** did not prevent the applicant's silence from being taken into account in assessing the prosecution's evidence provided there are sufficient safeguards. Further, in *Ibrahim v United Kingdom* **(Application No. 50541/08),** *European Court of Human Rights, 13 September 2016*, it was held that the **Terrorism Act 2000** struck an appropriate balance between the importance of a suspect's right to legal advice and the need in exceptional cases to enable the police to obtain information necessary to protect the public. This shows the Court's flexible approach in the context of terrorism charges.

The Court has also taken a liberal approach to the use of unlawfully obtained evidence (*Schenk v Switzerland* **(1988) 13 EHRR 242**). Thus, in *Khan v United Kingdom* **(2001) 31 EHRR 45,** it was held that although evidence used against the applicant in his criminal trial had been obtained in violation of **article 8**, and the applicant's conviction was based solely on the use of that evidence, the admission of such evidence did not violate **article 6**. This was because the trial court had carefully assessed the evidence to see whether its inclusion had caused substantive unfairness.

[6] The author now deals with the controversial and topical issues of legal aid and access to legal advice and representation.

The Court has been particularly damning where the applicant has been denied legal representation and legal aid. **Article 6(3)** states that a person has the right to defend himself against any criminal charge and specifically the right to the legal assistance of a person of his own choosing.[6] This right is not absolute, but in *Benham v United Kingdom* **(1996) 29 EHRR 293**, **article 6** was violated when the applicant had not been provided with legal representation when charged with 'culpable neglect' in failing to pay his community charge. This was because the charge was not legally straightforward and the applicant's liberty was at stake. The Court has also found a violation with respect to the denial of pre-trial legal assistance (*Brennan v United Kingdom* **(2002) 34 EHRR 18**). However, in *Ibrahim v United Kingdom*, it was held that the **Terrorism Act 2000** struck an appropriate balance between the importance of a suspect's right to legal advice and the need in exceptional cases to enable the police to obtain information necessary to protect the public..

In addition, **article 6(3)** specifically provides that if a person has not sufficient means to pay for legal assistance he should be given it free when the interests of justice so require. This provision was violated in *Granger v United Kingdom* **(1990) 12 EHRR 496**, where a person of limited intelligence had been refused legal aid and the right to be provided with counsel at appeal. Further, in *Steel and Morris v United Kingdom* **(2005) 41 EHRR 22** it held that the inability of the applicants to obtain expert legal representation in a long and complicated libel case was in violation of their right to a fair trial.

[7] The author chooses to deal with two leading cases in order to highlight the friction between ECHR and domestic law.

The Court's supervisory role can often cause friction between the Convention's enforcement machinery and domestic law.[7] For example, in *Al-Khawaja and Tahery v United Kingdom* **(2009) 49 EHRR 1**, the Court found a violation of **article 6** when the domestic courts accepted hearsay and uncontested witness statements at the defendants' trial. The Supreme Court subsequently refused to follow that judgment pending the government's appeal to the Grand Chamber (*R v Horncastle* **[2010] 2 WLR 47**). The conflict was avoided when the Grand Chamber recognised the member states' right to take a flexible approach in this area so as to reflect notions of justice in that state (*Al-Khawaja and Tahery v United Kingdom* **(2012) 54 EHRR 23**), confirmed in *Horncastle v United Kingdom* **(2015) 60 EHRR 1**. In other cases, however, the Court has insisted on a strict application of **article 6**. Thus, in *Othman (Abu Qatada) v United Kingdom* **(2012) 55 EHRR 1**, there was a violation of **article 6** when the applicant faced a criminal trial in Jordan where there would have been a real risk of the admission of evidence that had been obtained by torture. In this case the Court disagreed with the UK House of Lords, which had held that there would be no flagrant denial of justice if such evidence been used (*R (Othman) v Secretary of State for the Home Department* [2010] 2 AC 110).

In conclusion, there have been many instances where the European Court has had to correct the domestic law's willingness to compromise due process rights. This has caused friction between the Convention and the domestic authorities and decisions such as *Othman* have fired proposals for possible reform of the Convention system and repeal of the **Human Rights Act 1998**.[8] On the other hand, there have been other cases where UK law has complied with the basic principles of **article 6** and where the Court has been prepared to allow an element of flexibility as to how those principles are upheld in practice.

[8] The Conclusion neatly summarises the general themes of the case law and makes reference to the topical issue of subsidiarity and the possible repeal of the Human Rights Act.

➕ LOOKING FOR EXTRA MARKS?

- Show that you understand the scope and values of article 6 and the basic requirements for its compliance.

- Appreciate the dilemmas facing the UK legal system in complying with article 6 whilst operating an effective criminal and civil justice system.

- Use leading cases to illustrate those dilemmas and the tensions which exist between domestic legal systems and the role and power of the European Court of Human Rights.

Ⓠ QUESTION | 5

Why is article 7 of the European Convention so fundamental to due process? By the use of case law critically examine how effectively that article has protected individuals from retrospective criminal law and sanctions.

❗ CAUTION!

- This question requires a general knowledge of due process as it is protected by articles 6 and 7 of the Convention, but the answer should concentrate on article 7 and its role in securing due process, justice, and the rule of law.

- The question is asking you to *critically examine* how the Court has protected individuals from retrospective criminal law and sanctions, so ensure you understand the meaning and danger of retrospective criminal law and comment critically on the court's record in this area.

- You can use case law from both the European Court and the domestic courts in order to illustrate the effectiveness of that protection.

- The answer should, where relevant, include reference to other articles of the Convention, such as articles 6 and 15 (derogation).

DIAGRAM ANSWER PLANS

> Explanation of the wording and scope of article 7 of the Convention

> Explanation of the democratic and constitutional values embodied in article 7 and its relationship with other articles in the Convention

> Critical examination of the case law of the European Court and Commission with respect to applications brought under article 7 and other articles

> Critical analysis and conclusions of the effectiveness of article 7 and the relevant case law in upholding the rule of law and the principles against retrospectivity

SUGGESTED ANSWER

[1] The author applies a clear but essential overview of the article's wording together with the values it upholds.

A fundamental aspect of the rule of law and the protection of individual liberty is that law should be prospective, as opposed to retrospective.[1] In other words, it should regulate the *future* conduct of the individual and should not be applied retrospectively to regulate conduct which at the time of commission was not regulated by clear law. This is particularly fundamental in relation to the criminal law, where an individual's liberty and other rights are subject to sanction by the law. Accordingly, **article 7** of the European Convention upholds the principle that there shall be no punishment without law by stating that no one shall be held guilty of any criminal offence on account of any act or omission which did not constitute a criminal offence under national or international law at the time when it was committed. Further, it guarantees that the law does not impose a heavier penalty than the one that was applicable at the time the criminal offence was committed.

[2] The article's fundamental nature is stressed by reference to its non-derogable status under article 15.

The European Court has stated that **article 7** occupies a prominent place in the Convention system of rights protection (***SW and CR v United Kingdom* (1995) 21 EHRR 404**). Accordingly, it should be noted that **article 15**,[2] which allows states to derogate from its obligations in times of war or other emergency, does not apply to **article 7**. Further, it has stated that the article not only prohibits retrospective application of criminal law to the accused's disadvantage, but also embodies the principle that only the law can define a crime and prescribe a penalty (***Kokkinakis v Greece* (1993) 17 EHRR 397**).

Article 7 only applies with respect to 'criminal offences'; the European Court applying the same test as it has in relation to **article 6** in determining whether a person is facing a criminal charge

[3] The author deals with the legal difficulty in determining its scope and refers to similarities in interpretation of other Convention articles.

(*Engel v Netherlands* (1976) 1 EHRR 647).[3] Consequently, the Court has not restricted the scope of the article to cases which are formally recognised as criminal within domestic law, and has used the same flexible test in interpreting the phrase 'penalty' (*Jamil v France* (1996) 21 EHRR 65). The concept 'penalty' was considered in *Welch v United Kingdom* (1995) 20 EHRR 247, where the applicant had been convicted of a number of drug offences and where, in addition to imposing a custodial sentence, the trial judge had imposed a confiscation order under the **Drug Trafficking Act 1986**. These measures had come into force after the applicant's arrest but before his conviction and the applicant argued that this violated **article 7**. The Court held that in determining whether there existed such a penalty it should take into account whether the measure was imposed following conviction for a criminal offence, the nature and purpose of the measure (including how it is characterised under domestic law), the procedures involved in making and implementing the provision, and its severity. Applying those criteria, it held that there was a strong indication of a regime of punishment and that taking into account a combination of punitive elements involved in the measure, the confiscation order was a penalty within **article 7**.

In *Welch*, the Court held that the confiscation proceedings were clearly retrospective as they were made in respect of offences committed before the statutory provision came into force. However, this decision was distinguished in *Taylor v United Kingdom* [1998] EHRLR 90, which again concerned the use of confiscation powers under the 1986 Act. The applicant had been found guilty of drug offences with respect to offences committed between 1974 and 1979, and was subsequently convicted of similar offences committed between 1990 and 1993. At his subsequent trial the judge made a confiscation order in respect of all offences and the applicant argued that this contravened **article 7**. The European Commission declared his case inadmissible, finding that the penalties imposed on him in the proceedings were essentially for the later offences. Further, the applicant must have been aware that at the time of committing the later offences he was liable to a confiscation order covering the earlier proceeds, as the 1986 Act was then in force.

[4] The author critically analyses the courts' approach in certain cases where it could be argued that they have compromised article 7's values.

The decision in *Taylor* illustrates the danger of a restrictive interpretation of **article 7** and this concern is evident in the House of Lords' decision in *R (Uttley) v Secretary of State for the Home Department* [2004] 1 WLR 2278.[4] The case concerned the power of the domestic courts (under the **Criminal Justice Act 1991**) to impose licences on certain prisoners in addition to their fixed sentence, which it was alleged were incompatible with **article 7**. The Court of Appeal held that the imposition of a one-year licence on a prisoner who had served a 12-year sentence for rape and sexual assault was retrospective because the licence applied with respect to acts committed before the Act came into force. He had, therefore, been subjected to a heavier penalty within **article 7**. The Court of Appeal decision was then overturned by the House of Lords, who held that **article 7** referred to the maximum penalty prescribed by law for the offence in question at the time when it was committed, which in the prisoner's case was life imprisonment. In their Lordships' views **article 7** did not refer to the penalty that would *probably* have been imposed on a particular offender at the time. These decisions, it is argued, are based on semantics and ignore the true spirit of **article 7**. Similarly, in *R v Bowker* **[2007] EWCA Crim 1608**, the Court of Appeal held that it was not in violation of **article 7** to subject a defendant to a harsher penal regime than the one existing at the time of the offence, provided the law itself had not been changed.

A fundamental principle of **article 7** is that a person should foresee the consequences of his action. This principle is threatened when the law is uncertain and thus subject to novel interpretation and application by the courts. This situation would clearly offend against the principle of retrospectivity unless the new interpretation was the result of the natural and foreseeable development of a specific legal rule.[5] The European Court faced this problem in the famous case of *SW and CR v United Kingdom*, concerning the criminalisation of marital rape. The applicants had been found guilty of the rape of their wives as a result of a decision of the domestic courts that a husband could no longer rely on the traditional principle of marital immunity (*R v R* **[1991] 4 All ER 481**). They argued that this decision violated **article 7** as they had in effect been convicted of conduct that at the time of commission did not constitute a criminal offence. The Court held that **article 7** will not be violated if the constituent elements of an offence are not essentially changed to the detriment of the accused, and where the progressive development of the relevant legal rule is reasonably foreseeable. In the present case the Court found that the traditional immunity granted to husbands had been eroded by a steady number of case authorities. Thus, the decision in *R v R* had merely followed that pattern of cases. Consequently, as those cases had been well documented, the Court held that it was inconceivable that either applicant believed that the course of action he embarked upon was lawful.

Further, it held that the abandonment of the unacceptable idea of a husband being immune against prosecution for rape of his wife could not be said to be at variance with **article 7**.[6] In the Court's view, that was in conformity with the fundamental objectives of the Convention, based on the respect for human dignity and human freedom, and of the civilised concept of marriage. Accordingly, the protection afforded by **article 7** does not extend to conduct that violates the fundamental notions underlying the Convention. This is reflected in the second paragraph of the article, which does not provide protection for conduct that is criminal according to the general principles of law recognised by civil nations. This would apply to acts such as torture and genocide, and would appear to ensure the compatibility of legislation such as the **War Crimes Act 1991** with **article 7** (*Kononov v Latvia* (2010) **29 BHRC 137**), provided the law is sufficiently clear (*Korbelly v Hungary* (2010) **50 EHRR 48**).

[7] The author outlines the reasons for the Court's inevitable pragmatic approach with respect to the requirement of clarity in the law.

The decision in *SW and CR* accepts that the law will invariably be subject to interpretation and application to new cases, and that although this may act to the detriment of the accused, such an interpretation will not necessarily offend **article 7** and the principles of legal certainty.[7] Thus, in *Gay News v United Kingdom* (1983) **5 EHRR 123**, the European Commission confirmed that the domestic courts must not create new, retroactive criminal offences, or extend existing offences to encompass conduct which was lawful at the time of its commission. However, it was not in violation of **article 7** for the courts to clarify the requirements of an established offence. In that case the applicant's conviction for blasphemy had been upheld when the House of Lords had confirmed that liability for the offence was strict and did not rely on the intent of the author. In rejecting his application as inadmissible, the Commission held that the decision did not amount to the creation of new law. Rather, the House of Lords had clarified the law, and the applicants could have foreseen such an interpretation with appropriate legal advice.

In conclusion, **article 7** seeks to protect the most fundamental aspect of criminal justice by prohibiting retrospective law and penalties. This provision is strengthened by other Convention articles, which, along with **article 7**, ensure that any interference with a person's liberty and rights complies with the rule of law. However, the European Court has been prepared on occasions to take a pragmatic approach to the interpretation of these articles, which, it is suggested, has compromised the absolute character of these rights.[8]

[8] The Conclusion neatly summarises the importance of article 7 and the Court's robust, yet at times pragmatic approach to its application.

 LOOKING FOR EXTRA MARKS?

- Show that you understand the scope and character of article 7 and its general purpose—to uphold the rule of law and to ensure prospective and clear criminal law and liability.

- Appreciate the dilemma facing the courts in interpreting the article's wording and application and highlight where the courts have had to take a pragmatic approach.

- Use leading cases which illustrate those dilemmas and which allow you to employ your critical skills and conclude on the central question about the courts' success in upholding article 7 and it values.

TAKING THINGS FURTHER

- Emmerson, B, and Ashworth, A, *Human Rights and Criminal Justice*, 3rd edn (Sweet and Maxwell 2012), Part 2

  A specialist examination of the impact of human rights law on the criminal justice system

- Fenwick, H, 'Redefining the Role of TPIMs in Combatting "Home-Grown" Terrorism within the Widening Counter-terror Framework' [2015] 1 EHRLR 41

  A critical examination of TPIMs and their impact on human rights and the fight against terrorism

- Harris, DJ, O'Boyle, M, Warbrick, C, and Bates, E, *The Law of the European Convention on Human Rights*, 4th edn (OUP 2018), chs. 8, 9, and 10

  A comprehensive examination of the Convention's due process principles and their application to liberty and fair trials

- Mowbray, A, *Cases and Materials on the European Convention on Human Rights*, 3rd edn (OUP 2012), chs. 7, 8, and 9

  A thorough coverage of relevant European Court decisions relating to articles 5 and 6

- Salvert, J, 'Deprivation of Liberty and Persons with Incapacity: The Cheshire West Ruling' (2015) 19(1) Edin LR 129

  An analysis of the Cheshire case in terms of its impact on the meaning and scope of liberty

Online Resources   www.oup.com/uk/qanda/

Go online for extra essay and problem questions, a glossary of key terms, online versions of all the answer plans and audio commentary on how selected ones were put together, and a range of podcasts which include advice on exam and coursework technique and advice for other assessment methods.

8 Prisoners' Rights

ARE YOU READY?

In order to attempt questions in this chapter, which covers various aspects of the rights of incarcerated prisoners, you will need to have acquired a sound knowledge of the areas listed below during the course and your revision programme:

- A range of questions have been included to reflect the fact that different courses concentrate on different aspects of prisoners' rights, including the remedies available to prisoners and specific areas such as prison conditions and the right to vote, and to examine the jurisprudence of both the domestic courts and the European Court of Human Rights.
- The civil, public, and human rights' remedies available to prisoners in both domestic and European law.
- The availability and application of human rights law to specific areas such as prison conditions, prison discipline, prisoners' free speech and the right to vote, release from prison, and the right to private and family life.
- The political and constitutional dilemmas involved in the enforcement and restriction of prisoners' rights at both the national and European level.

KEY DEBATES

Prisoners' rights are the subject of much case law from both the domestic and European courts as well as great political debate; in particular the issue of the prisoner's right to vote has caused great political and diplomatic controversy. Thus, whilst politicians and the public often feel that prisoners should either not have rights, or should have them curtailed at the discretion of the government, civil libertarians feel that the rights of prisoners are essential for upholding the rule of law, and respecting the dignity and civil status of prisoners (and their families) in accordance with international standards. It is in this context that the courts—both domestic and European— have to resolve issues such as: whether prisoners have the right to vote; to what extent prisoners should continue to enjoy family and private life; and whether prison discipline should be subject to the requirements of a fair trial. Students need to appreciate these debates before analysing the substantive case law in this area.

Debate: Status of Prisoners' Rights

The extent to which incarcerated prisoners enjoy their legal and human rights, and the extent to which they can be restricted on grounds of their prisoner status and public order and safety, continues to attract legal actions, both in the domestic courts and before the European Court of Human Rights. Prisoners' rights have also been related to proposals for the repeal of the Human Rights Act 1998 and the curtailment of individual rights at the expense of social interests such as public safety. Thus, there is often a fierce debate as to whether prisoners should be exempt from some of the protection of the HRA, including the idea that a Bill of Rights and Responsibilities should involve the restriction of prisoners' and other criminals' rights with respect to family and private life, free speech and the right to vote, and their treatment in prison.

Debate: Prisoners and the Right to Vote

In particular, the prisoners' right to vote saga continues to attract judicial and political comment with the government refusing to alter the law. In addition, the area is affected by EU law and decisions of the ECJ. The European Court has been involved in a long battle with the UK Parliament with respect to the current ban on prisoner voting (*Hirst v UK (No. 2)*), and this has affected the approach taken by the domestic courts (*Chester*). The matter has now become a political one and any proposals for reform in this area will involve a conflict between public and political opinion and the need to comply with international human rights standards.

Debate: Whole Life Sentences and Prisoners' Rights

Cases concerning the sentencing and release of prisoners, including the imposition of whole life sentences and the possible review of such sentences, have caused great legal and political discussion and a conflict between European and domestic law. In particular, should domestic law be able to retain the concept of the whole life sentence (where the prisoner will die in prison), or does human rights law demand that there should be some possibility of review and release? The domestic and European judges have initially disagreed on this issues (*Vinter*), but eventually compromised (*Hutchinson*).

QUESTION 1

Critically examine the extent to which prisoners' rights have been protected by the domestic courts. By the use of case law explain how their protection has been enhanced in the post-Human Rights Act era.

CAUTION!

- This question requires a very sound overall knowledge of prisoners' rights, but the answer should concentrate on a *critical examination* of how they have been protected in domestic law, both before and after the passing of the Human Rights Act.

- The question employs the phrase *critical examination*, so you should take a critical approach having understood the importance of prisoners' rights and the controversies inherent in their recognition and enforcement; see the Key Debates section for guidance on the context of critical analysis.

- The question refers to protection in domestic law, but it is permissible to use cases from the European Court as well as domestic decisions in order to examine how such decisions have impacted on the domestic courts' case law and have led to any legislative changes.

- Use cases—from both eras—which examine the legal and constitutional dilemmas faced by the courts in upholding prisoners' rights and which allow you to assess the courts' performance in this area.

DIAGRAM ANSWER PLANS

> The definition and scope of, and justification for prisoners' rights

> Examples of prisoners' rights, using relevant European Convention and Human Rights Act provisions

> Critical account of the methods of enforcement in domestic law via actions in public and private law

> Critical examination of pre-Act efforts to recognise and protect prisoners' rights

> Examination of relevant case law under the Human Rights Act in comparison to pre-Act, including any relevant legislative changes as evidence of any enhanced protection of such rights

A   SUGGESTED ANSWER

[1] The author begins by defining prisoners' rights, providing examples of claims.

Prisoners' rights may refer to the prisoners' civil and political rights, such as the right to life and private and family life, which should be retained despite incarceration, save the inevitable interference with freedom of movement and personal liberty.[1] This claim is supported by both the European Court (*Golder v United Kingdom* (1975) 1 EHRR 524), and by the statement of Lord Wilberforce in *Raymond v Honey* [1983] AC 1 that a prisoner retains all basic rights save those which are taken away either expressly or by necessary implication. In addition, prisoners may claim basic human needs, such as the right to decent food, clothing, and accommodation in prison. This is because the state has a duty to protect the prisoners' dignity by providing those resources. Whatever the nature of prisoners' rights, they are justified on grounds such as the inherent dignity of the individual and the rule of law, requiring the prison authorities to be legally accountable for misuse of their powers.

[2] The author then begins to examine the traditional methods of protecting prisoners' rights, beginning with the availability of civil claims, before moving on to public law remedies.

Domestically, in the absence of a bill of rights and any clear and comprehensive system of statutory protection, such rights have principally fallen to be protected by the courts.[2] First, a number of private law actions are available to prisoners and, in *Ellis v Home Office* **[1953] 2 QB 135**, it was accepted that the prison authorities owed prisoners a duty to take reasonable care for their safety. It is also possible for the prisoner to sue in the tort of assault (*Rodrigues v Home Office* **[1989] Legal Action 14**) and misfeasance in a public office (*Racz v Home Office* **[1984] 2 AC 45**). However, in *R v Deputy Governor of Parkhurst Prison, ex parte Hague* **[1992] AC 58**, the House of Lords held that the fact of imprisonment precluded the prisoner from suing in the torts of false imprisonment and breach of statutory duty.

The prisoner is also allowed to bring proceedings in public law (judicial review) to ensure that the prison authorities act within their legal powers. Although early case law seemed to suggest that the decisions of such bodies were not reviewable (*Becker v Home Office* **[1972] 2 QB 407**), in *ex parte Hague* it was accepted that, at least in theory, all prison decisions affecting prisoners were reviewable.

Using judicial review, the courts have declared a variety of practices and policies *ultra vires*, often on the basis that the rule or decision was contrary to the prisoner's fundamental rights. For example, in *Raymond v Honey* a rule that stopped a prisoner from taking legal action until he or she had exhausted the internal procedures was declared *ultra vires* the **Prison Act 1952**. This was because the rule-making powers in the Act did not envisage a policy that interfered with the prisoner's right of access to the courts. This decision was influenced by the case law of the European Court of Human Rights (*Golder v United Kingdom*) and, in subsequent cases, rules which interfered with the prisoner's right of access to legal advice and access to the courts were declared void (*R v Secretary of State for the Home Department, ex parte Leech* **[1994] QB 198**). These powers continue to be used

[3] The author displays an awareness of how public law remedies can still be used in the post-Act era, using a very recent Supreme Court decision.

in the post-Human Rights Act era[3] and in *R (Bourgass) v Secretary of State for Justice* **[2015] UKSC 54** the Supreme Court declared unlawful the segregation of two prisoners by the prison's operational manager without the authority of the Secretary of State; see also *Shahid v Scottish Ministers* **[2015] UKSC 58**.

[4] The author now critically analyses the use of public law remedies in this area.

Judicial review has also been employed to protect the rights of prisoners with respect to release and recall and executive sentencing.[4] For example, in *R v Secretary of State for the Home Department, ex parte Venables and Thompson* **[1997] 3 All ER 97**, the House of Lords held that the Home Secretary could not take into account public opinion in setting the minimum term for two boys found guilty of murder. Again, in *R v Secretary of State for the Home Department,* *ex parte O'Brien and Simms* **[2000] 2 AC 115,** the House of Lords struck down a policy which stopped direct contact between journalists and prisoners on the basis that it interfered with the prisoners' right to use journalists to expose a possible miscarriage of justice. However, they were not allowed to use such principles or case law directly and, in *R v Secretary of State for the Home Department, ex parte Mellor* **[2002] QB 13,** a decision of the Home Secretary to refuse a prisoner's request to artificially inseminate his wife was upheld. That policy was later being declared disproportionate by the European Court (*Dickson v United Kingdom* **(2008) 46 EHRR 41**).

The passing of the **Human Rights Act 1998** made Convention rights enforceable in domestic courts and a prisoner may (under **s.7**) bring a direct action against the prison authorities (a public authority under **s.6**) claiming that Convention rights have been violated.[5] The prisoner can rely on Convention principles, such as proportionality and legality, and prisoners will also be entitled (under **s.8**) to 'just satisfaction' if the court decides that his or her Convention rights have been violated. In addition, the prisoner may use the Convention and its case law to strengthen their claim in private law (*Russell, McNamee and McCotter v Home Office*, **The Daily Telegraph, 13 March 2001**). **Articles 2 and 3** of the Convention will also be relevant in determining negligence claims brought by prisoners (*Orange v Chief Constable of West Yorkshire* **[2001] 3 WLR 736**).

There is some evidence that prisoners' rights have been enhanced by the Act.[6] In *R (Daly) v Secretary of State for the Home Department* **[2001] 2 AC 532** Lord Steyn noted that the doctrine of proportionality called for a much more intensive review on behalf of the courts. Thus, any interference with Convention rights had to be necessary and be proportionate to any legitimate aim. For example, in *R v Secretary of State for the Home Department, ex parte P and Q* **[2001] 3 WLR 2002,** a blanket policy which meant that female prisoners were separated from their babies after 18 months was declared unlawful as it gave too little weight to the mother's right to private and family life under **article 8** of the Convention. This should ensure that a proper balance is achieved and that prisoners' rights will not be so easily compromised on the grounds of prison discipline and public policy (as in *Mellor*).

The Act should also ensure that prisoners' rights are not violated purely on the grounds of incarceration.[7] In *O'Brien and Simms*, the House of Lords held that prisoners could not expect to enjoy the general right to freedom of expression. However, post-Act case law suggests that any interference with a prisoner's Convention rights needs to be justified solely on the grounds permitted by the Convention itself. For example, in *R (Hirst) v Secretary of State for the Home Department* **[2002] 1 WLR 2929**, it was held that a blanket policy forbidding prisoners from directly accessing the media was

[5] The author provides a clear account of how the 1998 Act operates in practice so as to enhance the rights of prisoners, before examining the relevant post-Act case law.

[6] The author now provides some case law evidence of how prisoners' claims are strengthened under the Act.

[7] The author now deals with the complex issues of implied restrictions on prisoners' rights, giving case examples of the courts rejecting, and then accepting, that concept.

disproportionate to the aim of achieving good order and discipline in prisons. This approach was also adopted in *R (BBC and others) v Secretary of State for Justice* **[2012] EWHC 13 (QB)**, where it was held that the refusal to allow the BBC to conduct a face-to-face interview with a prisoner awaiting deportation to face terrorist charges constituted a disproportionate interference with the prisoner's freedom of expression.

On the other hand, in *R (Nilsen) v Secretary of State for Home Affairs* **[2005] 1 WLR 1028** the Court of Appeal held that the prison authorities could take into account factors beyond prison order and discipline in deciding to restrict the claimant's right to freedom of expression. Equally, in *Hirst v Attorney-General*, *The Times*, 17 April 2001 the domestic courts referred to public policy arguments in deciding that the disenfranchisement of prisoners was not contrary to **article 3 of the First Protocol** of the European Convention, a decision overturned by the European Court in subsequent proceedings (*Hirst v United Kingdom (No. 2)* **(2004) 38 EHRR 40**). These domestic decisions appear to go against the principles laid down in cases such as *Golder* and *Raymond v Honey*. Further, the domestic courts' inability to overrule express primary legislation has left prisoners denied the right to vote without a remedy in domestic law (*R (Chester) v Secretary of State for Justice* **[2013] UKSC 63**).

With respect to prison conditions, the lack of any statutory protection in this area made it difficult for prisoners to challenge the legality of the conditions of incarceration. Now prisoners can rely directly on **article 3** of the Convention, which prohibits inhuman and degrading treatment, and the increasing case law of the European Court in this area[8] (*Peers v Greece* **(2001) 33 EHRR 51**). Thus, in *Napier v Scottish Ministers*, *The Times*, 13 May 2004 the Scottish Courts awarded damages to a remand prisoner who had been subjected to the harshness of prison conditions, including the regime of 'slopping out'. However, in *R (Gleaves) v Secretary of State for the Home Department* **[2011] EWHC 3379 QB** it was held that such practice was not automatically contrary to **article 3**.

In conclusion, the **Human Rights Act 1998** provides a more formal mechanism by which prisoners can vindicate their civil and political rights and prisoners can still rely on the principles of administrative justice and their civil law claims.[9] This enhanced judicial enforcement should also raise the public and political profile of such rights, perhaps persuading Parliament to recognise such rights. However, as *Nilsen* suggests, there is still some evidence of judicial reluctance in this area, which has not been affected by the Act's implementation. Further, Parliament had, until recently, refused to respond to the European Court's ruling in *Hirst* with respect to prisoner enfranchisement.

[8] The author uses the area of prison conditions to illustrate the courts' efforts to uphold prisoners' rights, highlighting the use by them of European Court case law.

[9] The Conclusion summarises the points made in the essay and in particular gives an overall impression of the successes and limitations of judicial protection.

LOOKING FOR EXTRA MARKS?

▨ Show that you understand the scope and importance of prisoners' rights and the reasons why they may have to be restricted.

▨ Appreciate the legal and constitutional dilemmas facing the courts in enforcing such rights, together with the political arguments created by certain claims (the right to vote, whole life sentences).

▨ Use leading and topical cases which illustrate those dilemmas and which allow you to employ your critical skills and conclude on the central questions.

QUESTION | 2

With particular reference to cases brought against the UK, critically examine how successful the European Court of Human Rights has been in protecting prisoners' rights.

CAUTION!

▨ This question requires a very sound overall knowledge of prisoners' rights cases decided by the European Court, but the answer should concentrate on a critical examination of cases brought against the UK.

▨ The question asks you to *critically examine* the European Court's jurisprudence, so you need to be aware of the standards expected by international and European human rights law and of any dilemmas involved in recognising and upholding those rights. See the Key Debates section for guidance.

▨ The question refers, specifically, to cases brought against the UK, so ensure that you highlight the impact of such cases on UK prison law and practice. However, you can refer to other cases that establish relevant principles and standards in this area.

▨ Use cases which highlight controversial areas—such as those affecting prison conditions, release of prisoners, and the very topical area of prisoner voting rights.

DIAGRAM ANSWER PLANS

> The definition of prisoners' rights and a brief consideration of the Convention rights relevant to prisoners

▼

> Case law demonstrating the areas of prisoners' rights that have been upheld by the European Convention machinery

▼

The effectiveness of the Court in upholding those rights in specific areas, including any relevant changes to domestic law and practice resulting from the Convention case law

▼

Identification of areas where the Convention machinery has been unsuccessful in protecting prisoners' rights

SUGGESTED ANSWER

Prisoners have used the European Convention to protect a wide range of human rights, including the right to life, freedom from torture and inhuman and degrading treatment and punishment, liberty and security of the person, the right to private and family life, and the right to vote. Many of these cases have been successful and have resulted in changes to domestic law and practice in areas such as prisoners' correspondence (*Silver v United Kingdom* (1983) 5 EHRR 347), the right to marry (*Hamer v United Kingdom* (1982) 4 EHRR 139), and the right of access to lawyers and the courts (*Golder v United Kingdom* (1975) 1 EHRR 524).

[1] The author explains the position of the European Court with respect to prisoners' rights under the ECHR; that there is no room for the implied exclusion of such rights.

The European Court has stated that prisoners retain their basic rights despite incarceration and have insisted that any restriction on the prisoner's Convention rights must be justified within the terms of the Convention.[1] For example, in *Golder* the Court stressed that there were no implied restrictions on the prisoner's right to correspondence under **article 8** of the Convention. Thus, any interference with the right has to be in accordance with law and necessary in a democratic society. This approach is taken in respect of other rights, such as freedom of expression (*Bamber v United Kingdom, Application No. 33742/96*), the right to vote (*Hirst v United Kingdom (No. 2)* (2004) 38 EHRR 40; *MT and Greens v United Kingdom, The Times*, 24 November 2010), and the enjoyment of private life (*Silver v United Kingdom*). However, the Court has recognised that the enjoyment of these rights may have to be compromised by reasonable prison regulations (*Boyle and Rice v United Kingdom* (1988) 10 EHRR 425). This general stance was also employed by the Grand Chamber in *Dickson v United Kingdom* (2008) 46 EHRR 41, where it was held that it was permissible for the authorities to take into account public confidence in the penal system in placing restrictions on the prisoner's right to family and private life. However, it insisted that before such rights are interfered with the authorities and the courts must adopt a suitable balance between the prisoner's right and the competing public interests.

[2] The author deals with the Court's success in guaranteeing prisoners access to the courts and to legal and other correspondence rights.

[3] The Court's decisions with respect to release and recall are explored, including the recent decision on the compatibility of whole life sentences with article 3.

With respect to the right of access to the courts and the protection of legal correspondence, in *Golder* the Court held that preventing a prisoner from writing to a solicitor in order to bring a civil action against a prison officer was a disproportionate interference with the prisoner's right of correspondence and access to the courts.[2] This was followed in *Silver v United Kingdom* and *Campbell v United Kingdom* (1992) 15 EHRR 137, where the Court held that any interference with the prisoner's right of correspondence with his lawyer had to be justified by a pressing social need, such as the need to ensure that such correspondence was genuine and not a threat to prison security. The Court has also upheld the prisoner's right of medical correspondence (*Szuluk v United Kingdom*, *The Times*, 17 June 2009) and of general correspondence (*Silver v United Kingdom*), insisting that any restrictions on prisoner's correspondence should be measured by clear and regular law rather than executive or judicial discretion (*Domenichini v Italy* (2001) 32 EHRR 4).

Prisoners have employed **article 5** of the Convention in challenging a number of rules regarding their release at the discretion of administrative officials.[3] In *Thynne, Wilson and Gunnell v United Kingdom* (1990) 13 EHRR 666 the Court held that there had been a violation of **article 5(4)** of the Convention—which guarantees the right to challenge the lawfulness of one's continued detention. In this case, three discretionary life-sentence prisoners had been denied release by the Home Secretary on the grounds that he still felt them to be a risk to the public. The Court held that once the punitive period of the sentence was complete the prisoners had the right for their continued detention to be determined by a court-like body, which should have the power to order, rather than recommend, release. This principle was upheld in the context of young offenders detained at Her Majesty's Pleasure in *Hussain and Singh v United Kingdom* (1996) 21 EHRR 1 and *V and T v United Kingdom* (2000) 30 EHRR 121, and in respect to mandatory sentences for murder in *Stafford v United Kingdom* (2002) 35 EHRR 32. Thus, in *Stafford*, the Court found that the power of the Home Secretary was inconsistent with the notion of the separation of powers and thus in violation of **article 5**. The Grand Chamber has also ruled that prisoners serving whole life sentences are entitled to have that sentence reviewed (*Vinter v United Kingdom*, *The Times*, 11 July 2013) This decision caused some conflict with the domestic courts (*R v Newell; R v Mcloughlin* [2014] EWCA Crim 188), which has now been resolved as the Court feels that current law can be interpreted in compliance with article 3 (*Hutchinson v United Kingdom*, *The Times*, 17 January 2017).

[4] The author explains how the Court has insisted on due process in relation to prisoners' disciplinary proceedings, providing relevant case law as authority.

With respect to *prison* discipline, the Court has held that prisoners will be entitled to the protection of **article 6**, guaranteeing the right to a fair trial by an independent tribunal, where the disciplinary charges amount to a 'criminal charge' (*Campbell and Fell v United Kingdom* **(1984) 7 EHRR 165**).[4] Further, in *Ezeh and Connors v United Kingdom* **(2004) 39 EHRR 1** the Grand Chamber held that there had been a similar violation of **article 6** when additional days (up to 40 days) had been imposed on the prisoners and their request for legal representation had been denied. Finally, in *Whitfield v United Kingdom* **(2005) 41 EHRR 44**, it held that a governor's disciplinary decision did not satisfy the requirement of impartiality laid down in **article 6**.

[5] The author now deals with prisoners' democratic rights, in particular the still topical and controversial right to vote debate.

The European Court has also been successful in recognising the democratic rights of prisoners.[5] The Court has recognised that the prisoner retains his fundamental right of free speech. Thus, in *Bamber*, it was accepted that a regulation which stopped a prisoner from contacting the media interfered with the prisoner's **article 10** rights. In addition, in *Hirst v United Kingdom (No. 2)*, the Grand Chamber recognised that prisoners have the *prima facie* right to vote and held that the blanket disenfranchisement of convicted prisoners under UK law was an arbitrary and disproportionate violation of **article 3 of the First Protocol** to the Convention. The Grand Chamber appeared to dilute the decision in *Hirst* when, in *Scoppola v Italy* **(2013) 56 EHRRR 19**, it suggested that the member state would have a wide margin of appreciation in this area. However, the basic tenor of *Hirst* was maintained and the UK remains in violation of the Convention (despite the domestic court's unwillingness, or inability to issue a declaration of incompatibility (*R (Chester) v Secretary of State for Justice* [2013] UKSC 63)).

[6] The author explains how the Court has been more deferential in respect of restrictions on the prisoner's enjoyment of private and family life, providing relevant case examples.

Despite these successes, a more hands-off approach has been adopted in other areas, such as challenges to prison conditions and various aspects of the prisoner's right to private and family life.[6] Thus, in *Boyle and Rice v United Kingdom*, it was accepted that the prisoner's visiting rights are necessarily curtailed in regulations which reflect the ordinary and reasonable requirements of imprisonment. Further, in *ELH and PBH v United Kingdom* **[1998] EHRLR 231** it was held that the denial of a prisoner's conjugal rights was not in violation of the prisoner's family and private rights. However, the Court's deference in this area is not absolute (*Dickson*), and in *Hamer v United Kingdom* the Commission held that the denial of the convicted prisoner's right to marry struck at the very essence of the right to marry as guaranteed under **article 12**.

[7] The author now deals with prison conditions, explaining how the Court's initial reluctance to interfere has been replaced by a more robust approach.

With respect to prison conditions, the early case law displayed a marked reluctance to apply **article 3** (*Hilton v United Kingdom* **(1981) 3 EHRR 104** and *B v United Kingdom* **(1987) 10 DR 87**). More recently, however, the Court has adopted a more positive approach.[7] Thus, in *Peers v Greece* **(2001) 33 EHRR 51** it was held that the subjection of the applicant to unsanitary, cramped, and dark conditions amounted to inhuman and degrading treatment. The Court has attempted to establish some basic, though flexible, standards (*Kalashnikov v Russia* **(2003) 36 EHRR 34)**, and the Court has taken a particularly robust approach with respect to mentally and physically disabled prisoners. The Court thus insists that such prisoners receive proper treatment and attention (*Keenan v United Kingdom* and *Price v United Kingdom* **(2002) 34 EHRR 53)**. The Court has also accepted that the state has a duty to protect the prisoner's life from attack by state officials, and that it must take steps to protect the prisoner from fellow inmates (*Edwards v United Kingdom* **(2002) 35 EHRR 19)**. In that case, the Court also found that the state has a duty to conduct a proper investigation into a prison death and that there had been no such effective investigation on the facts. In addition, liability under **article 2** might be engaged where a prisoner takes his own life due to the negligence of the prison authorities. Thus, in *Keenan v United Kingdom* **(2001) 33 EHRR 38** the Court accepted that the prison authorities would have a duty under **article 2** to ensure that prisoners do not take their own lives.

[8] The author concludes by reflecting that the Court has secured many rights for prisoners, before qualifying this by providing examples where they have been less hands on.

In conclusion, the case law of the European Court has resulted in a number of high-profile and successful claims being brought by UK and other prisoners, which have not only secured changes to domestic law, but have also led to a marked change in judicial attitudes in the domestic courts.[8] The Court has taken a robust approach in areas of prisoners' correspondence, access to the courts, prison discipline, and the release of life-sentence prisoners. There is also evidence that the Court is prepared to find certain conditions and practices inconsistent with **article 3**, especially where the prisoner has special physical or mental needs. However, the Court is still prepared to offer prison authorities a wide margin of error in certain areas, such as prison visits (particularly conjugal visits). Notwithstanding this area of discretion, the decision in *Hirst v United Kingdom (No. 2)* reflects the Court's view that prisoners are entitled to the enjoyment of their Convention rights and that such rights are not lost automatically on incarceration.

➕ LOOKING FOR EXTRA MARKS?

- Show that you understand the scope and values of prisoners' rights and the European Court's role in upholding them.
- Appreciate the legal and diplomatic dilemmas facing the European Court in applying Convention rights to prisoners, together with state claims as to their exclusion and limitations.
- Use leading cases (and academic arguments) which illustrate those dilemmas (prisoner voting rights, review of whole life sentences) and which allow you to employ your critical skills to conclude on the central question.

TAKING THING FURTHER

- Bates, E, 'Analysing the Prisoner Voting Saga and the British Challenge to Strasbourg' (2014) 14(3) HRLR 503

  A thorough and critical analysis of the UK's law on prisoner voting and its challenge in the domestic and European Courts

- Foster, S, 'The Effective Supervision of European Prison Conditions' in F Ippolito and S Iglesias Sanchez (eds.), *Protecting Vulnerable Groups: The European Human Rights Framework* (Hart 2015), ch. 18

  An examination of the various mechanisms responsible for monitoring prison conditions in Europe, including a critical analysis of the case law of the European Court of Human Rights in this area

- Livingstone, S, Owen, T, and Macdonald, A, *Prison Law*, 5th edn (OUP 2015)

  A comprehensive coverage of UK prison law and all aspects of prisoners' rights

- Van Zyl Smit, D, Weatherby, P, and Creighton, S, 'Whole Life Sentences and the Tide of European Human Rights Jurisprudence: What is to be Done?' (2014) 14(1) HRLR 59

  A critical analysis of the case law on whole life sentences and their compatibility with article 3 ECHR

Online Resources   www.oup.com/uk/qanda/

Go online for extra essay and problem questions, a glossary of key terms, online versions of all the answer plans and audio commentary on how selected ones were put together, and a range of podcasts which include advice on exam and coursework technique and advice for other assessment methods.

9 The Right to Private Life

KEY DEBATES

Privacy and the enjoyment of private and family life is the subject of much case law from both the domestic and European courts and moral and political debate with respect to privacy intrusions by the state and the press. This involves discussion regarding state surveillance, press intrusion into the private lives of celebrities and public figures, interferences with physical integrity, and restrictions on the right to marry.

Debate: Scope of Private and Family Life
The European and domestic courts are still interpreting the scope of privacy and other rights under article 8; in particular the extent of the state's positive obligations under article 8 to allow access

to personal information and the application of article 8 to the rights of self-determination and human dignity. Specifically, the assisted suicide/right to die cases have excited great moral and legal debate, and the domestic courts are still being asked to question the compatibility of domestic legislation which outlaws assisted suicide (**Conway**).

Debate: Privacy and Press Freedom

Phone-hacking and other press tactics prompted the Leveson Inquiry and changes to press regulation and the European and domestic courts continue to decide cases where privacy must be balanced with press freedom and the public right to know. Cases such as **PSJ** have raised concerns over the extent to which the press need to respect the private lives of public figures, and the limited extent to which the public interest in publication can be utilised in such cases. A wealth of case law from both the domestic courts and the European Court of Human Rights continues to inform the debate.

Debate: Privacy, Surveillance, and Retention of Personal Data

State surveillance continues to generate public and legal debate as to the correct balance between individual privacy and national security and the detection and prevention of crime. UK law has been informed by decisions of the European Court of Human Rights (**Malone**, **Khan**), and the domestic courts must interpret legislative powers in compliance with those judgments. In addition, the **Investigatory Powers Act 2016** introduces new surveillance powers and these have heightened this debate and started to generate case law when such powers have been challenged.

QUESTION | 1

Critically analyse the way in which the European Court of Human Rights has developed the right to private life as guaranteed by article 8 ECHR.

CAUTION!

- This question requires a very sound overall knowledge of article 8 and the case law of the European Court of Human Rights, but the answer should concentrate on the controversial aspects of the Court's case law so as to provide a critical analysis of how the Court has developed the right to private life.

- You should take a critical approach, assessing the extent to which the Court has upheld the values of privacy and its approach in developing the right so as to accommodate new challenges.

- The question refers to the case law of the European Court, but you may mention domestic decisions, where relevant, to stress the impact of the European Court's jurisprudence in this area.

- Use cases which highlight controversial areas and which examine the dilemma faced by the courts in developing the right to privacy and related rights.

- The answer can, where relevant, include reference to other articles of the Convention, such as freedom of expression, where the right to private life impacts on such.

DIAGRAM ANSWER PLANS

Definition and scope of privacy and private life and examination of privacy and related rights covered by article 8

▼

Critical analysis of relevant case law of the Court in order to examine the dynamic approach of the Court to the interpretation of article 8 and its scope

▼

Critical examination of relevant European Convention case law illustrating the extent of its protection of such rights when those rights are in conflict with other rights and the public interest

▼

Conclusions on the success or otherwise of the Court in developing article 8 rights and protecting it against undue interference

 SUGGESTED ANSWER

[1] The introduction explores the main values and characteristics of private life and what it can protect.

[2] The author uses the case of *Pretty* to illustrate how the Court has accepted the principle of self-determination within article 8.

The right to private life lies at the heart of the right to be free from arbitrary state interference. Privacy includes the right to be left alone and the right to enjoy one's individual space, which the state or other individuals should not penetrate, including the right to enjoy one's property and to be free from physical interference.[1] However, in ***Niemietz v Germany* (1992) 16 EHRR 97** the European Court held that the notion was not restricted to the person's inner circle, but includes the right to develop and establish relationships with other human beings.

Privacy or private life may also refer to the right of personal autonomy and human dignity. This demands that the individual has the right to make choices about their life, such as whom they marry, or whether they have the right to die.[2] Thus, in ***Pretty v United Kingdom* (2002) 35 EHRR 1**, the Court accepted that **article 8** recognises the right to self-determination. Equally, the right to private life can complement the right to be free from inhuman or degrading treatment and thus protect personal dignity (***Costello-Roberts v United Kingdom* (1993) 19 EHRR 112**).

Each state must ensure that an individual's right to private life is protected within its jurisdiction. Accordingly, **article 8** duly provides that everyone has the right *to respect* for his private and family life, his home, and his correspondence. **Article 8(2)** then stipulates that there may be no interference with the exercise of those rights *by a public authority* unless the restrictions are 'in accordance with law' and 'necessary in a democratic society' for the purpose of achieving legitimate aims, such as the prevention of disorder or crime.

Although this right is enjoyed primarily against the state, the state has a duty to protect these rights from violations by private individuals (*X v Netherlands* (1985) 8 EHRR 235). Further, the state has an obligation to provide the resources necessary for the enjoyment of these rights (*Marckx v Belgium* (1979) 2 EHRR 330).[3]

The Court has interpreted 'private life' to cover privacy issues relating to access to personal information (*Gaskin v United Kingdom* (1990) 12 EHRR 36), as well as interference with privacy by surveillance techniques (*Malone v United Kingdom* (1984) 7 EHRR 14) and press intrusion (*Von Hannover v Germany* (2005) 40 EHRR 1). The article also covers a variety of private and family interests, including the right to communicate private information with others (*Silver v United Kingdom* (1983) 5 EHRR 347), and the right to private sexual life (*Dudgeon v United Kingdom* (1982) 4 EHRR 149).

[4] The author explains the Court's robust approach in defending individual privacy from arbitrary interference.

Further, although interferences are permitted under **article 8(2)**, the Court has insisted on strict procedural safeguards (*Klass v Germany* (1978) 2 EHRR 214)[4] and has made it clear that the state will be allowed a narrow margin of appreciation when its law and practice have interfered with private rights (*Dudgeon v United Kingdom*). In this case, the Court recognised that the right to private life included the right to enjoy one's private sexual life, this being one of the most intimate aspects of private life. It also stressed that strong justification would be required to allow interference. Thus, in *Smith and Grady v United Kingdom* (2000) 29 EHRR 493 the dismissal of armed forces personnel due to their sexuality was held to constitute a disproportionate interference with their private lives. However, in *Laskey, Jaggard and Brown v United Kingdom* (1997) 24 EHRR 39 it upheld the applicants' convictions for assault for taking part in consensual acts of a sadomasochistic nature, noting that not every sexual activity carried out behind closed doors falls within the scope of **article 8**. On the other hand, the state's margin will be limited where the criminal law has been used exclusively against one particular group based on its sexual orientation (*ADT v United Kingdom* (2001) 31 EHRR 33; *Sutherland v United Kingdom, The Times*, 13 April 2001). The Court has adopted a flexible approach on abortion and in *A, B and C v Ireland* (2011) 53 EHRR 13, refused to grant a general right to an abortion in domestic law where there were strong moral grounds for its prohibition. It did however uphold the right to an abortion in cases where the woman's life and health was in question.

The Convention has also extended its protection to transsexuals, although earlier cases had refused to interfere with domestic law that refused to recognise the private rights of transsexuals to marry and to choose their new sexual identity (*Rees v United Kingdom* (1986) 9 EHRR 56). The Court revisited its stance in this area in *Goodwin v United Kingdom* (2002) 35 EHRR 18, where a violation of **articles**

8 and 12 was found where the applicants could not exercise their right to marry under **article 12** and were refused the right to change their sexual identity on various civil documents. This is evidence of the Court's dynamic approach to article 8; the Court noting that the government had not kept the need for legal reform under review so as to reflect the change of attitude in this area.[5]

The Court has also been instrumental in protecting the right of correspondence, recognising not only the right to communicate with friends or relatives, but also the right to carry on business communications (*Halford v United Kingdom* (1997) 24 EHRR 523 and *Amann v Switzerland* (2000) 30 EHRR 843). This protection has been notable in the context of prisoners' correspondence (*Golder v United Kingdom* (1975) 1 EHRR 524; *Silver v United Kingdom* (1983) 5 EHRR 347). Thus, a number of prison regulations were declared insufficiently accessible to be 'in accordance with law', and excessive and disproportionate in relation to maintaining prison order.

The problem of state interference with the right of communication is perhaps most acute with respect to its use of surveillance devices, and in *Klass v Germany* it was accepted that surveillance and other techniques struck at the heart of freedom of communication.[6] The Court has stressed that any such interference has to be justified in accordance with law and that the executive authorities should be subject to effective control, normally via the judiciary. The decision in *Klass* was applied in *Malone v United Kingdom*, where the domestic law on telephone tapping did not satisfy **article 8(2)** because it was not publicly accessible and did not indicate with sufficient certainty the scope and manner of the relevant authorities' discretion. Further, in *Liberty v United Kingdom* (2009) 48 EHRR 1, it was held that there had been a violation of **article 8** when Liberty had had their telephone calls and other communications intercepted by the MOD. This was because the power to intercept and read communications, under **s.3(2) of the Interception of Communications Act 1985**, gave an unlimited discretion and any safeguards against abuse were not made public or accessible.

The Court's primary concern in this area is with procedural safeguards as opposed to the substantive justification for such intrusions. Thus, in *Kennedy v United Kingdom*, *The Times*, **3 June 2010** it was satisfied that domestic law and the Investigatory Appeals Tribunal maintained a fair balance between the rights of the applicant and national security. Consequently, although the Court has succeeded in putting into place proper safeguards for the use of such techniques, it has been reluctant to interfere with the substantive balance between individual privacy and the prevention and prosecution of crime. This reluctance is also apparent in the Court's willingness to allow illegally obtained evidence to be used in subsequent criminal trials (*Khan v United Kingdom* (2000) 31 EHRR 45). The Court has also responded to the dangers of modern monitoring techniques, including closed-circuit television (CCTV). For example, in **Peck v United Kingdom** (2003) **36 EHRR 41**, it held that there had been a violation of **article 8** when CCTV footage of a person in a distressed condition had been released for use in various newspapers and television programmes without sufficient safeguards to ensure his anonymity. It has also held that the monitoring of an employee's use of emails and the internet was in violation of **article 8**, the practice not being in accordance with any law (**Copland v United Kingdom** (2007) **45 EHRR 37** and the recent decision in **Bărbulescu v. Romania** (Application No. **61496/08**).

The Court has stressed the necessity of not only regulating other people's access to the individual's private information, but also of allowing the individual to access such personal information. Thus, in **Gaskin v United Kingdom** it was held that a system that denied a person's access to information relating to his upbringing was an unnecessary restriction on the right to private life. It has also been active in protecting individual privacy from press intrusion.[7] In **Von Hannover v Germany**, the Court held that the publication of various photographs of the applicant, Princess Caroline Von Hannover, of her in her daily life clearly fell within the scope of her private life. The Court noted that the photographs had been taken without her consent and secretly, and that they made no contribution to a debate of public interest. In the Court's view, the protection of private life was essential to the development of every human being's personality. Accordingly, everyone, including people known to the public, had a legitimate expectation that his or her private life would be protected. The decision illustrates the Court's desire to protect individual privacy from press harassment and disclosure of confidential and private information. However, the Court will also consider the public right to know, where there is a clear public interest (**Von Hannover v Germany (No. 2)** (2012) **55 EHRR 15**).

In conclusion, **article 8** protects a vast array of privacy interests and the European Court has taken a dynamic approach to the protection of such interests.[8] Although the right to private life is clearly a conditional right, the Court has made it clear that interferences with individual privacy must be justified on strong grounds. This reflects the Court's recognition of the importance of individual privacy and the need to protect it from unwarranted and uncontrolled intrusion.

[7] The author now deals with access to and protection of private information, including the topical issue of press intrusion into the private lives of well-known figures.

[8] The Conclusion neatly summarises the issues of recognition of various privacy issues and the Court's control of arbitrary interference with private life.

LOOKING FOR EXTRA MARKS?

- Show that you understand the scope and values of article 8 and the right to private life—to recognise an individual's privacy and dignity and protect against *arbitrary* interference.
- Appreciate how the Court has developed the meaning and scope of private life since the Convention was drafted and how it has responded to new dilemmas.

- Illustrate how the Court has balanced private life with other's rights and interests such as the prevention of crime, and how that has compromised the enjoyment of private life.

- Use leading cases in controversial areas which illustrate those dilemmas and which allow you to employ your critical skills to conclude on the central question.

 QUESTION | 2

To what extent has the implementation of the Human Rights Act 1998 led to the development of a domestic law of privacy? Do you agree that the current law provides adequate protection against intrusions into an individual's private life?

 CAUTION!

- This question requires a very sound knowledge of various areas of privacy protected at the domestic level, but the answer should use those areas to prove whether or not domestic law has provided *adequate protection* of privacy from intrusion.

- You should take a critical approach, particularly in the second part of the question, having understood the scope of protection afforded under the European Convention and by the European Court of Human Rights.

- The question refers to the development of domestic law, but it is permissible to use cases from the European Court where those decisions have informed the domestic law.

- Use cases and other examples which highlight the development of the law in line with the ECHR and which allow discussion on the level of protection afforded by domestic law.

- The answer should, where relevant, include reference to other articles of the Convention, such as article 10 (freedom of expression).

DIAGRAM ANSWER PLANS

Definition of privacy and its values; the scope of the right to privacy

↓

Relevant and brief explanation of traditional common law position and the inadequacy of that protection

↓

Critical account of the effect of the implementation of the Human Rights Act 1998 and various developments in the common law and under statute

↓

Analysis of the efficacy of the present legal position and its compatibility with the European Convention and privacy values

[1] The author begins with a general explanation of privacy and what it entails.

The right to privacy includes the right to be left alone and the right to enjoy one's individual space as well as being free from physical interference and is guaranteed under **article 8** [1] of the European Convention. It ensures the protection of personal autonomy (*Pretty v United Kingdom* **(2002) 35 EHRR 1**), the right to choose and practise one's sexual orientation (*Dudgeon v United Kingdom* **(1982) 4 EHRR 149**), and to be free from press intrusion (*Von Hannover v Germany* **(2005) 40 EHRR 1**).

[2] The author explains how domestic law lacked a general law of privacy before the HRA.

Although various aspects of English law protected privacy interests such as property, and confidential information, it failed to recognise the right to privacy as such. [2] Consequently, in *Malone v Metropolitan Police Commissioner (No. 2)* **[1979] Ch 344**, it was held that the plaintiff had no remedy when the police had tapped his telephone because no domestic law had been breached on the facts. As a consequence the individual had to take proceedings under the European Convention (*Malone v United Kingdom* **(1984) 7 EHRR 14**). Similarly, individuals dismissed from the armed forces on grounds of their sexual orientation could not rely on **article 8**, and needed to seek a remedy from the European Court (*Smith and Grady v United Kingdom* **(2000) 29 EHRR 493**).

The absence of a general right to privacy was most notable in the area of press intrusion (*Kaye v Robertson* **[1991] FSR 62**). Thus, individuals had to rely on specific domestic laws to protect their privacy interests, such as the **Data Protection Acts 1988 and 1998** and the law of confidentiality, which was developed so as to be consistent with the right to privacy (*HRH Princess of Wales v MGN Newspapers* **(Unreported, 8 November 1993)**). Even after the passing of the **Human Rights Act 1998**, the courts confirmed that there is still no specific common law action in privacy (*Secretary of State for the Home Department v Wainwright and others*

[3] The author now explains the potential for privacy protection under the HRA.

[2004] 2 AC 406). However, the Act allows the courts to enhance the protection of private life. [3] First, because **article 8** has now been 'incorporated' into domestic law, and a victim of a violation carried out by a *public authority* can bring an action under the Act. Secondly, in *Wainwright* the House of Lords confirmed that the Act will have a horizontal effect. As a consequence, the courts (as 'public authorities') have developed the law to ensure that **article 8** rights are not unduly interfered with. More specifically, under **s.12(4)** of the 1998 Act the courts have a duty to take into account the contents of any privacy code in deciding whether to grant relief regarding any affected freedom of expression.

[4] The author provides examples where the courts began to recognise and develop privacy rights under the HRA.

After the Act came into force the courts began to use their powers to develop a law of privacy.[4] For example, in ***Douglas and others v Hello! and others* [2001] 2 WLR 992,** Sedley LJ stated that the domestic law was now in a position to respond to an increasingly invasive social environment by affirming that everybody has the right to some private space. This duty to provide a Convention-like protection of privacy was confirmed by the European Court in ***Wainwright v United Kingdom* (2007) 44 EHRR 40,** where it found that there had been a breach of **article 13**—the right to an effective remedy at domestic law—when a victim of an unlawful search had not been able to rely on **article 8** in domestic proceedings.

Thus, whether domestic law has in effect developed an effective law of privacy depends largely on the extent to which the law of confidentiality, and other legal areas, have filled the gaps evident in the pre-Act era. Certainly, surveillance powers, contained in various legislation passed as a result of cases such as ***Malone***, can now be considered as part of a privacy law, as they contain restrictions on the use of such powers in line with **article 8**, as upheld by the domestic courts (***Liberty and others v Secretary of State for Foreign and Commonwealth Affairs* [2015] UKIP Trib 1377H2).**

[5] The author explains how the law of confidentiality has been developed in line with privacy principles.

Further, with respect to the law of confidentiality, the courts have developed the law consistently with the basic notions contained in **article 8**.[5] Accordingly, the courts have refused to give freedom of expression an enhanced status over and above the right to private life (***Douglas v Hello!***). With respect to press intrusions into privacy, the courts were initially unwilling to interfere with press freedom when individual privacy has been invaded (***A v B plc and another* [2002] 3 WLR 542).** This situation was redressed to some extent by the House of Lords in ***Campbell v MGN Newspapers* [2004] 2 AC 457,** where it was held that the revelation of detailed information relating to the claimant's drug addiction constituted an undue interference with her right of enjoyment of private life. This decision was upheld by the European Court in ***MGN Ltd v United Kingdom* (2011) 53 EHRR 5.** Further, as a result of the European Court's decision in ***Von Hannover v Germany* (2005) 40 EHRR 1,** domestic case law effected a shift from the public right to know to individual privacy (***McKennitt v Ash* [2007] 3 WLR 194).** This has attracted some criticism of the judiciary who have been accused of developing a law of privacy to the detriment of press freedom. Notwithstanding, there is little doubt that the current legal situation has enhanced the pre-Act protection in cases such as ***Kaye v Robertson***. The courts also now have the power to subject public authority interference with privacy to greater scrutiny and must now strike a correct balance between individual privacy and the public interest. For example, in ***Wood v Commissioner of the Police of the Metropolis* [2010] 1 WLR 123,** the Court of

Appeal found that the taking and retention by the police of an individual's photograph as he left an area of protest was disproportionate because the police could provide no cogent reason for retention. However. the courts took a more deferential approach to the challenge of such powers in *R (Catt) v Commissioner of Police of the Metropolis* **[2015] 1 AC 1065**. Here it was held that the retention by the police of records of an elderly and non-violent man's participation in demonstrations organised by an extremist protest group was proportionate to the aim of preventing crime and protecting people from harassment.

[6] The author provides examples of the courts' attempts to include privacy protection in their application of various domestic laws.

Under the 1998 Act the courts have interpreted various laws in the context of privacy claims.[6] This has included cases involving physical and personal integrity (*Munjaz v Mersey Care NHS Trust; S v Airedale NHS Trust* **[2006] 2 AC 148**); and the retention of DNA samples (*R v Chief Constable of South Yorkshire, ex parte LS and Marper* **[2004] 1 WLR 2196**); the latter case was successfully challenged in *S and Marper v United Kingdom* **(2009) 48 EHRR 50**, and then modified by the Supreme Court in *R (GC) v Commissioner of the police of the Metropolis* **[2011] UKSC 21**. Further, both the courts and Parliament ensured that laws relating to sexual privacy are consistent with **article 8** of the European Convention. For example, following the decision in *Goodwin v United Kingdom* **(2002) 35 EHRR 18** the House of Lords declared that the refusal of the law to recognise a transsexual's post-operative gender was contrary to **articles 8 and 14** of the Convention (*Bellinger v Bellinger* **[2003] 2 AC 467**). Further, the **Gender Recognition Act 2004** now regulates such rights in a Convention-compliant manner. Similar protection has been afforded by the courts in respect of those discriminated against on grounds of sexual orientation (*Mendoza v Ghaidan* **[2004] 2 AC 557** and the **Civil Partnership Act 2004**).

[7] The author now examines some cases which have been less protective of privacy claims.

However, despite the availability of privacy actions in domestic law, some recent cases have highlighted the law's inability, or unwillingness, to offer full protection to privacy interests.[7] Thus, in addition to the wide area of discretion afforded to the police in *Catt*, in *R (Nicklinson) v Ministry of Justice* **[2015] AC 657** the Supreme Court refused to declare **s.2** of the **Suicide Act 1961** incompatible with **article 8**, despite its discriminatory impact on a disabled person's choice to end their life. The Supreme Court agreed with the European Court of Human Rights in *Pretty* that such a law was within the state's margin of appreciation in protecting the sanctity of life. A further challenge to the law was dismissed in *Conway v Ministry of Justice* **[2017] EWHC 2447**. Further, in *Re JR38's Application for Judicial Review* **[2015] 3 WLR 155,** it was held that the publication by the police of images of a 14-year-old boy apparently committing public order offences did not violate his **article 8** rights. It was held that he could not have had a reasonable expectation that photographs of him committing the offences—taken for the limited purpose of identifying him—would not be published so as to engage **article 8**. The decision was criticised for applying the general test of reasonable expectation of privacy to a minor, thus ignoring the special protection that should be given in such cases.

[8]The author concludes by stating that the HRA has improved the situation with respect to legal certainty.

At the very least, in the post-Human Rights Act era both the courts and Parliament must ensure that provisions empowering public authorities to encroach upon individual privacy are sufficiently clear, accessible, and certain.[8] Thus, following defeats in Strasbourg in cases involving telephone tapping (*Malone*) such powers are now contained in relatively clear statutory form (**Regulation of Investigatory Powers Act 2000** and the **Investigatory Powers Act 2016**). Also, these laws must strike a reasonable balance between the protection of privacy and competing legitimate aims. Despite the absence of a distinct law of privacy in domestic law, there is in place a flexible framework for the protection of privacy interests. These laws may not always achieve consistency with the European Convention (*S and Marper v United Kingdom*), although such conflict may occur even where the state possesses a distinct law of privacy.

➕ LOOKING FOR EXTRA MARKS?

- Show that you understand the scope and values of article 8 and the need for domestic law to provide adequate protection of privacy rights and protection from arbitrary intrusion.
- Appreciate the failures of the traditional system in this area and the need to develop a coherent and human rights friendly system of protection in the post-HRA era.
- Use leading cases which illustrate those developments and which allow you to assess the adequacy of the current system for protecting and balancing privacy rights.

ⓠ QUESTION | 3

Critically examine how the European Convention and the Court of Human Rights has protected individuals from unlawful and arbitrary surveillance by police and other authorities.

❗ CAUTION!

- This question requires a very sound knowledge of the case law of the European Court of Human Rights in this area, but the answer should concentrate on the Court's case law with respect to the protection from unlawful and arbitrary interference by such techniques.

- The question employs the phrase *critically examine*, so you should take a critical approach with respect to what protection the Court should provide (in accordance with principles of legality and proportionality) and the protection that has been achieved by the Court.

- The question refers to the European Convention and the European Court, so the case law will be from the Strasbourg Court; although it is permissible to use domestic cases and developments to see how Convention principles have been adopted and applied.

- Use the cases in a way which illustrates how the Court has upheld, or failed to uphold, principles of legality and proportionality and provided safeguards with respect to the abuse of such state powers.

DIAGRAM ANSWER PLANS

Explanation of various surveillance techniques, their utility, and the potential danger to individual liberty

Examination of relevant Convention articles and case law of the European Court and Commission in the area

Identification of the central principles and values evident from the cases and a critical evaluation of the scope and effectiveness of the Convention's protection

Reference to relevant domestic statute and case law in illustration of the above principles

Conclusions on the success of the Convention, the European Court (and domestic law) in protecting individuals from surveillance techniques

A   SUGGESTED ANSWER

[1] The author begins with a warning against the use of surveillance techniques with respect to individual privacy.

The employment of covert surveillance techniques (such as telephone tapping, 'bugging', and the modern use of closed-circuit television surveillance), involve a specifically sinister and grave interference[1] with individual privacy and the enjoyment of such rights. In these cases, it is essential that such practices are only carried out with proper legal safeguards which restrict their use and which provide the individual with a remedy in cases of their illegal use.

Article 8 of the European Convention provides protection against interference with private life, home, and correspondence and in ***Klass***

[2] The author cites the *Klass* judgment to stress the breach of privacy caused by such techniques.

***v Germany* (1978) 2 EHRR 214** the European Court confirmed that the mere existence of legislation allowing telephone tapping by state authorities struck at freedom of communication.[2] Accordingly, the power to carry out surveillance must be 'in accordance with law' so that executive authorities are subjected to effective control. Although the Court suggested that there should, ideally, be a system of judicial control, it was prepared to take a flexible approach, provided the domestic legislation had inbuilt safeguards against abuse.

The law should be couched in terms which give both the individual and the authorities sufficient guidance as to the scope of the powers. Consequently, in *Amann v Switzerland* **(2000) 30 EHRR 843**, it was held that tapping violated **article 8**, because the national law was not sufficiently clear to clarify the scope and conditions of the authorities' discretionary powers in this area. The principles in *Klass* and *Amann* were applied in *Malone v United Kingdom* **(1984) 7 EHRR 14.** Here the European Court held that the law regulating the practice of telephone tapping, contained in government circulars that were not publicly accessible, did not satisfy **article 8(2)**. Telephone tapping required clear and accessible legal rules and in the present case it could not be determined what powers were incorporated in legal rules and what elements remained within the discretion of the executive and the police force. As a consequence, Parliament passed the **Interception of Communications Act 1985**, which at least put telephone tapping on a statutory basis. These provisions are now contained in the **Regulation of Investigatory Powers Act 2000** and the new **Investigatory Powers Act 2016**,[3] and such methods are supervised by an independent, and legally qualified, Interception of Communications Officer.

[3] The author states that such provisions are now embedded in domestic statutes, before mentioning the potential impact of the recent draft Bill.

However, recent reforms contained in the **Investigatory Powers Act 2016**, have given rise to concerns over the control of arbitrary use in this area. This is particularly so in respect of the powers of bulk collection and data collection. These powers will be subject to challenge before the European Court of Human Rights (*Big Brother Watch v United Kingdom* **(Application No. 58170/13)**) on the grounds that such collection and retention should be for limited purposes (serious crime) and that such data should be subject to access requests.

The Court has extended protection to practices other than the tapping of telephones in the private home. Thus, in *Halford v United Kingdom* **(1997) 24 EHRR 523**, it held that telephone calls made from business premises were covered by the notion of private life and correspondence under **article 8**. Accordingly, as such practices were not covered by legislation passed to conform to the decision in *Malone*, the interference was in breach of **article 8**. Further, in *Copland v United Kingdom* **(2007) 45 EHRR 37** it was held that **article 8** applied to the monitoring of the employees' use of email and internet facilities at work.

[4] The author summarises some of the cases affecting the UK and challenges to its law.

With respect to covert surveillance in the UK,[4] in addition to the decisions in *Malone* and *Halford*, the Court has also made rulings with respect to surveillance carried out by intelligence agencies such as MI5 (*Harman and Hewitt v United Kingdom* **(1992) 14 EHRR 657**). This led to the passing of the **Security Services Act 1989**. Further challenges were made in respect of the placing of bugging devices on individuals and their property (***Khan v United Kingdom* (2001) 31 EHRR 45**). These powers are now contained in the **Police Act 1997** and the **Regulation of Investigatory Powers Act 2000**. Further, in ***Perry v United Kingdom* (2004) 39 EHRR 3** the Court held that the secret filming of the applicant in a prison cell engaged the applicant's right to respect for his private life. In these cases, the Court not only found violations of **article 8**, but also held that the lack of regular domestic law in this area meant that the victim had been denied an effective legal remedy, as required by **article 13** of the Convention.

Despite the Court's insistence that such activities have a clear legal basis, it would appear that it will afford a member state a good deal of discretion[5] when adjudicating upon the necessity and proportionality of such measures. Thus, in ***Klass***, the Court accepted that such techniques were vital in protecting societies from sophisticated forms of espionage and terrorism. Consequently, states are in general justified in resorting to such methods. This approach follows ***Leander v Sweden* (1987) 9 EHRR 433**, where it was held that the state has a wide margin of appreciation when deciding the best means of securing a balance between individual privacy and national security. Thus, the Court's fundamental concern is with procedural safeguards rather than challenging the necessity of individual measures and their application (***RE v United Kingdom*, decision of the European Court of Human Rights, 27 October 2015**). For example, in ***PG and JH v United Kingdom*, *The Times*, 19 October 2001**, the police had placed a covert listening device in the applicant's flat, using such information in subsequent criminal proceedings. The Court noted that the police lacked the statutory power to carry this out and thus found a violation of **article 8** with regard to the use of the applicant's telephone, at this stage unregulated by domestic law. However, it held that had there been regulation, and as the information had been obtained and used in the context of an investigation and trial concerning a suspected robbery, the measures would have been justified under **article 8(2)**. The Court also validated UK law in this area in ***Kennedy v United Kingdom*, *The Times*, 3 June 2010**. Here it held that the laws on interception were sufficiently clear and that the appeal proceedings before the Investigatory Appeals Tribunal maintained a fair balance between the rights of the applicant and national security. In contrast, in ***Liberty and others v United Kingdom* (2009) 48 EHRR 1**, it was held that the law had failed to set out in a form accessible to the public any indication of the procedure to be followed for examining, sharing, storing, and destroying intercepted material.

Further, the Court is not prepared to find a violation of the applicant's right to a fair trial under **article 6** simply because such information has been used against the applicant in subsequent criminal proceedings[6] (***Schenk v Switzerland* (1988) 13 EHRR 242**). Thus, in ***Khan v United Kingdom* (2001) 31 EHRR 45**, it held that the absence of domestic law regulating the use of bugging devices meant that there had been an unjustified interference with the applicant's private life and correspondence. However, it then held that although his conviction was based solely on the use of that unlawfully obtained evidence, there were sufficient safeguards in place to ensure that such information would not be admissible if it seriously prejudiced the applicant's right to a fair trial. Consequently, the European Court concerns itself with the overall fairness of the proceedings, rather than adopting a dogmatic exclusionary rule.

[7] The author moves on to the interesting and controversial area of CCTV.

The Court has also had the opportunity to rule on the legality of closed-circuit television surveillance.[7] In **Perry v United Kingdom**, it held that the secret filming of a prisoner in his cell, and the subsequent use of such images for identification purposes, amounted to an interference with his right to private life. The filming was not in accordance with law as the police had failed to follow the procedures set out in the relevant code and had not obtained the applicant's consent or informed him of his rights. Further, the filming had gone beyond the normal use of that type of camera and was thus disproportionate.

Although the Court appears to accept that such television surveillance is a necessary and increasingly normal practice, it is prepared to subject it to close scrutiny to ensure that it is not carried out unlawfully or unnecessarily. The legality of such techniques was challenged in **Peck v United Kingdom (2003) 36 EHRR 41**, concerning the use by local authorities of closed-circuit television for the purposes of protecting public safety in the community. The applicant had been filmed by closed-circuit television walking down the street with a kitchen knife and attempting to commit suicide. The Council then issued a press feature in its CCTV News, containing photographs from the footage, which were later published in a local newspaper and used in a number of local and national television programmes, without the applicant's face being specifically masked. The European Court held that the disclosure of that footage constituted a serious interference with the applicant's right to respect for private life. The Court accepted that the interference was prescribed by law and that it had a legitimate aim—public safety, the prevention of disorder and crime, and the protection of the rights of others. It also held that the interference was not necessary or proportionate. The Court stressed that the disclosure of private and intimate information could only be justified by an overriding requirement in the public interest and that such disclosure without the consent of the individual called for the most careful scrutiny. In the present case the disclosure of the material was not accompanied by sufficient safeguards to ensure anonymity and thus constituted a disproportionate and unjustified interference. The decision in **Peck** suggests that the Court is willing to rule on the necessity and proportionality of these particular surveillance techniques, albeit in exceptional cases.

The European Court has provided essential safeguards against unlawful and arbitrary use of surveillance, insisting that such measures are controlled by the law, and this has led to domestic legislation, which places the techniques on a statutory footing and provides some element of judicial (or quasi-judicial) supervision. However, it has displayed a good deal of deference to the state authorities in this area. Consequently, although the Convention and its case law have insisted on procedural protection from abuse, such practices appear to be regarded as essential to the protection of the public and their extent is, generally, best determined by the authorities themselves. This may be particularly pertinent given the content of the recent **Investigatory Powers Act 2016** which, inter alia, controversially requires[8] telecommunications and information service providers to provide access to encrypted information and data stored on customers' websites.

[8] The author refers to the controversial new Act of Parliament to stress the need for effective supervision and control of such powers.

LOOKING FOR EXTRA MARKS?

- Show that you understand the necessity for surveillance and threat of such techniques to individual privacy and the regulation of state power.

- Appreciate the dilemma facing the European Court and the general law in balancing state and individual interests in this area and in upholding basic principles of accountability, the rule of law, and individual privacy.

- Use leading cases which illustrate those dilemmas and which allow you to employ your critical skills to conclude on the central question.

- Allude to the continuing political and legal debates in this area, together with recent proposals for legislative reform.

QUESTION | 4

Part A

Critically examine how domestic law has attempted to balance the right of press freedom with the enjoyment of private life?

Part B

Sheila is a former girl band member with the group Witchiz! She left the group three years ago and is now 28 and has been married for three years, although she has been separated for the last six months. One year ago she had an affair with a 17-year-old schoolboy who now wishes to tell his story to the *Daily Scum*. Sheila was telephoned by the newspaper, stating that next week it was to publish this story and another (true) story about her past affairs with several young men, along with photographs of her naked in a hotel room. For the next two days Sheila was persistently followed by the newspaper's photographers, who took photographs of her and her current boyfriend.

Advise Sheila as to the chances of her suppressing the stories, or suing for damages with respect to the stories or other tactics adopted by the newspaper.

CAUTION!

- The first part of the question requires a very sound overall knowledge of press freedom and private life, but the answer should concentrate on the *balance* between the two and how domestic law has *attempted to achieve* that balance.

- The question employs the phrase *critically examine*, so you should take a critical approach, having understood the importance of both claims and the manner in which human rights law measures the legitimacy of that balance.

- The question refers to *domestic* law, but it is permissible to use cases from the European Court if those cases have informed domestic law.

- Use cases which highlight controversial areas and which examine the dilemma faced by the courts in achieving the balance.

- The answer to the second part should rely on the cases and principles identified in your answer to the first part of the question, in addition to giving advice on the facts of the scenario.

DIAGRAM ANSWER PLANS

Part A

> Explanation of privacy and press freedom and its importance in a democratic society

> Consideration of the domestic law of confidentiality and misuse of private information, both pre- and post-Human Rights Act, affecting the balance between press freedom and private life

> Conclusions on how the courts have balanced the rights

Part B

Identify the issues	▪ The legal issues and the claims made by the claimant ▪ Action in confidentiality/misuse of private information
Relevant law	▪ Outline the rules and cases relating to the claim, remedies, and any possible defences
Apply the law	▪ Application of the rules and cases together with any defences to the facts
Conclude	▪ Conclude on whether the action, or any defence, would be likely to succeed

SUGGESTED ANSWER

Part A

[1] The Introduction notes that domestic law must now accommodate the right to privacy in its various laws.

The giving effect to European Convention rights in domestic law has allowed the courts to develop traditional legal principles, most notably the law of confidentiality/misuse of private information, in line with **article 8**.[1] This law often involves a conflict between the protection of privacy interests and freedom of expression and must be applied in a manner which strikes an appropriate balance between such rights.

This dilemma is most acute when press freedom comes up against the private lives of 'public' figures. Accordingly, in the post-Human Rights Act era the courts have confirmed that this area should be dealt with primarily within the law of confidentiality/misuse of private information, rather than the development of a separate law of privacy[2] (*Campbell v MGN* **[2004] 2 AC 457**). Thus, in *Douglas and others v Hello! and others* **[2001] 2 WLR 992** Sedley LJ stated that English law now recognised and protected a right of personal privacy and that the courts had a duty to protect the individual's right to some private space. This required the courts to take into account any countervailing Convention right, such as freedom of expression. **Section 12** of the **Human Rights Act** requires the Court to have special regard to **article 10** when granting relief that affects freedom of expression. Further, **s.12(4)** orders the court to consider both the public interest and the contents of any relevant privacy code. Accordingly, in *Douglas* Sedley LJ held that both rights were to be balanced by the principles of legality and proportionality. Also, in *Re S (Publicity)* **[2005] 1 AC 593**, in deciding whether to grant an interim injunction a court should consider the magnitude of the interference proposed and whether there was a clear and proper interest in revealing the information.

This balance has tended to favour the protection of privacy when the claim of privacy is accompanied by a threat of physical harm to the claimant (*Venables and Thompson v MGN Ltd* **[2001] 2 WLR 1038**). On the other hand, in less crucial cases, the courts have shown a reluctance to grant interim injunctions where violation of the claimant's privacy could be remedied at full trial (*Douglas v Hello!*), unless the injunction is needed to protect intimate aspects of the claimant's private life (*CC v AB* **[2007] EMLR 11***)*.

[2] The author explains that this has been done by the development of the common law and the provisions of the HRA.

[3] The author traces the development of domestic case law in this area, covering the major cases (including persuasive ECHR case law).

In particular, the courts have had to decide whether, and to what extent, a public figure enjoys the right to private life, and whether the public's right to know should override any such interest.[3] Early case law suggested that press freedom and the public right to know would generally prevail. Thus, in *A v B plc and another* **[2002] 3 WLR 542**, it was held that although a celebrity was entitled to a private life, he must expect that his actions would be more closely scrutinised by the media. This was because the public had an understandable and legitimate interest in being told such information. However, later cases favoured individual privacy. For example, in *Campbell v MGN* **[2004] 2 AC 457** the House of Lords held that the revelation of detailed information relating to the claimant's drug addiction, including photographs of her visiting a rehabilitation clinic and details of her treatment, constituted an interference with her right of enjoyment of private life. Further this was not justified on grounds of public interest. Although there was a genuine public interest in receiving the information—the claimant had lied to the press about her drug addiction— the revelation of these specific details was held to be unwarranted. The decision was upheld by the European Court in *MGN Ltd v United Kingdom* **(2011) 51 EHRR 5**, which followed *Von Hannover v Germany* **(2005) 40 EHRR 1**.

[4] The author notes the move towards a greater recognition of privacy rights by the domestic courts.

Subsequently, in *McKennitt v Ash* **[2007] 3 WLR 194** it was noted that there was a significant shift taking place between freedom of the press and individual privacy.[4] Thus, even where there was a genuine interest in the media publishing articles and photographs, sometimes such interests would have to yield to the individual's right to private life. In this case, the court stressed that there was a clear difference between publication in the public interest and publication of matters that the public were interested in or curious about.

The courts will continue to take into account all the circumstances, including the extent of any intrusion and the importance of the public interest. For example, in *Jagger v Darling* **[2005] EWHC 683** the court granted an injunction to stop the publication of CCTV footage showing the claimant engaged in sexual activities. The court found that repeated publication of the images would only serve to humiliate the claimant, although in *Browne v Associated Newspapers* **[2007] 3 WLR 289** the court allowed the publication of some details of the claimant's homosexual affair. Here the court recognised that there was a genuine public interest because of the claimant's position as a director of a global company and of allegations of abuse of the company's funds and facilities. The courts have also recognised that the private lives of well-known individuals, such as sportsmen, can be a matter of public interest if the person in question holds a special position, such as captain of the national team (*Ferdinand v MGN Ltd* **[2011] EWHC 2454 (QB)**). However, the courts may side with the claimant when disclosure would damage the interests of children. For example, in *PJS v News Group Newspapers* **[2016] UKSC 23**, the Supreme Court upheld an injunction forbidding the publication by the press of an adulterous relationship despite the fact that the story had leaked to many on social media. The court reasoned that the extra humiliation caused to the claimant and his family by press disclosure justified the order.

[5] The author examines the controversial and topical issue of injunctions and anonymity orders, using recent cases and developments in this area.

Much controversy has been created by attempts by public figure to prevent the publication of private details[5] and to gain either anonymity orders to hide their identities or 'super' injunctions to prevent the publication of the fact that such orders are being sought. Such orders were refused in the case of *LNS v Persons Unknown (John Terry)* **[2010] EMLR 16**, because the claimant was seeking to protect his commercial reputation rather than his private and family life. However, anonymity orders have been granted in appropriate cases where the details are intimate (a sexual affair) and there is no public interest in publication (*MNB v News Group Newspapers Ltd* **[2011] EWHC 528 (QB)**). In *JIH v News Group Newspapers* **[2011] EWCA Civ 42** it was held that as a general rule the parties' names in an action should be disclosed and an anonymity order constituted a departure from the principles of open justice. The court held that in general the media and the public interests would be better served by an order granting anonymity but allowing limited details of the case into the public domain, as opposed to publishing the claimant's name with little else. The *Report of the Committee on Super-Injunctions: Super-Injunctions, Anonymised Injunctions and Open Justice*, 20 May 2011, suggests that 'super' injunctions should only be granted where they are strictly necessary and that anonymised injunctions should be kept to a minimum. In addition, the European Court held that it is not necessary for the press to notify potential claimants in advance of publication, so that they can seek prior restraint (*Mosley v United Kingdom* **(2011) 53 EHRR 30**).

Present case law appears flexible and to some extent inconsistent, and although the existence of a *genuine* public interest in disclosure is

[6] The author concludes that the domestic courts now tend to favour individual privacy over press freedom and the public right to know.

vital, many of the above decisions expose the courts' desire to protect individual privacy from press intrusion and public exposure.[6]

Part B

The publication of the story and the photographs

[1] The author identifies the appropriate legal areas and actions that will need to be considered when giving advice.

As the information to be published by the newspaper appears true, Sheila must pursue an action in confidentiality/misuse of private information,[1] which has been used by the domestic courts to protect privacy interests (*Campbell v MGN* **[2004] 2 AC 457**). Further, the law of harassment will be considered with respect to the subsequent press tactics. In particular, she may seek an interim injunction in order to prohibit the publication of the stories and the photographs. This may be combined, with an anonymity order to prevent her identity, and/or a 'super' injunction to hide the mere fact that such an order is being sought.

[2] The author now examines the first requirement of a successful action: has S a reasonable expectation of privacy?

First, the court will need to be satisfied that the information she is seeking to protect has a sufficient quality of confidence and that she has a reasonable expectation of privacy.[2] Details of sexual encounters, even outside marriage, may attract protection (*Stephens v Avery* [1998] Ch 499). In *A v B plc and another* [2001] 1 WLR 2341 Lord Woolf CJ stated that there was a significant difference between confidentiality attaching to sexual relations in transient relationships as opposed to those within marriage or other stable relationships. Despite this, such relationships are still worthy of protection (*CC v AB* [2007] EMLR 11; *PJS v News Group Newspapers* [2016] UKSC 23). Thus, in *Mosley v News Group Newspapers Ltd* [2008] EMLR 20 it was accepted that the publication of video footage showing the claimant taking part in sexual activities with prostitutes was private and confidential. Mosley had a reasonable expectation of privacy in those sexual activities, despite them being unconventional. Sheila's case would, therefore, appear to pass this test, and the fact that the boy was 17 does not appear to make the relationship illegal or iniquitous in the absence of any betrayal or abuse of trust.

[3] The author now considers the rules on granting of injunctions, considering the relevant statutes and case law.

Secondly, the court would need to decide whether it would grant an interim injunction,[3] and in doing so would need to consider both the strength of Sheila's claim and any defence of public interest raised at full trial. **Section 12** of the **Human Rights Act 1998** requires the courts to have particular regard to freedom of expression in considering whether to grant relief. Further, **s.12(3)** provides that no relief shall be granted so as to restrain publication before trial unless the court is satisfied that the applicant is likely to establish that publication should not be allowed. This involves determining the strength of the parties' respective arguments (*Re S (Publicity)* [2005] 1 AC 593), and whether the claimant can be adequately compensated by compensation at full trial (*Douglas v Hello!*).

[4] The author now considers both arguments for granting a remedy in this particular scenario before giving an opinion based on the law and the facts.

Applying those principles to the present case, it is debatable whether Sheila will prevent publication of the stories.[4] On the one hand, they relate to extra-marital and transient affairs. Thus, it could be argued that as she is a well-known figure there may be some public interest in publication, at least pending the full trial; although the defendant would have to show more than mere public curiosity. On the other hand, the strength of the claimant's interests may also be diminished by the fact that one boy now wishes to exercise his right to freedom of expression (*A v B plc*). Nonetheless, recent cases appear to indicate that the courts will uphold sexual and family privacy in these cases, and will not judge the morality of the claimant's behaviour unless there is a strong element of public interest (*Mosley v News Group Newspapers* [2008] EWHC 687 (QB)). In that case it was held that the footage was private and confidential and that there was no legitimate public interest in further publication of the video. Again, there appears to be no strong public interest, or acts of true iniquity, to justify publication in this case.

Moreover, Sheila may also be able to gain an anonymity order, preventing the revelation of her identity as well as any details of the relationship (*MNB v News Group Newspapers Ltd* [2011] EWHC 528 (QB)). Such orders were granted in the recent Ryan Giggs affair, even after the relevant information was released on Twitter and in Parliament (*CTB v News Group Newspapers* [2011] EWHC 1326 (QB); *CTB v News Group Newspapers* [2011] EWHC 1334 (QB)) because the court felt that publication in the newspapers was more intrusive of private and family life. This factor might be particularly relevant if Sheila's children or family would be affected (*PJS v News Group Newspapers* [2016] UKSC 26).

[5] The author notes the courts' approach to privacy and photographs, giving leading cases in illustration.

Sheila should also be successful in stopping the publication of the photographs.[5] Thus, in *Theakston v MGN Ltd* [2002] EMLR 22, the Court granted an injunction in respect of photographs taken of the claimant in a brothel, finding that there was a reasonable expectation that such photographs taken without consent would remain private. Such a finding would reflect the domestic courts' concern over the public dissemination of intimate and private detail (*Campbell v MGN*). Failing any attempt to prevent publication, the court could award damages and in *Mosley* the court awarded £60,000 to represent the humiliation and distress caused by the publication of intimate photographs.

The photographing of Sheila and her boyfriend

[6] The author considers the legal position of photographing the boyfriend, considering the leading case law.

Taking a person's photograph without their consent may amount to a *prima facie* breach of confidence (*HRH Princess of Wales v MGN* (Unreported, 8 November 1993)) and may also constitute a misuse of private information (*Campbell*).[6] We are not told where the photographs were taken, and the court must decide whether Sheila and her boyfriend were in a private place and had a reasonable expectation of privacy (*Weller v Associated Newspapers Ltd* [2016] EMLR 7). More generally, the court would need to consider whether a fair-minded person would consider it offensive to disseminate such information (*Campbell*). It would appear that the press behaviour in this case does not impact on individual privacy to the same extent as the photographs taken in *Campbell* and *Theakston*. Nevertheless, taking into account the decision in *Von Hannover*, it is possible that the courts would regard this tactic as an unnecessary method of exposing a public interest story and thus award damages.

[7] The author now examines the possible application of the 1997 Act to the scenario.

Sheila may also bring proceedings under the **Protection from Harassment Act 1997**.[7] **Section 2** makes it an offence to pursue a course of conduct that amounts to harassment of another. Further, **s.3** provides a civil remedy for breaches of the Act, including damages for any anxiety and other loss caused, and for the award of an injunction to restrain such conduct. In our case, the newspaper has pursued a course of conduct against Sheila and her boyfriend. Whether that conduct is unreasonable or not depends on the circumstances of the case, and would depend on the court's findings on whether the invasion was reasonable and in the public interest. Certainly, the taking of a person's photograph without their permission may amount to a breach of confidence or harassment (***Murray v Express Newspapers [2008] 3 WLR 1360; Weller***), and the court's assessment on the press's tactics and the effect of such on the privacy of the individuals would be fundamental to the outcome of the case.[8]

[8]In the Conclusion, the author attempts to gauge the court's reaction to the press tactics in this scenario.

LOOKING FOR EXTRA MARKS?

- For Part A show that you understand the importance of both protecting privacy and upholding press freedom and the public right to know.
- Appreciate the dilemma facing the courts in balancing those rights and the complexity of employing various principles and factors in each case.
- Use leading cases which illustrate that dilemma and which allow you to conclude on the central question.
- For Part B use your appreciation of the cases and principles explained in Part A, together with your interpretation and analytical skills, to analyse the facts and come to logical conclusions on those facts.

TAKING THINGS FURTHER

- Amos, M, *Human Rights Law*, 2nd edn (Hart 2014), ch. 11
  A thorough coverage of article 8 as it has been interpreted under the HRA, together with relevant case law
- Anderson, D, 'The Investigatory Powers Review: A Question of Trust' [2015] 4 EHRLR 331
  A useful overview of surveillance law as it impacts on data protection and other privacy issues, written in the context of the draft Investigatory Powers Bill
- Cobb, J, 'Casting the Dragnet: Communications Data Retention under the Investigatory Powers Act [2018] PL 10
  A critical analysis of the Act with respect to its compatibility with both the ECHR and EU law
- Coleman, L, '"Thou Shalt Not Kill; But Needst Not Strive Officiously to Keep Alive": A Study into the Debate Surrounding Euthanasia and Assisted Suicide' (2015) 3(1) NELR 113
  An interesting and thought-provoking examination of the central debate and the case law
- Harris, D, O'Boyle, K, Warbrick, C, and Bates, E, *The Law of the European Convention on Human Rights*, 4th edn (OUP 2018), chs. 12 and 16
  A thorough coverage of the essential issues under articles 8 and 12 as they have been interpreted by the European Court of Human Rights

Phillipson, G, 'Leveson, the Public Interest and Press Freedom' (2013) 5(2) Journal of Media Law 220

A post- Leveson Inquiry debate on the balance between press freedom and privacy and the role of public interest

Sanderson, MA, 'Is Von Hannover a Step Backward for the Substantive Analysis of Speech and Privacy Interests?' [2004] 6 EHRLR 631

An interesting discussion on the balance between the two rights which can be supplemented by the study of subsequent case law

Online Resources   www.oup.com/uk/qanda/

Go online for extra essay and problem questions, a glossary of key terms, online versions of all the answer plans and audio commentary on how selected ones were put together, and a range of podcasts which include advice on exam and coursework technique and advice for other assessment methods.

10 Freedom of Expression

ARE YOU READY?

In order to attempt questions in this chapter, which covers various aspects of freedom of speech and expression, you will need to have acquired a sound knowledge of the areas listed below during the course and your revision programme:

● A range of questions have been included to reflect the fact that different courses concentrate on different aspects of freedom of expression, including protection under the HRA and the ECHR, press freedom, free speech and national security, free speech and defamation, and contempt of court.

● The various criminal, civil, and other regulations which potentially restrict free speech.

● The underlying values of free speech and expression (and press freedom) together with the requirements for lawful and proportionate restrictions of those rights.

● The legal and constitutional dilemmas involved in the enforcement and restriction of free speech and expression.

KEY DEBATES

Freedom of expression is the subject of much case law from both the domestic and European courts as well as great political and moral debate; in particular with respect to the balancing of free speech and press freedom with the rights of others and matters such as public safety and national security.

Debate: The Scope and Values of Free Speech

What amounts to free speech, and the values it upholds, has become particularly controversial with respect to the restriction of free speech which causes offence, attacks individual rights or sensibilities, or which threatens national security. In particular, speech on social media which causes offence and distress has caused a great deal of debate as to whether we have the right to shock and offend and whether regulation of such speech, under the **Communications Act 2013**, is an unwarranted and dangerous attack on freedom of expression. Equally, speech which causes racial, religious, or sexual offence has been raised in both public debate and in the courts: these cases (*Ngole*) are relevant not only in relation to freedom of expression, but also to the protection of religious and other views considered in Chapter 11.

Debate: Press Freedom and Free Speech

The right of the press to report on matters of public interest gives rise to much legal and social debate as to the role of the press (and its behaviour) and how it should be balanced with matters such as the right to privacy (see Chapter 9), the reputation of others, and other interests such as national security and the administration of justice. Thus, areas such as contempt of court, misuse of private information, official secrecy laws and defamation law impinge on free speech, press freedom, and the public right to know. All such laws need to maintain a balance between press freedom and the preservation of those individual or public interests, and specific 'public interest' defences are essential in maintaining that democratic balance.

QUESTION 1

'Freedom of expression constitutes one of the essential foundations of a democratic society . . . This means that every formality, condition, restriction or penalty imposed in this sphere must be proportionate to the legitimate aim pursued.'

(European Court of Human Rights in *Handyside v United Kingdom* (1976) 1 EHRR 737)

By the use of the case law of the European Court of Human Rights explain how freedom of expression has been upheld, and how the Court has used the 'margin of appreciation' to limit that freedom.

CAUTION!

- This question requires a very sound overall knowledge of article 10 ECHR, but the answer should concentrate on the underlying values of freedom of expression and how they have been protected by the European Court of Human Rights when expression has been limited by state laws and practices.

- In particular, it requires you to comment on the use of the margin of appreciation by the Court in this area and whether that detracts from the enjoyment of free speech values.

- The question does not use the phrase *critically examine*, but you should still take a critical approach having understood the importance of freedom of expression and the danger of over regulation and sanctions on free speech.

- The question refers to the case law of the European Court, but it is permissible to use cases from the domestic courts to illustrate the impact the European Court's jurisprudence may have had.

- Use cases which illustrate the Court's success, or failure, to uphold freedom of expression and which illustrate the way in which the margin of appreciation has been used by the Court to restrict its review of laws that restrain free speech.

DIAGRAM ANSWER PLANS

> Explanation of the values of freedom of expression and its importance in democratic societies

▼

> Explanation of how article 10 of the European Convention seeks to protect freedom of expression

▼

> Examination of the requirements of legitimacy and necessity employed by the Convention with respect to the restriction of that freedom

▼

> Examination of relevant case law of the European Court to explain how and to what extent free speech has been upheld

▼

> Explanation of the doctrine of margin of appreciation and its application in cases of free speech adjudication, together with conclusions

SUGGESTED ANSWER

[1] The author begins by identifying the underlying values of free speech and its importance to liberty.

In *Handyside v United Kingdom* **(1976) 1 EHRR 737** it was recognised that freedom of expression formed one of the essential foundations of any democratic society, forming one of the basic conditions for its progress and for the development of every man. This dictum recognises the value of free speech in achieving individual autonomy and self-fulfilment.[1] Consequently, the Court stressed that the protection afforded by **article 10** is applicable not only to information or ideas that are favourably received or regarded as inoffensive or as a matter of indifference. Accordingly, it applies to those that offend, shock, or disturb the state or any sector of the population. In the Court's view, this accords with the demands of pluralism, tolerance, and broadmindedness without which there is no democratic society.

[2] The author also identifies the democratic value of free speech.

However, the reference to 'a democratic society' recognises that freedom of expression also promotes democracy, allowing the free flow of views on matters of public interest.[2]

Article 10 includes the right to 'hold opinions and to receive and impart information and ideas'. The European Court has extended its protection to various types of expression, including commercial speech (*Autronic AG v Switzerland* **(1990) 12 EHRR 485**), and obscene and blasphemous expression (*Müller v Switzerland* **(1991) 13 EHRR 212** and *Otto-Preminger Institut v Austria* **(1994) 19 EHRR 34**). However, **article 10** does not protect racist speech, particularly if it is aimed at the destruction of the rights of others as prohibited by **article 17** (*Glimerveen and Hagenbeek v Netherlands* **(1980) 18 DR 187)**.

[3] The author clearly states the requirements for any interference with free speech.

Article 10, paragraph 2 allows interference with the right provided the restriction is 'prescribed by law', pursues one of the legitimate aims listed within paragraph 2, and is 'necessary in a democratic society' for the furtherance of that legitimate aim.[3] Freedom of expression, therefore, carries with it duties and responsibilities and has to be balanced against other rights. These could include an individual's privacy (*Von Hannover v Germany* **(2005) 40 EHRR 1;** *MGN Ltd v United Kingdom* **(2011) 51 EHRR 5)** as well as a number of social interests, such as public morality (*Handyside v United Kingdom*). Nevertheless, any interference must possess the qualities of legality and necessity laid down in **article 10(2)**. Further, the Court is not faced with a choice between two conflicting principles, but with a principle of freedom of expression subject to a number of exceptions. Importantly, these must be restrictively and narrowly construed (*Sunday Times v United Kingdom* **(1979) 2 EHRR 245)**.

The Court must be satisfied that any interference is 'prescribed by law', insisting that the law must be identified and established (either in statute or the common law (*Sunday Times v United Kingdom*)). Further, it must be accessible and formulated with sufficient certainty to enable people to regulate their conduct by it (*Silver v United Kingdom* **(1983) 5 EHRR 347)**. Thus, although the Court has accepted that laws are inevitably couched in vague terms (*Sunday Times v United Kingdom*), it has refused to accept rules which are so vague that their meaning cannot be reasonably predicted. For example, in *Hashman and Harrap v United Kingdom* **(1999) 30 EHRR 241**, the power to order a person to desist in conduct which is seen as wrong in the eyes of the majority of contemporary citizens failed to give sufficient guidance to protestors. Further, the restriction must be imposed for a legitimate aim recognised by **article 10(2)**; although it will recognise a measure despite it being unequal in its application (*Gay News v United Kingdom* **(1983) 5 EHRR 123)**.

Crucially, any violation of **article 10** must be 'necessary in a democratic society' for achieving the legitimate aim. Thus, there must be a pressing social need for the restriction and that restriction must constitute a proportionate response to such a need (*Barthold v Germany* **(1985) 7 EHRR 383)**. Further, in *Handyside* it was held that the word 'necessary' did not mean 'useful' or 'convenient'. This protects free speech from violations based on spurious and unsubstantiated grounds.[4] Thus, any restriction needs to be strictly proportionate to its aim and it should not go beyond what is strictly required to achieve that purpose (*Barthold*).

[4] The author explores the meaning of 'necessary' restrictions in the debate on balancing free speech with other interests.

However, this review goes hand in hand with the doctrine of the 'margin of appreciation',[5] which leaves a certain margin of discretion

[5] The author introduces the nature of the doctrine in order to discuss the second part of the question.

to domestic authorities when passing, interpreting, and applying domestic laws that interfere with free speech (*Handyside*). This doctrine assumes that each state might take a variety of measures in attempting to balance free speech with other rights and interests. Accordingly, the Court should respect those measures provided they generally comply with free speech principles in **article 10**.

[6] The author stresses the fact that the doctrine is flexible depending on the context of the restriction.

The doctrine has been used cautiously and the margin of appreciation can be narrowed or widened depending on the circumstances of the case.[6] The state's margin of appreciation has been quite broad with respect to expression that conflicts with public morality, and the Court has been prepared to defer to the member state on such measures. Thus, in *Handyside* it stated that it was not possible to find a uniform conception of morals within the Council of Europe. Accordingly, states, by reason of their direct and continuous contact with the vital forces of their countries, were in a better position than the international judge to give an opinion on the exact content of the requirements of morals, as well as to the necessity of any restriction. The Court has taken a similar stance with respect to blasphemous speech (*Otto-Preminger Institut v Austria* and *Wingrove v United Kingdom* **(1996) 24 EHRR 1**) and has held that it is within each state's discretion to pass and maintain such laws (*Gay News v United Kingdom*). These cases reflect the fact that it may be difficult to apply a common European standard in this area, and that the Court regards shocking and offensive speech as less important than other speech, such as political expression (*Müller v Switzerland*).

[7] The author identifies the limited role of the doctrine with respect to public interest speech.

In contrast, the Court has offered a much narrower margin of appreciation to speech that promotes the wider public interest[7] and, in *Sunday Times*, it held that account must be taken of any public interest aspect of the case. In that case, it held that the granting of injunctions to stop a newspaper discussing impending litigation on the thalidomide disaster should not have been permitted unless it was *absolutely* certain that it would interfere with legal proceedings. That decision can be explained on one of two bases. First, as the Court pointed out, the laws of contempt, as opposed to the laws of obscenity and indecency, displayed a much more common approach. This allowed the Court to more easily judge the necessity of any particular interference and, in such a case, a more extensive European supervision corresponds to a less discretionary power of appreciation. Secondly, the duty of the press to inform the public on matters of great public interest was essential to democracy, and the Court will thus subject the measure to more intense scrutiny.

[8] The author highlights the Court's role in safeguarding press freedom.

The Court is thus prepared to afford special protection to freedom of speech in the context of press freedom.[8] For example, in *Thorgeirson v Iceland* **(1992) 14 EHRR 843** it held that when journalists publish articles directed at a matter of serious public interest in an attempt to draw popular attention to matters of legitimate public concern, any penalty imposed on such a person had to be strictly proportionate. This suggests that excessive penalties, including excessive damages in defamation actions (***Tolstoy v United Kingdom* (1995) 20 EHRR 442**), might have a chilling effect on press freedom, and should be subjected to very close scrutiny. Similarly, in ***Jersild v Denmark* (1994) 19 EHRR 1,** the conviction and fining of an employee of a broadcasting company for assisting the expression of unlawful racist speech on a television show was held in violation of **article 10**. Although the views of the group were not protected by **article 10**, the punishment of a journalist for assisting in the dissemination of such statements would seriously hamper the contribution of the press in discussion of matters of public interest.

[9]The author refers to US jurisprudence to support the protection of political debate.

As with the United States Supreme Court (***New York Times v Sullivan* (1964) 376 US 254**), the European Court has given enhanced protection under **article 10** to those who question and criticise government and public officials.[9] For example, in ***Castells v Spain* (1992) 14 EHRR 445** it stressed that in the democratic system, the actions or omissions of the government must be subject to close scrutiny not only by the legislative and judicial authorities but also via the press and public opinion. Thus, in ***Lingens v Austria* (1986) 8 EHRR 407** it noted that freedom of the press afforded the public the best means of discovering and forming an opinion of the ideas and attitudes of political leaders. As a consequence, the limits of acceptable criticism of an individual are wider with respect to a politician than as regards a private individual. However, the Court has not gone so far as to prohibit public figures or large corporations from taking actions in defamation (***Steel and Morris v United Kingdom* (2005) 41 EHRR 22**). The Court will also allow a narrow margin of appreciation if the restriction takes the form of prior restraint (***Observer and Guardian v United Kingdom* (1991) 14 EHRR 153**).

[10]The author provides a neat summary of the European Court's stance on freedom of expression and its regulation.

The European Court has extended the protection of **article 10** to almost all forms of expression and has, despite the doctrine of the margin of appreciation, required strong justification for any restriction with that right.[10] However, the Court is more likely to offer states more deference where the speech does not genuinely serve the public interest. This is evident in the judgment in ***Von Hannover v Germany***, where it held that a celebrity's privacy had been violated when the paparazzi persistently photographed her whilst shopping and socialising. In the Court's view, the public did not have a genuine public interest in receiving such information, distinguishing this case from those such as ***Lingens***. From this case, it appears that some speech may be more important than others, and that such a factor will dictate the margin of appreciation afforded to the domestic authorities.

LOOKING FOR EXTRA MARKS?

▦ Show that you understand the values of free speech and its democratic importance to the individual and the public interest.

▦ Appreciate the legal and diplomatic dilemma facing the European Court in upholding such rights, and in judging the necessity and proportionality of any state restrictions.

▦ Use leading and topical cases which illustrate that dilemma and which allow you to identify any themes which can define the Court's jurisprudence in this area.

QUESTION | 2

To what extent does English common law protect freedom of expression? How has the passing of the Human Rights Act 1998 enhanced free speech and do you feel that domestic law is now consistent with the case law of the European Court on Human Rights?

CAUTION!

▦ This question requires a sound overall knowledge of freedom of expression in UK law, but the answer should concentrate on addressing the extent to which domestic law has and does recognise the notion and values of freedom of expression and whether that law is consistent with the protection offered by the European Court.

▦ The question does not employ the phrase *critical examination*, but nevertheless you should take a critical approach having understood the democratic importance of free speech and the protection offered to it under the ECHR.

▦ The question refers to protection in domestic law, but you will need to refer to cases from the European Court to examine the second part of the question: the law's compliance with the European Convention case law.

▦ Use cases and other domestic law which examine the legal and constitutional dilemmas faced by the courts and the law-makers in upholding freedom of expression and which allow you to assess the domestic law's compatibility with free speech values and the ECHR.

DIAGRAM ANSWER PLANS

Brief explanation of the theory of free speech protection and its constitutional importance

▼

Examination of the status of free speech at common law and examples of its recognition, enforcement, and the limitations of that protection

▼

Explanation of the 'incorporation' of article 10 of the Convention into domestic law by the 1998 Act, in particular via s.12 of the Act

Critical examination of the post-Human Rights Act case law to examine the effectiveness of free speech protection

Analysis of present domestic law to assess its compatibility with the European Convention with respect to the values and principles of free speech upheld by article 10 of the Convention, along with relevant case law

SUGGESTED ANSWER

Before the **Human Rights Act 1998**, freedom of expression existed as a residual freedom. This allowed everyone freedom of speech provided that it did not infringe restrictions in statute or the common law, such as the criminal laws of obscenity and indecency, and civil laws such as defamation and confidentiality. Although freedom of expression was not protected in a bill of rights, the courts accepted it as a fundamental constitutional right,[1] protecting it from arbitrary and unnecessary interference by interpreting legislative and common law restrictions to ensure its greatest possible enjoyment (***Wheeler v Leicester County Council* [1985] AC 1054**).

The courts would thus insist on substantial justification for any interference and, in ***R v Secretary of State for the Home Department, ex parte O'Brien and Simms* [2000] 2 AC 115**, a policy restricting journalists visiting prisoners and publishing of such interviews was declared *ultra vires* the **Prison Act 1952**. Lord Steyn noted that the starting point was freedom of expression, which in a democracy is a primary right and without which an effective rule of law is not possible. The courts thus insisted that freedom of expression was as well protected at common law as under **article 10** of the European Convention on Human Rights.[2] For example, in ***R v Secretary of State for the Home Department, ex parte Brind* [1991] AC 696** the House of Lords stressed that the courts would start with the presumption that any interference with freedom of expression was unlawful. Similarly, in ***Attorney-General v Guardian Newspapers (No. 2)* [1998] 3 All ER 852** the House of Lords held that an injunction could not be granted restraining the publication of information on matters of government unless there was evidence of an overriding public interest outweighing the public interest in the free dissemination of information.

Despite this approach, the position of freedom of expression was regarded as unsatisfactory. In **Brind** the courts had rejected the possibility of relying on **article 10** of the Convention directly[3] and subjecting restrictions to the doctrine of proportionality. This led to defeats

[1] The author begins by asserting free speech as a common law right in the UK.

[2] He then examines the proposition that common law protection is as effective as that under the ECHR.

[3] The author now examines the weakness of common law protection.

before the European Court of Human Rights in areas such as contempt of court (*Sunday Times v United Kingdom* (1979) 2 EHRR 245), the disclosure of press sources (*Goodwin v United Kingdom* (1996) 22 EHRR 123), and prior restraint (*Observer and Guardian v United Kingdom* (1991) 14 EHRR 153). This displayed the inconsistency of domestic judges in protecting free speech and the need for reform.

[4] The author stresses the potential importance of the HRA in safeguarding free speech against arbitrary interference.

With the passing of the **Human Rights Act 1998**, domestic courts were allowed to refer to relevant Convention case law when resolving free speech disputes[4] and in deciding whether any interference is 'necessary in a democratic society'. This was intended to ensure that the domestic courts were applying the same weight to freedom of expression as does the European Court. In addition, **s.12** of the **Human Rights Act** requires the courts to have particular regard to freedom of expression where it grants relief that might affect the exercise of freedom of expression. More specifically, **s.12(2)** encourages open discussion on free speech restrictions and stresses the need for both parties to be present and represented in free speech proceedings before relief is granted. Further, the *Report of the Committee on Super-Injunctions: Super-Injunctions, Anonymised Injunctions and Open Justice*, 20 May 2011, recommended that the press should receive pre-notification of anonymity orders and 'super' injunctions.

[5] The author now deals with the important issue of prior restraint and its regulation.

The Act also seeks to control interferences with free speech via prior restraint, viewed by the European Court as the most dangerous form of restriction[5] (*Observer and Guardian v United Kingdom*). **Section 12(3)** provides that a court should not restrain publication before trial unless it is satisfied that the applicant is likely to establish that publication should not be allowed. This is intended to favour publication by modifying the rule in *American Cyanamid v Ethicon Ltd* [1975] AC 396—the balance of probabilities test. In *Cream Holdings v Banerjee and another* [2005] 1 AC 253 it was held that this set a higher threshold for granting interim orders against the press; although controversially the Supreme Court granted an injunction in *PJS v News Group Newspapers* [2016] UKSC 26 to protect the claimant's private and family life, despite the information already having, partially, reached the public domain.

[6] The author stresses the courts' rejection of any 'trump' status for free speech.

However, the courts have recognised that freedom of expression is not an absolute right.[6] Thus, although **s.12** provides that the courts must have *particular regard* to the importance of this Convention right, this does not give free speech an absolute or even superior status over and above other Convention rights. For example, in *Douglas v Hello!* [2001] 2 WLR 992 the Court of Appeal held that **s.12(4)** requires the court to consider **article 10** of the Convention in its entirety. It must not, therefore, give freedom of speech additional weight over and above any competing right, such as the right to private life. Equally, the court's task under **s.12(3)** was to apply its mind to how one right was to be balanced against another right, without building in additional weight on the one side (*Re S (Publicity)* [2005] 1 AC 593). For example, in *PNM v Times Newspapers Ltd* [2017] UKSC 49, a judge had properly assessed the competing rights of the press and the public against those of a man who had been arrested but not formally charged following an investigation into allegations of child sex grooming and prostitution. In refusing an interim non-disclosure order, the court ordered that the appellant was to be referred to in the proceedings by his real name.

This reflects the wording of **s.12(4)**, which requires the court to consider whether it would violate any relevant privacy code. Nevertheless, the courts start with the premise that any interference with free speech is unlawful and that the grounds for interference have to be established convincingly (*Venables and Thompson v MGN* [2001] 2 WLR 1038).

Whether freedom of expression has been enhanced in the post-Human Rights Act era, can only be answered by examining the relevant case law. In many areas, such as national security, the courts appear to remain deferential.[7] For example, in *R v Shayler* [2002] 2 WLR 754 the House of Lords refused to imply a public interest defence into the **Official Secrets Act 1989**. This was because it believed that the special position of those employed in the security and intelligence services made it inappropriate to offer such a defence, even where the information in question was of great public interest. This is consistent with the European Court's stance in this area (*Leander v Sweden* (1987) 9 EHRR 433). More positively, in *Corporate Officer of the House of Commons v Information Commissioner, The Times*, 22 May 2008, it was held that the Information Commissioner and the Information Tribunal were entitled to disclose further details of the information provided by the House of Commons with respect to allowances claimed by MPs. On the other hand, in *Kennedy v Information Commissioner* [2015] AC 455 the Supreme Court upheld the absolute rule under **s.32 of the Freedom of Information Act 2000** on the public disclosure of documents relating to public inquiries.

Further deference was shown in *R (Prolife) v BBC* [2004] 1 AC 185, where the courts upheld a ban on a proposed election broadcast on the grounds that it violated taste and decency. In that case the House of Lords stressed that the courts should be reluctant to interfere with the broadcasting authority's decision in balancing the requirements of political speech and the protection of the public from undue distress. Further, in *R (Animal Defenders International) v Minister of Culture, Media and Sport* [2008] 2 WLR 781 it was held that the **Communications Act 2003**, which prohibits political advertising, was compatible with **article 10**. This was despite the Minister making a declaration of incompatibility when introducing the Bill, believing it to be inconsistent with the European Court's case law (*VgT Verein gegen Tierfabriken v Switzerland* (2002) 34 EHRR 4). This decision, however, was upheld in the European Court (*Animal Defenders*

[7] The author now examines areas where the courts have continued with traditional deference.

International v United Kingdom (2013) 57 EHRR 31). Similar deference has been shown in cases where free speech might endanger either international relations or public safety; and where the judgement of the executive authorities is unlikely to be challenged (*R (Lord Carlile of Berriew) v Secretary of State for the Home Department* [2015] AC 945; *R (Geller) v Secretary of State for the Home Department* [2015] EWCA Civ 45). An equal deference was given recently to educational bodies when restricting anti-gay speech which was inconsistent with the claimant's intention to enter the social work profession (*R (Ngole) v University of Sheffield* [2017] EWHC 2669 (Admin)).

[8] The author now examines the more favourable protection of public interest speech under the HRA.

The courts have been more liberal in cases where they are satisfied that there is a true public interest in publication,[8] allowing them to refuse interim injunctions in cases where free speech conflicts with the commercial confidences of the claimant (*Cream Holdings*). However, they have been less generous where freedom of expression has conflicted with individual privacy, stating that the public have a very limited interest in publication of details of such individuals' private lives, even if they are well known (*McKennitt v Ash* [2007] 3 WLR 194; *HRH Prince of Wales v Associated Newspapers Ltd* [2007] 3 WLR 222). Despite this, a more positive approach was taken in *R (on the application of Evans) v Attorney General* [2015] UKSC 21, where it was held that **s.53 of the Freedom of Information Act 2000** did not entitle an accountable person to issue a certificate to override a Tribunal decision that communications between the Prince of Wales and government departments should be disclosed. So, too, the courts have extended the defence of qualified privilege to the press where there is a true and strong public interest in publication (*Jameel v Wall Street Journal Europe* [2007] 1 AC 359), and this approach was adopted in the **Defamation Act 2013**, which liberalised the law in this area.

In conclusion, domestic law is now equipped to apply the principles of legality and necessity that are employed by the European Court to ensure that interference with free speech is not incompatible with **article 10**. In some areas there is evidence that freedom of expression is given greater weight than in the past, particularly with respect to the granting of temporary injunctions. However, in areas such as national security and public morality, there appears to be little evidence of fundamental change.

[9] The author comes to a guarded and balanced conclusion as to whether the HRA has impacted positively on free speech.

This probably justifies the conclusion that, on the whole, freedom of expression has not been greatly enhanced in the post-Human Rights Act era,[9] but that some speech at least is better protected.

LOOKING FOR EXTRA MARKS?

- Show that you understand the scope and importance of free speech (and press freedom) in a democracy and the reasons why restrictions have to be kept to a minimum.

- Appreciate the legal and constitutional dilemmas facing the domestic courts in recognising free speech rights, together with the impact of the Human Rights Act 1998 on that role.

- Use leading and topical cases which illustrate the extent to which the law and the courts have upheld free speech values in particular contexts, allow you to employ your critical skills, and conclude on the central question of the status of free speech in domestic law and its compliance with the ECtHR.

QUESTION | 3

Part A

To what extent are the laws of defamation a justifiable interference with free speech and freedom of the press?

Part B

Arnold, a freelance journalist, began investigating the private and professional affairs of Sir Graham Forrester, an MP and former government minister. On the basis of information given to him by Sir Graham's ex-personal secretary, Arnold submitted an article to the *Sunday Scum*, which alleged that, whilst chairman of the 'Family Values' Committee, Sir Graham had been involved in an affair with the 18-year-old daughter of a neighbour. Acting on the same source, he also submitted an article to the same newspaper, which alleged that his wife allowed him to entertain prostitutes in the family home. Sir Graham was telephoned by the newspaper's editor and asked for his comments on the allegations, but he simply told them that he had no comment, other than he would sue if they published 'these lies'. Sir Graham now wishes to sue the newspaper in defamation in connection with these articles.

Advise Sir Graham as to what remedies are available to him and the likelihood of him succeeding in an action for defamation.

CAUTION!

- This question requires a very sound overall knowledge of defamation law, but the answer should concentrate first on an examination of the law in terms of its compatibility with free speech; and then, in Part B, an application of those laws to a particular scenario.

- The first question does not employ the phrase *critical examination*, but you should take a critical approach having understood the importance of the balance between the protection of free speech and reputation and the basic principles established by the ECHR in this area.

- In the first part it is permissible to cite cases from the European Court as well as domestic decisions in order to examine that balance; use cases which illustrate that balance and allow you to judge the compatibility of domestic law with ECHR principles.

- In the second part of the question apply the relevant law and cases (including ECHR cases if relevant) to the facts so as to allow you to give clear and appropriate advice to both parties.

DIAGRAM ANSWER PLANS

Part A

> Explanation of the aims of defamation laws and their impact on freedom of expression

▼

> Explanation and analysis of the extent of those laws, the penalties for infringement, and any available defences, including the new law under the Defamation Act 2013

▼

> Conclusions as to the necessity and proportionality of those laws and defences and their compatibility with the Human Rights Act 1998 and the European Convention on Human Rights

Part B

| Identify the issues | ■ The legal issues and the claims made by Sir Geoffrey and any defences employed by the journalist
■ Action in defamation and remedies; defences of truth, honest opinion, and public interest |

| Relevant law | ■ Outline the rules and cases relating to the claim, remedies, and any defence |

| Apply the law | ■ Application of the rules on remedies and defences to the facts |

| Conclude | ■ Conclude on whether the action, or any defence, would be likely to succeed |

 SUGGESTED ANSWER

Part A

[1] The author identifies that defamation laws are required for the protection of reputation and human rights.

[2] The author now stresses that such laws have to be proportionate so as not to stifle free speech.

Article 10(2) of the European Convention provides that freedom of expression can be restricted to protect the rights or reputations of others; a person's right to reputation being part of his or her private life[1] (*Tammer v Estonia* **(2003) 37 EHRR 43**). However, such laws must strike a proper balance between these competing fundamental rights and domestic law should not unreasonably halt the flow of political and other public interest discussion[2] (*Lingens v Austria* **(1986) 8 EHRR 407**), or award damages and costs so excessive as to impose a chilling effect on free speech (*Tolstoy v United Kingdom* (1975) **20 EHRR 442;** *MGN Ltd v United Kingdom* (2011) **51 EHRR 5**). Further, in *Steel and Morris v United Kingdom* (2005) **41 EHRR 22** the Court stressed the importance of equality of arms between those who publish and powerful claimants.

The domestic law protects an individual's reputation from untrue statements that either subjects them to ridicule, hatred, or contempt, or which lower that person's reputation in the eyes of right-thinking members of society (*Sim v Stretch* (1936) **52 TLR 669**). However, in an attempt to protect free speech, the law may in some cases not allow such actions to be taken.[3] Thus **article 9 of the Bill of Rights 1689** protects parliamentary debates by providing that freedom of speech and debates or proceedings in Parliament cannot be impeached or questioned; upheld by the European Court (*A v United Kingdom* (2003) **36 EHRR 51**). Further, in *Derbyshire County Council v Times Newspapers* [1993] **AC 534**, it was held that democratically elected bodies were not able to sue in defamation as such an action would stifle public criticism of its activities; although individuals within public bodies can sue in defamation if adequately identified (*McLaughlin v Lambeth LBC* [2011] **EMLR 8**).

The common law also protects freedom of expression in this area from prior restraint. Thus, in *Bonnard v Perryman* [1891] **2 Ch 269** it was held that no temporary orders pending full trial will be given where the defendant intends to raise any available defence, unless it was clear that such a defence would fail at the trial. This has been accepted as a necessary safeguard to free speech and thus compatible with **articles 8 and 10** of the Convention (*Green v Associated Newspapers* [2005] **3 WLR 281**). The presumption against prior restraint is, however, offset by the threat of large damages awards, which may have a chilling effect on freedom of expression. This danger was recognised in *Tolstoy Miloslavsky v United Kingdom* where it was held that an award of £1.5m constituted a disproportionate interference with freedom of expression. The domestic courts are now empowered to give juries strict guidance on the acceptability of damage awards (*Grobbelaar v News Group Newspapers* [2002] **1 WLR 3024**). However, in *Independent News and Media plc and another v Ireland* (2006) **42 EHRR 46**, the European Court held that high awards are acceptable provided domestic law provides sufficient safeguards against disproportionate damages. Further, under **s.1 of the Defamation Act 2013** claimants must show that they have suffered serious harm before suing for defamation, with companies having to show serious financial harm (*Lachaux v Independent Print Ltd* [2015] **EWHC 2242 (QB)**). Thus, in *Barron and Healey v Caven Vines* [2016] **EWHC 1226 (QB)** it was held that damages of £40,000 each for defamatory allegations against two MPs, to the effect that

[3] The author examines instances where actions in defamation are barred in order to encourage free speech.

they had known about the large-scale sexual abuse of children in Rotherham and had allowed it to continue, was proportionate. The award struck the right balance between the need to vindicate their reputations and the need to avoid over-chilling freedom of speech in the political arena.

Because the law has such a potentially damaging impact on free speech, it is essential that suitable defences are available in such actions.[4] The **Defamation Act** now provides a defence of truth (formerly justification) and honest opinion (fair comment) and also provides a defence of public interest (together with the defence of qualified privilege, which will be lost if the defendant has acted maliciously or in bad faith). These defences apply, *inter alia*, to fair and accurate reports of both parliamentary proceedings and *bona fide* public meetings held for a lawful purpose and to discuss matters of public concern. Thus, in *Turkington v Times Newspapers Ltd* [2001] 2 AC 277, a press conference attracted qualified privilege, recognising that such forums had become an important vehicle for promoting discussion on matters of public concern.

The defence is also available where the defendant has a legal or moral duty to impart information (*Beech v Freeson* [1972] 1 QB 14), and in *Reynolds v Times Newspapers* [1999] 4 All ER 609 it was held that the defence might be used by the press in appropriate circumstances to justify the publication of public interest information. Whether the defence was available depended on factors such as the seriousness of the allegation, the nature of the information (including the urgency of the matter), and the extent to which the subject matter was of public concern. In addition, they stressed the need for the press to display responsible journalism, requiring it in most cases to check its sources and to seek the comments of the potential claimant before publication. The courts applied the defence with caution and in *Loutchansky v Times Newspapers Ltd and others (No. 2)* [2002] 1 All ER 652 it was held that the press had a corresponding duty to act responsibly. Thus, to set the standard of journalistic responsibility too low would encourage too great a readiness to publish defamatory material (*Galloway v Telegraph Group Ltd* [2005] EMLR 7). However, in *Jameel v Wall Street Journal* [2005] 2 WLR 1577 the House of Lords held that the defence should not be denied simply because the press had departed from one of its obligations to ensure professional journalism. The main factor was whether the public interest test had been satisfied, and this more liberal approach is now reiterated in statutory form by **s.4 of the Defamation Act 2013**.[5]

Outside the defence of qualified privilege/public interest, the press will have to rely on the defences of honest opinion (fair comment) and truth (justification), involving the press proving the substantial truth of the statement. For example, in *Begg v BBC* [2016] EWHC 2688

[4] The author stresses the need for effective and liberal defences in order to protect free speech and press freedom.

[5] Having examined the application of the qualified privilege defence by the courts, the author displays his awareness of recent statutory changes in this area.

(QB) it was accepted that words spoken by the presenter of a current affairs television programme were substantially true in their meanings that the imam was an extremist Islamic speaker who espoused extremist Islamic positions and had recently promoted and encouraged religious violence by telling Muslims that violence in support of Islam would constitute a man's greatest deed.

Although the European Court has accepted that this burden of proof is not necessarily inconsistent with **article 10** (*McVicar v United Kingdom* **(2000) 35 EHRR 22**), it has stressed that the law of defamation should provide greater protection to speech which attacks politicians (*Lingens*), and large corporations (*Steel and Morris v United Kingdom*), particularly where the statements are part of general public discussion.

[6] The author concludes by referring to the potential effect of the Defamation Act 2013 in further liberalising the law of defamation; referring specifically to a high-profile case.

It is hoped that the **Defamation Act 2013** will further enhance free speech in this area[6] and achieve an even more coherent balance between press freedom and the protection of individual reputation. The 'plebgate' controversy—*Mitchell v News Group Newspapers Ltd* **[2014] EWHC 4014 (QB)**—suggests that the courts will be less tolerant of public figures using defamation actions to suppress public discussion, although the law will have to be more tolerant in other cases so as to secure the right to defend one's reputation against unreasonable attacks.

Part B

Sir Graham would need to establish that the allegations contained in the stories would lower Sir Graham's reputation in the eyes of right-thinking members of society (*Sim v Stretch*) and would cause him serious harm (under **s.1 of the Defamation Act 2013**). There would appear to be little doubt that such allegations would so harm Sir Graham's reputation, ruining his career as an MP and causing him to be castigated in the eyes of the public.[1] Further, this could cause him serious financial harm, as he may find it difficult to hold a position of authority and responsibility in the future.

[1] Having defined defamation the author comes to a sensible conclusion as to whether there is a defamatory statement on the facts.

If Sir Graham sought an interim injunction, prohibiting the publication of the allegations pending the full trial of the action, the courts will not grant such an order where the defendant relies on any relevant defences at the trial (*Bonnard v Perryman* and *Green v Associated Newspapers*). The injunction will be refused unless the court is satisfied that the defences are bound to fail at the full trial,[2] which given the fact that the information was received from an ex-employee, appears unlikely.

[2] The author explains the prior restraint rule before applying that test to the facts.

[3] The author now examines the damages claim, then outlining the basic principles of any such award.

Accordingly, Sir Graham is advised to maintain an action in defamation for damages.[3] This will compensate him for the harm caused to his reputation. Such damages could also reflect any interference with his right to private life, as guaranteed by **article 8**, and can be substantial in a case such as the present where great financial and other harm is likely to be caused (***The Gleaner Company and another v Abrahams* [2004] 1 AC 628**). However, any award must not be so great as to have a chilling effect on freedom of expression (***Tolstoy Miloslavsky v United Kingdom* (1995) 22 EHRR 442**).

[4]The author now examines the defences available to the defendant before considering whether they are available on these facts.

The newspaper would seek to rely on a number of defences at full trial.[4] First, it will seek to rely on the defence of truth (justification). The newspaper will have to prove the truth of the sting of the allegation, rather than the truth of every allegation made in the stories (***Begg v BBC***). Thus, if the neighbour's daughter was 20 rather than 18, that would not defeat a defence, whereas if the affair was with a mature woman who was not a neighbour's daughter, the defence would fail. Similarly, under **s.2 of the Defamation Act 2013**, where more than one defamatory comment is made and not all of them are justified, the defence is still available if the words not proved to be true do not materially injure the claimant's reputation having regard to the truth of the remaining charges. Thus, if the allegations about the prostitutes are proved to be true, then the newspaper could rely on **s.2** even if the story about the neighbour's daughter was untrue, the reputation of Sir Graham already being irreparably damaged.

As the newspaper's allegations could not be described as opinion, it could not rely on the defence of honest opinion (fair comment)—

[5]The author identifies the need to consider an alternative defence and proceeds to explain its scope and limitations, using relevant cases.

***Spiller v Joseph* [2010] UKSC 53**—and it would have to rely on the defence of public interest under **s.4**.[5] The defence is not available if it can be proved that the defendant has acted maliciously or in bad faith, which is unlikely in the present circumstances because the newspaper at least relies on information given by a third party.

Since ***Reynolds v Times Newspapers***, the press has been allowed to rely on the defence provided the 'duty-interest test' had been satisfied. The court would first need to be satisfied that there was a sufficient public interest in the publication. This seems to be clear, as the claimant is a current MP, a former cabinet minister, and a former chairman of a Family Values Committee, making the allegations particularly appropriate for public debate. The court would also consider factors such as the seriousness of the allegation—in this case it is particularly serious, which might act against the newspaper. Equally, it would consider the nature of the information and the extent to which the subject matter was of public concern, which in the present case would favour publication.

To rely on this defence, newspapers must exercise the attributes of professional journalism (***Loutchansky v Times Newspapers Ltd and others (No. 2)***), although the essential question is whether there is a public interest in publication (***Jameel v Wall Street Journal Europe***)—an aspect stressed in **s.4 of the 2013 Act**. Although the courts will pay regard to particular factors such as the source and status of the information, the steps taken to verify it, the urgency of the matter, and the tone of the article, these are subject to the ultimate test of public interest. In any case, these factors appear to favour the press in our case as the source appears reliable, and the public interest would be best served by the instant publication of the matter.

More specifically, regard can still be had as to whether the defendant had sought comment from the claimant, and whether the article contained the gist of the claimant's side of the story. Sir Graham was approached and told the editor that he had nothing to say, apart from his threat to sue. Thus, given the public interest in the information, and the facts that the newspaper appears to be relying on a reliable source and to have given the claimant an opportunity to comment, Sir Graham would be advised that his action in defamation would be met with a successful defence of public interest.[6]

[6] The author's conclusion is based on a sound knowledge of the principles and cases and careful consideration of the facts.

LOOKING FOR EXTRA MARKS?

- For Part A, show that you understand the dilemma involved in balancing free speech with the need to protect reputation and private life.
- Use leading and topical cases which illustrate that dilemma and which allow you to employ your critical skills and conclude on the central question of whether the law achieves an appropriate balance and is thus justified.
- For Part B, ensure that you appreciate the court's role in balancing the two rights when you are applying the relevant law and cases to the factual scenario.
- Be careful to look at the facts carefully and to make suitable comparisons with previous cases.

QUESTION | 4

Critically assess the extent to which the domestic law relating to government confidentiality and official secrets provides for a defence of 'press freedom' and the public right to know.

CAUTION!

- This question requires a very sound knowledge and appreciation of free speech and press freedom as it is affected by official secrecy and confidentiality laws.
- The question asks for an analysis of that law, but in particular the extent to which the laws provide for defences of press freedom and the public right to know; a good appreciation of the need for such defences to protect free speech is thus essential.
- The question refers to protection in domestic law, but it is permissible to use cases from the European Court in order to examine how such decisions have impacted on the domestic law.
- Use cases and statutory provisions to examine the law's recognition of the necessity of such laws and the need to accommodate press freedom and the public right to know in such laws.

DIAGRAM ANSWER PLANS

> Explanation of the rules and aims of the common law of confidentiality and the Official Secrets Acts

> ▼

> Consideration of the need to balance national security with press freedom and the public right to know

> ▼

> Consideration of the extent to which the above laws accommodate any press freedom defence

> ▼

> Conclusions as to whether the present law adequately protects press freedom and the public right to know

SUGGESTED ANSWER

[1] The author provided the reader with a neat summary of the legal and political dilemmas in this area.

Although the workings and activities of government and other public agencies are undoubtedly in the public interest, the disclosure of such information may be detrimental to effective government and national safety.[1] The law will, therefore, have to balance these issues. Under **article 10(2)** of the European Convention freedom of speech can be compromised on grounds of national security, territorial integrity, public safety, the prevention of disorder and crime, and the prevention of the disclosure of information received in confidence. All these potentially promote the machinery of government, but such restrictions

[2] The author now stresses the need to insist on the strict review of laws relating to secrecy and confidentiality.

have to be prescribed by law and necessary in a democratic society.[2] However, in *Leander v Sweden* **(1987) 9 EHRR 433** it was accepted that the state would be given discretion not only with respect to the necessity and proportionality of such laws, but also as to their clarity and certainty.

The government's power to defend national security is contained in specific official secrets and confidentiality laws, which can be employed by public authorities to criminalise the disclosure of sensitive information. Alternatively, it can employ the civil law to obtain prior restraint to stop its dissemination. Equally, it is important to provide the public with access to public information, a right which is not specifically protected under **article 10** of the Convention (*Leander v Sweden*), but which is now covered under the **Freedom of Information Act 2000**, which came into force in 2005.

[3] The author explains the purpose and scope of the Official Secrets Act 1989.

The **Official Secrets Act 1989** was passed in order to liberalise the **1911 Act**.[3] The earlier Act made it an offence for specified persons to disclose any official information without lawful authority, irrespective of the nature or content of the information or of any potential damage caused on disclosure. The Act was discredited in *R v Ponting* [1985] **Crim LR 318**, and the **1989 Act** creates particular categories of information that might attract liability—security and intelligence, defence, international relations, and crime and special investigation powers. Significantly, it imposes liability only where the disclosure of the information would be damaging to those interests. It was hoped that this would create a defence of public interest, allowing the defendant to argue that any breach, for example, exposed government incompetence; a claim clearly rejected in *Chandler v DPP* [1964] **AC 763**.

However, although the law of confidentiality has allowed defences of public interest and prior publication (*Attorney-General v Guardian Newspapers (No. 2)* [1990] **1 AC 109**), the **1989 Act** does not recognise a public interest defence. This rule was established in *R v Shayler* [2002] **2 WLR 754**,[4] where a former member of the security service had been charged with unlawful disclosure of documents and information, contrary to **ss.1 and 4**. The defendant had argued that his disclosure was justified in the public interest because he alleged that the security services had been involved in a plot to kill a head of state and that they had been guilty of gross incompetence. The House of Lords held that there was no right for the defendant to show that the disclosure was, or, in his opinion, might be, in the public interest. Further, such a finding was not incompatible with **article 10** of the European Convention or its case law (*Leander v Sweden* and *Klass v Germany* (1978) **2 EHRR 214**).

The House of Lords recognised the special duties owed by persons employed in the services as justifying the lack of any public interest defence. However, it added that despite such deference the courts would insist on adequate safeguards to ensure that any restriction on free speech did not exceed what was necessary to achieve national security. Thus, the ban on disclosure was not absolute and was tempered by the right under **s.7(3)(a)** of the Act to make disclosure to appropriate staff if one had concerns about illegality, maladministration, or incompetence. Further, a person had the right under **s.7(3)(b)** to seek official authorisation to make disclosure, any refusal being subject to judicial review. Given that the European Court's principal concern is to ensure procedural safeguards against abuse (*Klass*), the decision is probably consistent with the case law of the Convention. On the other hand, the reverse burden of proof contained in the **1989 Act** was held incompatible with the right to a fair trial in *R v Keogh* [2007] **1 WLR 1500**.

The courts have been more receptive to the notion of press freedom when interpreting the common law of confidentiality.[5] The

[4] The author explains the conservative approach adopted in *Shayler*.

[5] A more liberal approach in confidentiality laws is now used in contrast.

government relies on the duty of confidentiality to ensure that its servants do not breach their duties of loyalty (*Attorney-General v Blake* [2001] 1 AC 268; *Blake v United Kingdom* (2007) 44 EHRR 29). Further, this duty can be imposed on the press if it intends to disclose such information, making it guilty of contempt if it publishes. Such publications are subject to prior restraint in the form of interim injunctions; although, in *Attorney-General v Guardian Newspapers (No. 2)*, it was held that a public body could only maintain an injunction if it could prove that there was an overriding public interest justifying an interference with freedom of expression. Further, if information has entered the public domain it can no longer be the basis of an injunction to preserve confidentiality. This was evident in that case, where Peter Wright's book *Spycatcher* had already entered the public domain. The position was clarified by the European Court in *Observer and Guardian v United Kingdom* (1991) 14 EHRR 153, where it was held that the granting of injunctions before the book entered the public domain was necessary to preserve national security—as the domestic courts had weighed the conflicting public interests before granting the orders. However, injunctions granted after the information had entered the public domain were unnecessary and disproportionate to the need to protect the efficiency and reputation of the security service.

The European Court accepted that those injunctions prevented the newspapers from carrying out their right and duty to inform the public about matters of great and legitimate public concern. However, the decision suggests that judges, both domestic and European, will be loath to interfere when there is a *true* conflict between the public interest in defending national security and the public interest in receiving information on governmental matters. Thus, the European Court did not appear to conduct a full inquiry into whether prohibiting any breach of confidence would be offset by the public interest in receiving information about possible illegal conduct on behalf of the government. Nevertheless, the decision is more favourable to press freedom than the ruling in *Shayler*, which upholds the restriction on dissemination because of the position of the informant, irrespective of any public interest in publication. Further, the domestic courts have taken a liberal view with respect to the disclosure of confidential correspondence between states.[6] Thus, in *R (Binyan Mohamed) v Secretary of State for Foreign and Commonwealth Affairs* [2010] 3 WLR 554, the Court of Appeal ordered the publication of documents passed between the UK and the US authorities relating to a suspected terrorist's detention and treatment so that they could be used in legal proceedings. In refusing the claim of public interest immunity, it held that

[6] The author uses a high-profile intelligence case to support the argument that the courts are willing to protect the public right to know, before providing a less liberal case example.

confidentiality as to working arrangements between allied intelligence services was not absolute. In this case those reports should be included as they did not contain any information which would pose a risk to national security but did contain information that it was in the public interest to disclose. A less liberal approach was evident in *R (Lord Carlile of Berriew) v Secretary of State for the Home Department* [2015] AC 945, where the Supreme Court refused to gainsay the executive's assessment of a threat to international relations when upholding the exclusion of a political activist into the country.

[7] The author now examines the application of contempt laws in this area and the chilling effect on press freedom.

The law of contempt can be employed in conjunction with confidentiality to prevent the disclosure of information covered by an existing injunction safeguarding confidentiality.[7] In *Attorney-General v Times Newspapers* [1992] 1 AC 191 it was held that the publication of such matter could constitute an interference with the administration of justice. Thus, the publication of extracts of *Spycatcher*, after two newspapers had been injuncted for breach of confidence, constituted contempt of court. These actions can deny the press a public interest defence under the law of confidentiality, and the public interest defence under **s.5** of the **Contempt of Court Act 1981**. This threat was mitigated by the decision in *Attorney-General v Newspaper Publishing Ltd* [1997] 3 All ER 159, where it was held that a trivial breach of a court order was insufficient to attract liability for contempt. However, in *Attorney-General v Punch and Steed* [2003] 1 All ER 301 the House of Lords held that a breach of an order did not have to cause a risk of damage to national security. The purpose of any order was the prevention of publication pending the confidentiality proceedings, so that a deliberate breach would prejudge the issues and thus constitute contempt.

[8] The author concludes the essay by stating that the law still takes a guarded approach when national security is challenged, but also by pointing to some evidence of free speech protection.

Thus, the courts have fallen short of establishing any clear defence of press freedom[8] where the threat to national security can be balanced proportionally with freedom of expression and the public right to know. This has been exacerbated by the absence of a right to freedom of information, both in domestic law and under the European Convention. Thus, in *Leander v Sweden*, the European Court held that **article 10** does not require the facilitation of free speech and does not impose an obligation on government to provide an open forum to achieve the wider dissemination of views. Press freedom, therefore, will continue to be protected on a limited basis, allowing publication where no identifiable harm has been caused by the dissemination of government information. This does not always permit a true balance between press freedom and national security, although it does not appear to be in violation of **article 10**.

LOOKING FOR EXTRA MARKS?

- Show that you understand both the need for official secrecy and confidentiality laws and the importance of defences of public interest and press freedom to regulate the enforcement of such laws.

- Appreciate the legal and constitutional dilemmas facing the courts in balancing state secrecy with such rights, together with the reason for the trend for judicial deference in this area.

- Use leading and topical cases which illustrate those dilemmas and which allow you to employ your critical skills to conclude on the central question of whether the laws give adequate recognition to press freedom and the public right to know.

QUESTION | 5

Part A

What deficiencies of the domestic law of contempt were exposed by the decision of the European Court of Human Rights in *Sunday Times v United Kingdom*? To what extent are those laws now consistent with article 10 of the European Convention on Human Rights?

Part B

In June 2018, Sir Joseph Cranberry, a former Cabinet Minister, was facing charges of fraud connected with his financial and political dealings. His trial was due to take place on 22 June and, on 2 June, the *Daily Tribune* published an article about corruption in public life. The article focused on a number of incidents over the previous 10 years, involving politicians and other public officers who had been charged with offences involving fraud. The article concluded that 'fraud and deceit in public life is of epidemic proportions' and that 'many politicians had been proved to be constitutionally incapable of telling the truth'. The article also referred to a case last year when a well-known politician had been acquitted of a variety of theft and deception charges and concluded, 'Let us hope that juries have learnt from that lesson, and do not let abusers of public office off the hook'. On reading the article, the trial judge decided to abandon the trial and referred the matter to the Attorney-General. The *Daily Tribune* has now heard that they will face contempt charges in connection with the article.

Advise the newspaper as to any defences it might have and the likely outcome of the proceedings.

! CAUTION!

- Part A requires a sound overall knowledge of contempt laws, but the answer should concentrate on an examination of the deficiencies of the old law as exposed by the European Court and the present law's compatibility with free speech and the ECHR.

- The question does not employ the phrase *critical examination*, but you should take a critical approach having understood the importance of the *Sunday Times* case and the need for the law to strike an appropriate balance between the administration of justice and freedom of speech.

- Use statutory provisions and cases which examine the law's compatibility with the judgment and the ECHR.

- Part B requires a clear application of the law to the facts, but you need to appreciate the role of the domestic courts in ensuring consistency between domestic law and the ECHR.

DIAGRAM ANSWER PLANS

Part A

Brief examination of the aims of contempt law and its impact on freedom of expression and the public right to know

Explanation of the pre-1981 Act situation, the 'thalidomide' litigation, and the changes made to the law by the 1981 Act

Critical analysis of the Act's provisions and their application in post-1981 Act case law to consider their compatibility with the Convention and the decision in *Sunday Times*

Conclusions as to the compatibility of present law with article 10 of the Convention and relevant case law

Part B

Identify the issues	■ The legal issues and the claims ■ Prosecution for contempt of court and whether the offence has been committed and if any defences are available
Relevant law	■ Outline the rules and cases relating to the scenario, ss.2 and 5 of the Contempt of Court Act 1981, and accompanying cases
Apply the law	■ Application of the rules on liability and defences to the facts
Conclude	■ Conclude on whether the charge of contempt, or any defence, would be likely to succeed

Part A

[1] The author begins with a clear explanation of the purpose of contempt laws.

The law of contempt of court safeguards the individual's fundamental right to a fair trial and protects the public's confidence in the impartiality and independence of the judicial process.[1] These aims are contained in **article 10(2)** of the European Convention—the rights of others and the impartiality and independence of the judiciary—and must be balanced with the fundamental right of public debate on impending judicial proceedings.

[2] The author moves swiftly on to the *Sunday Times* case, which highlighted the deficiencies of the old law and the need for reform.

The domestic law of strict liability contempt came under attack as a result of the decision of the European Court in *Sunday Times v United Kingdom* **(1979) 2 EHRR 245**.[2] The case involved the publication of two articles commenting on the thalidomide affair before impending litigation between parents and a company had been resolved. The House of Lords granted injunctions, finding that one of the articles had prejudged the case (*Attorney-General v Times Newspapers* **[1974] AC 273**). The European Court held that the injunctions were not 'necessary in a democratic society' and that English law had formulated an absolute rule that made it unlawful to prejudge issues in pending cases. The Court recognised that the issue was a matter of undisputed public concern. Thus, the public and the families could only be deprived of this information if it appeared absolutely certain (as opposed to there being a 'real risk') that its diffusion would have presented a threat to the authority of the judiciary.

[3] The author now examines the purpose and provisions of the 1981 Act in order to tackle the second part of the question.

The judgment led to the passing of the **Contempt of Court Act 1981**, which addressed the strict liability rule,[3] and in particular the questions of the necessary risk of prejudice and the lack of a defence where prejudice is caused by public interest discussion. **Section 2** now provides that the strict liability rule only applies in relation to publications that create a *substantial* risk that the course of proceedings in question will be *seriously* impeded or prejudiced.[4]

[4] The author then moves to the new test, considering its wording and the relevant case law.

In *Attorney-General v News Group Newspapers* **[1987] 1 QB 1**, it was noted that both elements, although overlapping, must be met in each case. In particular, it was held that a substantial risk was one that was 'not minimal' or 'not insubstantial', rather than one that was 'weighty'. In addition, the effect of the publication on the particular proceedings had to be potentially serious. Thus, there must be some risk that the proceedings in question will be affected and, if so, that likely effect must be serious. The courts have tended to apply the test liberally in favour of free speech. For example, in this case it held that the *News of the World* was not in contempt when it published an article about an individual's behaviour that was the subject of a libel trial due to take place in 10 months' time. On the facts, it was not possible to say that there was a serious risk that the course of justice would be seriously prejudiced by such publication.

Equally, the courts have taken a liberal approach in deciding whether there is evidence of serious prejudice. Thus, in *Attorney-General v ITN and others* **[1995] 2 All ER 370** it was held that the defendants were not guilty of contempt when they published the fact that a person arrested for murder and attempted murder had recently escaped from jail in Belfast where he was serving a life sentence for murder. Given that the trial would not take place for nine months, and the ephemeral nature of a single news item on TV news, no contempt had been committed. In contrast, in *Attorney-General v MGN Ltd and others* **[2011] EWHC 2074 (Admin)**,[5] the *Sun* and *Daily Mirror* newspapers were found guilty of contempt of court for publishing a series of 'extreme' articles about a suspect who had been arrested by police investigating the murder of a young woman. The High Court ruled that the papers posed a 'substantial risk' of 'serious prejudice' to the course of justice. The vilification of a suspect under arrest and the publication of such material might discourage or deter witnesses from coming forward and providing information helpful to the suspect's defence.

The courts have thus taken a flexible approach, considering all the circumstances. Thus, in *Attorney-General v Times Newspapers, The Times*, **12 February 1983**, the *Sun* newspaper was not in contempt when they referred to someone facing charges of theft from Buckingham Palace as 'a glib liar with a long-standing drug problem'. However, the *Daily Star* was in contempt when they asserted that he had admitted to stealing wine from the Queen. More recently, however, in *Attorney-General v Conde Nast Publications* **[2015] EWHC 3322 (Admin)**, a publisher was found in contempt[6] after a magazine article headed 'HACKING SCANDAL' published during a phone hacking trial was found to have created a substantial risk that the course of justice in the trial would be seriously prejudiced or impeded.

The law is only likely to be tested where the publication serves a strong and genuine public interest, as in the *Sunday Times* case. In these cases, s.5 provides a public interest defence by giving protection to publications constituting a discussion in good faith of public affairs or other matters of general public interest.[7] However, in these cases, the risk of impediment or prejudice must be merely incidental to the discussion. Again, the provision has been interpreted quite liberally and in *Attorney-General v English* **[1983] 1 AC 116** the Court of Appeal held that it was not appropriate to ask whether an article could have been written without the offending words. Further, it accepted that a discussion of public affairs could take place beyond abstract debate and could include examples drawn from real life. Thus, in *Attorney-General v Times Newspapers* an article about

[5] The author uses a high-profile case to explain the relevant part of the test.

[6] The author includes another recent and high-profile case in illustration of the other requirement.

[7] The author now raises the defence under s.5, then examines the case law and its application in the context of the question.

someone who broke into the Queen's bedroom fell within **s.5** even though the person was named, as it formed part of a discussion of public concern, namely the Queen's personal safety. However, where the article relates clearly and closely to the legal proceedings it will be easier for the Attorney-General to show that the risk of prejudice is more than merely incidental (*Attorney-General v TVS Television Ltd and Southey and Sons, The Times*, 7 July 1989).

It should be noted that *Sunday Times* does not give absolute protection to press freedom and in *Worm v Austria* (1998) 25 EHRR 454 the Court stressed that it was essential that the public had confidence in the courts' capacity to carry out that function. Accordingly, the press must not overstep the bounds imposed in the proper administration of justice and prejudice the chances of a fair trial.[8] Equally, the domestic courts must construe **s.5** very liberally in order to comply with Convention case law.

[8] The author concludes by highlighting that both the courts and the press have a duty to ensure that the balance between the administration of justice and free speech is maintained.

Part B

[1] The author identifies which offences the press are likely to be charged with.

The newspaper will either face contempt charges under the **Contempt of Court Act 1981**, where liability for contempt is strict, or under the common law for intentional contempt.[1] Liability is based on interfering with the impartiality and independence of the judicial system and not simply on the individual's right to a fair trial. Thus, the fact that in our case the criminal trial has been abandoned as a result of the judge's assessment of the pre-trial publicity on Sir Joseph's right to a fair trial is a relevant, though not decisive, factor (*Attorney-General v MGN* [1997] 1 All ER 456).

[2] The author briefly outlines the offence under s.2, noting both ingredients.

Under the **1981 Act**, the court will need to be satisfied under **s.2** that the article created a substantial risk that the criminal proceedings would be seriously impeded or prejudiced.[2] There is no question that the criminal proceedings were not active, as such proceedings start with the issue of a warrant and end with the discontinuance of the trial. It is not sufficient if one of those factors exists, but not the other (*Attorney-General v News Group Newspapers*). Thus, in the context of criminal proceedings the court would have to be satisfied that not only would the article have a likely influence on the jury, but that such an influence would materially and substantially prejudice the defendant's, or prosecution's, case.

In *Attorney-General v News Group Newspapers* the Court of Appeal stated that for a risk to be substantial it had to be 'not minimal or insubstantial'. Further, it held that in assessing whether that substantial risk would cause serious prejudice, it was permissible to take into account factors that were considered at the first stage. Thus, some factors, such as the proximity of the article to the trial, are relevant at each stage. The court in our case would ask whether there was a substantial risk that one or more of the jury would encounter the article, remember it, and be affected by it, so that they could not put it out of their mind during the trial. The court could then refer to a number of factors such as the likely readership of the article, the proximity of publication of the article to the trial, whether the case had attracted the public interest, and the language used in the article. Because the article is written in a national newspaper, discusses a matter of public interest, is written in a strident manner, and appears only three weeks before the trial, there would appear to be a substantial risk that the jurors would encounter the article and remember it at the time of the trial.[3]

[3] The author gives an opinion on the likely application of the first element, based on the relevant case law.

The court would then address the question of whether the article would cause the jury to be *prejudiced* against Sir Joseph and whether that prejudice would be *serious*.[4] The court would consider similar factors to those considered at the first stage as well as the public profile of the defendant and the issue under discussion, as well as the tone and language used in the publication. In *Attorney-General v Conde Nast Publications*, a publisher was in contempt after a magazine article headed 'HACKING SCANDAL'—published during a phone hacking trial—was found to have created a substantial risk that the course of justice in the trial would be seriously prejudiced or impeded; see also *Attorney-General v MGN Ltd and others*. In our case, although the defendant is not specifically mentioned, the tone of the article is quite strong as is the potential for serious prejudice,[5] particularly as it appears to call upon juries to convict politicians facing criminal charges. Further, the timing of the article is critical, as opposed to *Attorney-General v ITN and others*, where the publication appeared nine months before the murder trial.

[4] The author now moves to the central question of whether the other element in s.2 is satisfied, carefully explaining the essential ingredient.

[5] The author concludes on the liability of the press under s.2 having examined the cases and the facts in the scenario.

If the court finds the newspaper in contempt, it may rely on **s.5** of the **1981 Act** if the publication was made as part of a discussion in good faith of public affairs,[6] or other matters of general public interest. However, it must be shown that any prejudice to the proceedings was merely incidental to that discussion. In *Attorney-General v English* it was held that a discussion of public affairs could take place beyond abstract debate and could include examples drawn from real life. In our case, therefore, the use of specific examples, including the allusion to Sir Joseph's case, might be acceptable. However, in *Attorney-General v TVS Television Ltd and Southey and Sons* it was stressed that the main thrust of the article must not consist of a discussion of the proceedings. In our case, the article does discuss wider issues over and above the impending trial. However, the warning given to the jury not to acquit might be seen as unacceptable and make the likelihood of prejudice central to, rather than incidental to, the discussion. Accordingly, a court might reject a public interest defence in such circumstances.[7]

[6] The author now introduces the s.5 defence, explaining its scope.

[7] The author concludes that the defence is unlikely to succeed after a careful examination of the facts and the case law.

Such is the tone of the article that it may be regarded as an intentional interference with the administration of justice under common law. In such a case the newspaper would not be able to avail itself of any public interest defence, although the court would have to be satisfied that the defendants intended to prejudice proceedings or saw such interference as an inevitable consequence of the publication (***Attorney-General v News Group Newspapers***). It is uncertain that the newspaper saw with virtual certainty that Sir Joseph's trial would be prejudiced[8] (***Attorney-General v Sport Newspapers* [1991] 1 WLR 1194**), unless there is evidence of a personal or other vendetta, as in ***Attorney-General v Conde Nast Publication***.

[8]The author concludes by stating it is unlikely that there has been intentional interference.

LOOKING FOR EXTRA MARKS?

- For Part A, show that you understand the importance of the law of contempt of court but equally the danger to free speech and the public right to know.
- Appreciate the significance of the *Sunday Times* judgment and its impact on the domestic law of contempt.
- Use leading cases which illustrate the extent of any changes effected by the judgment and the 1981 Act.
- For Part B, appreciate the significance of the cases mentioned in Part A and the effect they are likely to have on the court's decision on the facts.
- Apply those cases carefully to the scenario.

QUESTION | 6

Critically evaluate the extent to which English law on the disclosure of press sources is consistent with notions of press freedom and article 10 of the European Convention on Human Rights.

CAUTION!

- This question requires a very sound knowledge of disclosure of press sources, but the answer should concentrate on a *critical evaluation* of how that principle is protected in domestic law, and how the law is consistent with values of press freedom and the values in article 10 ECHR.
- The question employs the phrase *critical evaluation*, so you should take a critical approach having truly understood the importance of non-disclosure to democracy and the public right to know.
- The question refers to protection in domestic law, but it is essential to examine the case law of the European Court in conjunction with domestic decisions in order to examine whether domestic law and decisions are consistent with ECHR values in this area.
- Use cases which examine how domestic law and cases balance the conflicting rights in such cases and which allow you to assess the compatibility of domestic law in this area.

DIAGRAM ANSWER PLANS

> Explanation of the values of press freedom, the dangers of the disclosure of press sources, and the cases where it might be necessary to do so

▼

> Examination of the domestic legal position under s.10 of the Contempt of Court Act 1981

▼

> Critical examination of the domestic case law under s.10, both pre- and post-Human Rights Act 1998

▼

> Examination of the principles underlying article 10 of the Convention and the case law of the European Court of Human Rights in this area

▼

> Conclusions as to the compatibility of the domestic law with the principles and case law of the European Convention

SUGGESTED ANSWER

The European Court of Human Rights has offered special protection to press freedom and the right of the press to impart information (*Sunday Times v United Kingdom* **(1979) 2 EHRR 245**). This recognises the importance of press freedom to the maintenance of a democratic society, the press having a duty to inform the public (*Jersild v Denmark* **(1994) 19 EHRR 1**).

An essential aspect of press freedom is that journalists are not forced to divulge their sources. Otherwise the confidence between the press and those who supply information to it is compromised and the disclosure has a chilling effect on the free flow of information. Thus, the European Court has noted that the protection of journalistic sources is one of the basic conditions for press freedom[1] (*Goodwin v United Kingdom* **(1996) 22 EHRR 123**; *Financial Times and others v United Kingdom* **(2010) 50 EHRR 46**; *Telegaaf Media Nederland Landeijke Media BV v Netherlands, decision of the European Court, 22 November 2012*).

On the other hand, there will be cases where such disclosure will serve both the public interest, such as the detection of crime (*BBC v United Kingdom* **(1996) 84-A DR 129**), and the rights of individuals, who may, for example, wish to identify a source with a view to taking civil action against that source or other persons. Consequently, both **article 10** of the Convention and domestic law will allow the principle of non-disclosure to be compromised; although disclosure should be ordered only in exceptional cases.[2] Accordingly, the state is given a

[1] The author highlights the importance attached to journalistic sources by the European Court.

[2] The author highlights that the rule against disclosure is not absolute but exceptions must comply with article 10 and strict requirements.

very narrow margin of appreciation in this area (**Goodwin v United Kingdom** and, more recently, **Becker v Norway (Application No 21272/12), 5 October 2017 (ECHR)**, where the right to non-disclosure was upheld despite the source identifying himself).

[3] The author begins to examine s.10 of the 1981 Act and its wording.

Under **s.10 of the Contempt of Court Act 1981** no court may require a person to disclose (nor is any person guilty of contempt of court for refusing to disclose)[3] the source of information contained in a publication unless the court is satisfied that disclosure is *necessary* in the interests of justice or national security or for the prevention of disorder or crime. Thus, in **Re an Inquiry under the Company Securities (Insider Dealing) Act 1985 [1988] 1 All ER 203** it was held that s.10 required that the disclosure was 'really needed' to achieve any of those listed reasons. Despite this, in **Secretary of State for Defence v Guardian Newspapers [1985] AC 339** the House of Lords ordered a newspaper to disclose the source of a leaked document containing allegations that Parliament had been misled on the issue of the storing of nuclear weapons. This was despite there being no evidence of any harm caused to national security and where the ministry had failed to carry out internal investigations into the leak.

[4] The author examines some pre-Act cases which may have been in breach of article 10.

Such cases suggested that the domestic courts were not prepared to give sufficient weight to press freedom[4] and that their approach was not consistent with the principles of free speech expounded by the European Court in cases such as **Sunday Times**. For example, in **X v Morgan Grampian (Publishers) Ltd [1991] AC 1**—challenged before the European Court in **Goodwin v United Kingdom**—an individual had disclosed a company's financial affairs to a journalist and the company had obtained an injunction prohibiting its publication. The company then sought an order forcing the journalist to disclose the source of his information so that it could take legal action against the informant. When he refused he was committed for contempt. The House of Lords held that the phrase 'the interests of justice' included contemplated legal proceedings and that the claimants had established the need to identify the informant; the public having no legitimate interest in the business of the claimants.

That decision was successfully challenged in **Goodwin**, the European Court stressing that without legal protection of the right of the press to protect its sources, its ability to provide reliable and accurate information would be adversely affected. Accordingly, any interference with that right would require an overriding requirement in the public interest. Although the interference in this case related to the legitimate aim of preserving the company's legal claim, the restriction was not necessary because the main element of damage to the company had already been redressed by the original injunction. The additional benefit of unmasking the culprit and allowing the legal action against him was not sufficient to outweigh the vital public interest in maintaining the confidentiality of the source.

The decision suggested that the domestic courts were attaching too little significance to the notions of press freedom and to violations of the principles of non-disclosure. This was borne out in *Centaur Communications v Camelot* [1998] 2 WLR 379. In this case, an employee of Camelot supplied a journalist with detailed information on the company's accounts. The company sought the return of the document in order to identify and take necessary legal action against the employee. The Court of Appeal held that the interests of the company in ensuring the loyalty of its employees and ex-employees outweighed the public interest attached to the protection of press sources, distinguishing *Goodwin* on the grounds that in *Camelot* there was a *continuing* threat of damage caused by the presence of a disloyal employee, which needed to be addressed in order to restore confidence within the company and its employees.

The decision in *Camelot* was criticised for attaching too much weight to the company's commercial interests and neglecting to promote a wider public interest in allowing the free flow of information. Specifically, the courts were often prepared to order such disclosure before the claimant had conducted a full inquiry into the breach of confidence (*Secretary of State for Defence v Guardian Newspapers* and *Camelot*). In contrast, in *Saunders v Punch* [1998] 1 WLR 986, the domestic courts followed *Goodwin* and refused a further order requiring the defendant to reveal its sources. The court found that although there was a great public interest in preserving the confidentiality of legal correspondence, the original injunction had gone a long way in protecting the claimant's interests.

[5] The author stresses the need for domestic courts to comply with article 10 ECHR when applying s.10.

In the post-Human Rights Act era the courts must develop the law in compliance with Convention rights,[5] and **s.12** of the **1998 Act** requires the courts to have special regard to freedom of expression when granting any relief. This duty is heightened when the information is of a journalistic nature (**s.12(4)**). In *John v Express Newspapers* [2000] 3 All ER 257 a journalist had destroyed a confidential legal document that had come into his possession, but an order requiring the newspaper to disclose the identity of the source was still sought. The court ordered disclosure even though the firm had failed to conduct an internal inquiry. However, on appeal it was accepted that the judge had attached insufficient significance to the failure to conduct an internal inquiry and too much significance to the threat posed to legal confidentiality. The Court stressed that when the press was being required to depart from its normal professional practice, the public interest in such an order had to be clearly demonstrated.

This approach was adopted in *Ashworth Security Hospital v MGN Ltd* [2002] 1 WLR 2033, where the House of Lords stated that any court should be satisfied that the case for disclosure was so important that it overrode the public interest in protecting journalistic sources. In *Ashworth*, disclosure was ordered when a hospital employee had supplied medical information on a mental patient to a third party and the defendants had published an article detailing confidential information. The House of Lords held that the present case was exceptional and was the only means of discovering the source of the information, an internal inquiry having failed to identify the employee.

[6] The author proceeds to examine the, inconsistent, case law in this area.

The question of whether disclosure will be ordered will be determined on a case-by-case basis, which has led to some inconsistency in this field.[6] For example, in *Interbrew SA v Financial Times and others* [2002] EMLR 24 an order was granted ordering a newspaper to produce documents identifying a person who had provided the newspaper with deliberately misleading financial material relating to the claimants. It was accepted that the court must start with a presumption that it is contrary to the public interest to require disclosure. However, here the right of the claimant to identify a disloyal employee overrode the general interest in non-disclosure. This decision was effectively overturned on appeal to the European Court (*Financial Times and others v United Kingdom*). The European Court held that the interference was not necessary in a democratic society because the company had not sought an injunction and there was no evidence that it had tried to identify the source. Noting the chilling effect of identification of anonymous sources, it concluded that the threat of damage to the company and the interest in gaining damages for such was insufficient to outweigh the public interest in the protection of journalistic sources.

[7] The author reviews the modern case law by suggesting that disclosure is only ordered exceptionally.

Although the domestic courts are still prepared to order disclosure, most cases (most notably *Ackroyd*) indicate that such disclosure will be exceptional.[7] Thus, the courts are no longer willing to grant such orders simply because they would assist the claimant in furthering their commercial or other interests. This stance may, of course, waiver in cases involving terrorism, where one would expect the courts to show more deference to national security and other public interest claims. However, in *An Application by D* [2009] NICty 4, the Northern Ireland High Court refused to order the disclosure of a journalist's sources when that would have put her life at risk.

[8] The author neatly summarises the current situation in the context of addressing the question of whether it is compatible.

In general, however, the current situation compares favourably with the traditional stance[8] taken by the courts in this area (*Guardian Newspapers*). Provided the courts use the orders in only exceptional cases, unlike the *Interbrew* case, it would appear that the law is generally compatible with **article 10**.

 LOOKING FOR EXTRA MARKS?

- Show that you appreciate and understand the importance of press freedom and the principle of non-disclosure of sources, together with the cases where disclosure may be necessary.

■ Appreciate the contrast between the traditional stance taken by the domestic courts and the one adopted by the European Court of Human Rights.

■ Use leading cases which illustrate that contrast and which allow you to employ your critical analysis in concluding on the central question.

TAKING THINGS FURTHER

■ Hooper, D, Waite, K, and Murphy, O, 'Defamation Act 2013—What Difference Will It Really Make?' [2013] 24(6) Entertainment Law Review 199

A succinct but incisive analysis of the new Act and its likely impact on free speech and defamation actions

■ Foster, S, 'Tell Us Something that We Don't Know: Celebrity Privacy, Interim Injunctions and Information in the Public Domain' (2016) 21(1) Coventry Law Journal 57

A critique of the decision in PJS v News Group Newspapers with respect to the public right to know and the protection of family and privacy issues

■ Khan, A, 'A "Right Not to be Offended" under Article 10(2) ECHR' [2012] 2 EHRLR 191

An interesting analysis of the extent to which human rights law should and does accommodate the right not to be offended and the impact of such on free speech values

■ Korpisaari, P, 'Balancing Freedom of Expression and the Right to Private Life in the European Court of Human Rights' (2017) 22(2) Communications Law 39

An analysis of the balancing act carried out by the Strasbourg Court with respect to privacy protection, press freedom, and the public right to know

■ O'Fathaigh, R, 'Article 10 and the Chilling Effect Principle' [2013] 3 EHRLR 304

An analysis of the likely chilling effect on free speech of various laws that impact on the effective protection afforded by article 10

■ Rowbottom, J, 'To Rant, Vent and Converse: Protecting Low Level Digital Speech' [2012] 71(2) CLJ 355

An analysis of the controversy surrounding the question of whether to protect various speech on social media

■ Wragg, P, 'Leveson's Vision for Press Reform: One Year On' [2014] 19(1) Communications Law 6

An analysis of the impact of the Leveson Inquiry on press freedom and responsible journalism

Online Resources   www.oup.com/uk/qanda/

Go online for extra essay and problem questions, a glossary of key terms, online versions of all the answer plans and audio commentary on how selected ones were put together, and a range of podcasts which include advice on exam and coursework technique and advice for other assessment methods.

11

Freedom of Religion, Association, and Peaceful Assembly

KEY DEBATES

Religious freedom and its restriction, especially in the areas of free speech and religious dress, have been the subject of much legislation and case law from both domestic law and the European Court of Human Rights as well as great political debate; where a balance has to be struck between religious freedom and the rights of others and public safety. So too the control of associations (including terrorist groups) and of demonstrations gives rise to much legal and political debate, both in the context of the fight against terrorism and in the need to ensure public safety during public assemblies and marches.

$\odot$

Debate: Religious Freedom and Religious Dress

The banning of religious symbols and dress in various European countries has caused intense political and moral debate and there has been much case law in this area (see SAS v France). The debate involves the balancing of religious freedom and expression with issues of safety, secularism, and social unity. This conflict may arise in public spaces (SAS) or in the context of employment, where employers seek to impose dress codes. In particular, a religious follower's beliefs may be compromised by the need to maintain equality and a conflict will arise between religious beliefs and the protection of sexual minorities from discrimination (for example, whether an employee should be forced to officiate at a same-sex wedding).

Debate: Police Powers and the Right to Demonstrate

The right of the police to regulate and restrict demonstrations has always been a controversial area and the courts continue to rule on the appropriate balance between the fundamental and democratic right to protest (and of free speech) and the need to preserve public order and the rights of others. Demonstrations involve 'direct action' and thus the threat to public safety and the rights of others is more tangible. How the courts regulate police discretion in this area is fundamental in preserving the democratic right of public assembly, and often a wide discretion is given by the courts in this area.

QUESTION | 1

Critically examine how effective article 9 of the European Convention on Human Rights has been in upholding the objectives and values of freedom of religion?

CAUTION!

- This question requires a very sound overall knowledge of article 9 and the case law of the European Court in this area, but the answer should concentrate on how *effective* article 9 has been in upholding the *objectives and values* of that article.

- The question employs the phrase *critical examination*, so you should take a critical approach having understood the importance of religion to individual liberty and choice together with the controversies inherent in both its recognition and restriction.

- The question refers to article 9, so it is permissible to use cases from both the European Court and the domestic courts in order to examine the extent to which freedom of religion has been upheld.

- Use cases—from both jurisdictions—to examine the legal and moral dilemmas faced by both courts in establishing the extent to which religious rights can be recognised by the law, and the extent to which it is permissible to restrict or compromise them.

DIAGRAM ANSWER PLANS

Explanation of the wording and scope of article 9 of the European Convention and the objectives and values of the right to freedom of religion (and thought and conscience)

▼

Critical consideration of the case law of the European Court on article 9 and assessment of the effectiveness of its protection in this area in safeguarding against arbitrary interference

▼

Critical examination of post-Human Rights Act case law in the domestic courts on article 9 and its restriction (in areas such as religious dress)

▼

Conclusions as to the effectiveness of article 9 in achieving religious freedom and protecting it from unnecessary interference and compromise

SUGGESTED ANSWER

Article 9 of the European Convention provides that everyone has the right to freedom of thought, conscience, and religion, including the freedom to change one's religion or belief, either alone or in community with others. This aspect of **article 9** is absolute and the qualifying provision in **article 9(2)** does not apply to the enjoyment of this basic right. The first element of **article 9** is thus concerned with the prohibition of religious or other persecution based solely on one's beliefs.[1] The article then provides the right of an individual (in public or private) to *manifest* his religion or belief, in worship, teaching, practice, and observance. This aspect is subject to **article 9(2)**, which allows for interferences provided they are prescribed by law and necessary in a democratic society in the interests of public safety, the protection of public order, health or morals, or the protection of the rights and freedoms of others. This recognises that in a democratic society, where several religions coexist, it may be necessary to place restrictions on the right to manifest one's religion in order to ensure that everyone's beliefs are respected.[2] This is complemented by **article 17** of the Convention, which safeguards against the destruction of other persons' Convention rights; in this context by one religious group obstructing another group's beliefs.

Article 9 complements the right to private life, freedom of expression, and freedom of association and public assembly. Thus, in ***Kokkinakis v Greece* (1993) 17 EHRR 397** the European Court stated that it was one of the most vital elements that go to make up the identity of believers and their conception of life. This gives special protection to religious views, although in ***Kokkinakis*** the Court stressed that the values underlying **article 9** were also essential for

[1] The author stresses the absolute and fundamental nature of the right to religion.

[2] The author now stresses the need to place restrictions on the manifestation of such views.

atheists, agnostics, and sceptics. **Article 9** is thus essential to the maintenance of a pluralist society.

[3]The author explores the scope of article 9 and when views are regarded as coming within it.

Not all views and opinions fall within the scope of **article 9** and the Court has stressed that it does not cover every opinion and conviction of the individual, such as temporary political views (***Arrowsmith v United Kingdom* (1978) 3 EHRR 218**).[3] Further, in ***Pretty v United Kingdom* (2002) 35 EHRR 1** it rejected the applicant's claim that her belief in the right to die fell within **article 9**, stressing that the term 'practice' did not cover each act that was motivated or influenced by a religion or belief. The applicant's views merely reflected her commitment to the principle of personal autonomy under **article 8**.

[4]The author introduces the reader to the question of balance and the requirements of necessity and proportionality.

Any interference with the right to manifest one's religion or beliefs needs to be prescribed by law and necessary in a democratic society for the achievement of one of the legitimate aims laid down in **article 9(2)**.[4] Thus, in ***Kokkinakis***, the Court held that **article 9** included the right to convince others of one's religion. Accordingly, proselytism could only be restricted if it took the form of exerting improper pressure on people in distress or in need, or the use of violence or brainwashing. Further, any interference will not be justified simply on the grounds that the applicant's beliefs are contrary to the established religion in that country (***Manossakis v Greece* (1996) 23 EHRR 387**).

The Court has offered a wider margin of appreciation in cases where the manifestation of religious or other views are inconsistent with fundamental democratic features of that society. Thus, in ***Kalac v Turkey* (1997) 27 EHRR 552** the dismissal of the applicant from the armed forces for voicing religious views conflicting with national principles of secularism was justified under **article 9**. In this case the applicant owed a particular allegiance to the state because of his position.

[5]The author now uses the controversial area of religious dress and symbols to illustrate the balance.

Much controversy has been caused by the state's rules on manifesting religion in public places or in employment, and the Convention is thus faced with maintaining a delicate balance between individual and state interests.[5] In ***Sahin v Turkey* (2005) 41 EHRR 8** the Court held that there had been no violation of **article 9** when the applicant had been suspended for wearing a Muslim headdress at university, contrary to that university's rules. In the Court's view, the ban on religious wear was proportionate to the protection of the rights of others and of public order, and necessary to preserve secularism in the country's educational institutions. More recently, in ***SAS v France* (2015) 60 EHRR 11**, it was held that a law forbidding concealing one's face in public was justified despite it restricting the wearing of full Muslim dress. This was on the basis that the rule promoted social inclusion, there being insufficient evidence of such dress posing a threat to public safety, as claimed by the state. Further, in ***Ebrahimian v France* (Application No. 64846/11***)* the Court upheld the right of the state to dismiss a social worker for her refusal to stop wearing the Muslim veil. The national authorities had not exceeded their margin of appreciation in finding that there was no possibility of reconciling her religious convictions with the obligation to refrain from manifesting them. Equally, they were entitled to give precedence to the requirement of neutrality and impartiality of the state and to observe the principle of secularism within article 1 of the French Constitution.

These cases suggest that the Court is not prepared to interfere with state practices unless they are arbitrary, even though they leave individual religious views unprotected.

A conservative approach has also been taken by the domestic courts and, in *R (Begum) v Denbigh High School* [2007] 1 AC 100, the House of Lords upheld a school uniform policy that precluded the wearing of the Muslim jilbab. The essential question was whether that policy struck a fair balance between the girl's interests and the interests of others, including the school and its other pupils. In the present case, it was found that the policy pursued a legitimate aim and accommodated the views and practices of all religions. However, the courts will interfere if the restriction is clearly disproportionate. Thus, in *R (Watkins Singh) v Aberdare Girls' High School Governors* [2008] EWHC 1865, it was held that the refusal of a school to allow a girl to wear a 'Kara'—a slim bracelet expected to be worn by Sikhs at all times—was contrary to the **Race Relations Act 1976**. This was because the Kara was less visible and ostentatious and did not interfere with the general uniform policy.

The European Court is prepared to uphold national laws and practices at the expense of individual beliefs, provided the individual is not treated arbitrarily or oppressively. Thus, in *Lautsi v Italy* (2012) 54 EHHR 3, it was held that there had been no breach when the applicant's children had to attend school where crucifixes were displayed in the classroom. In this case, its presence did not amount to proselytism or indoctrination, or put undue pressure on non-Christians. The crucifix was a symbol of not only religion but of democracy and it was within the state's margin of appreciation to display it as presenting the state's main, although not exclusive, religion and faith. Similar approaches are taken with respect to dress codes at work, which will be upheld if enforced for health and safety reasons (*Chaplin v United Kingdom* (2013) 57 EHRR 8). However, they have not been enforced in cases where the employer cannot show a sufficient harm to the sensibilities of the workforce (*Eiweda v United Kingdom* (2013) 57 EHRR 8).

[6] The author now illustrates the domestic courts' hands-off approach when religion conflicts with others' rights.

Equally, the domestic courts have been prepared to compromise freedom of religion when it is in conflict with the public interest or the rights of others.[6] For example, in *R (Williamson) v Secretary of State for Employment* [2005] 2 AC 246 it was held that a ban on corporal punishment in all schools did not violate the rights of teachers and parents under **article 9** and **article 2 of the First Protocol**, which guarantee the rights of parents to have their children educated in conformity with their religious and philosophical convictions. Parliament was entitled to make an exception to those rights on the basis that they interfered with the child's right not to be subject to inhuman and degrading treatment contrary to article 3. A similar approach has been taken in other cases where there has been a conflict between religious practice and public health or safety (*R (Swami Suryanada) v Welsh Ministers* [2007] EWCA Civ 893).

[7] The author moves to the positive duty imposed on the state to ensure that religious rights are not violated by other individuals or groups.

Article 9 imposes a positive obligation on the state to allow individuals the right to manifest and enjoy their beliefs peacefully and without undue interference[7] (*Dubowska and Skup v Poland* (1997) 24 EHRR CD 75). Thus, the Court has imposed strict obligations on the state to ensure that religious observers are protected against violent attacks from counter-religions (*Members of the Gldani Congregation of Jehovah's Witnesses v Georgia* (2008) 46 EHRR 30). States must also ensure that private employers allow employees to enjoy thought, conscience, and religion. For example, in *Ahmed v United Kingdom* (1981) 4 EHRR 126 it was accepted that an employer should not place unreasonable obstacles in the way of their employee's right to manifest his religion. However, an employee will in general have to take into account their contractual obligations in carrying out those rights. Accordingly, a wide area of discretion has been given in cases where the employee refuses to carry out instructions which conflict with their religious beliefs, but which are essential in terms of promoting equality, such as carrying out same-sex ceremonies[8] (*McFarlane v United Kingdom* (2013) 57 EHRR 8).

[8] The author uses a recent and controversial case to illustrate the dilemma of accommodating religious beliefs in the workplace.

With respect to defending religious sensibility, the Court has accepted that a state may impose criminal liability for blasphemy and that such law can be compatible with **article 10(2)** for protecting 'the rights of others'—that is the right to enjoy one's religion (*Gay News v United Kingdom* (1983) 5 EHRR 123 and *Otto-Preminger Institut v Austria* (1994) 19 EHRR 34). However, it has held that **article 9** does not impose a positive obligation upon states to protect religious sensibilities. Thus, followers had no right to demand that the state operated a law of blasphemy so as to protect their religious beliefs and activities (*Choudhury v United Kingdom* (1991) 12 HRLJ 172).

[9] The author provides a neat conclusion on the issue of recognising religious rights and balancing them with the interests of society.

In conclusion, although **article 9** is accepted as central both to the enjoyment of individual liberty and to the principles of a modern democracy, the courts have allowed states a generous margin of appreciation when balancing religious rights with other rights or social interests.[9] This approach, based on deference and the rights of the majority, may leave religious and other views of minority groups inadequately protected.

LOOKING FOR EXTRA MARKS?

- Show that you understand the scope of and values underpinning freedom of religion and its importance in a democratic society; including arguments based on secularism and public order as reasons for its restriction.

- Appreciate the legal and moral dilemmas facing the courts in enforcing religious rights, together with the arguments for its compromise, by employing principles of proportionality, equality, and tolerance.

▨ Use leading and topical cases (and academic opinion) which illustrate those dilemmas (religious dress and religious free speech) which allow you to employ your critical skills and conclude on the central questions.

QUESTION | 2

To what extent does both the European Convention on Human Rights and English law provide sufficient protection to religious groups and followers against blasphemous and other offensive or harmful speech?

! CAUTION!

▨ This question requires a sound overall knowledge of article 9 ECHR and the right to religion, but the answer should concentrate on whether the Convention and domestic law provides *sufficient* protection to religious followers *against speech* which attacks their religion or religious beliefs.

▨ The question does not employ the phrase *critical examination*, but you should take a critical approach having understood the importance of religious freedom and the controversies inherent in protecting religious followers from such speech.

▨ The question refers to protection in both domestic law and under the ECHR, so you must use both domestic legal provisions as well as cases from the European Court and the domestic courts in order to examine the extent of the law's protection to religious groups and followers.

▨ Use statutory provisions (including ones which have been repealed) and cases which examine the dilemmas faced by the law and the courts in balancing religious freedom with freedom of expression.

☐ DIAGRAM ANSWER PLANS

Appreciation and consideration of the potential conflict between articles 9 (freedom of religion) and 10 (freedom of expression) of the Convention

⬇

Consideration of the (now abolished) domestic law of blasphemy and other offences seeking to regulate religiously offensive speech in the context of a critical examination of relevant case law of the European Court and Commission where articles 9 and 10 are in conflict

⬇

Critical commentary on the scope of domestic law and Convention case law and whether they provide sufficient protection against such speech

⬇

Conclusions on the extent to which the law and the cases have achieved an appropriate and proportionate protection of religious rights

SUGGESTED ANSWER

[1] The author begins the essay by referring to a controversial and well-publicised event which highlights the dilemma.

[2] The author explains that free speech might conflict with religious rights and may need restricting.

[3] The author identifies that blasphemy laws may protect the enjoyment of religion.

[4] The author stresses the wide margin of appreciation given to states in protecting religious or other sensibilities.

The violent attacks by religious groups on the offices of Charlie Hebdo for publishing allegedly blasphemous material highlight the conflict between free speech and the right to enjoy one's religious views free from attack.[1] In a democratic, tolerant, and pluralist society freedom of expression will include the right to impart information and ideas that shock and offend (*Handyside v United Kingdom* (1976) **1 EHRR 737**). However, freedom of expression may be compromised provided any such restriction serves a legitimate aim and is necessary and proportionate. In this respect religious freedom, guaranteed under **article 9**, is identified as a legitimate aim in **article 10(2)**—the 'protection of the rights of others'.[2] This appears to legitimise domestic state laws that regulate speech or conduct which attacks either a religion or the right of individuals to practise their religion. Indeed, the absence of such laws might seriously affect the right to religious observance, arguably imposing a duty on the state to provide protection in this area (*Members of the Gldani Congregation of Jehovah's Witnesses v Georgia* (2008) **46 EHRR 30**).

Some legal systems will attempt to protect either the tenets of the country's religion or the sensibilities of its members via a specific law of blasphemy. Such a law not only protects public safety and prevents disorder or crime, but also, more specifically, guarantees freedom of religion and religious enjoyment. A domestic law of blasphemy might, therefore, offer some protection to religious followers against grossly offensive or outrageous expression. However, principles of free speech and tolerance insist on a proportionate balance between speech that questions or attacks religion and the rights of its followers.[3] For example, in *Otto-Preminger Institut v Austria* (1994) **19 EHRR 34** the European Court held that religious followers could not expect to be exempt from all criticism and must tolerate and accept the denial by others of their religious beliefs; and even the propagation by others of doctrines hostile to their faith. However, it also noted that the state must ensure the peaceful enjoyment of **article 9** rights by the holders of those beliefs; recognising that the effect of certain criticism might inhibit such believers from exercising their rights. In that case, therefore, it held that a film that depicted God as senile, Jesus as feeble-minded, and Mary as a wanton woman constituted a provocative portrayal of objects of religious veneration. Accordingly, the seizing of the film was a proportionate response to ensure religious peace in that region and to protect some people from an unwarranted and offensive attack on their religious beliefs.

Furthermore, the Convention machinery has offered each state a wide margin of appreciation with respect to whether, and how, it wishes to regulate blasphemous speech.[4] Thus, in *Otto-Preminger* it held that the state is better placed than the international judge to assess the need for blasphemy laws and of their application in particular circumstances. This was because it was not possible to discern a common European conception of the significance of religion in society. Further, it noted that the concept of blasphemy could not be isolated from the society against which it is being judged, as well as the population where publication was to take place, which in that case were strongly Catholic (see, also, *IA v Turkey* (2007) 45 EHRR 30).

[5] The author continues with examples illustrating this discretion and its limits.

This approach does not force the state to pass and maintain blasphemy laws. However, in cases where religious beliefs are recognised under such laws, one can expect a generous level of protection when that right comes into conflict with freedom of expression.[5] For example, in *Gay News v United Kingdom* (1983) EHRR 123, it was held that it might be necessary to attach criminal sanctions to material that offends against religious feelings, provided the attack is serious enough. Furthermore, it upheld the applicant's convictions (in *R v Lemon* [1979] AC 617) even though the offence was based on strict liability, thus ignoring the intention of the author and publisher in publishing the work. This approach was maintained in *Wingrove v United Kingdom* (1996) 24 EHRR 1, where the Court upheld the domestic authorities' refusal to give a video licence to a short film that described the ecstatic and erotic visions of Jesus Christ of a sixteenth-century nun. In that case, the authority felt that the video would risk violating domestic blasphemy laws, and the Court held that the interference corresponded to a legitimate aim—the protection of Christians against serious offence in their beliefs—and was proportionate despite the fact that the law did not treat all religions alike. This would suggest that the European Court would back any reasonable restriction on blasphemous speech imposed by regulatory agencies such as broadcasting authorities, who have a power to regulate material on grounds of taste and decency. Indeed, the domestic courts have indicated that they would provide these agencies with a wide area of discretion in this area (*R (Prolife) v BBC* [2004] 1 AC 185). However, it will not sanction restrictions which are simply hostile to a religion without being abusive (*Tatlav v Turkey*, Application No. 50692/99, judgment of the European Court, 2 May 2006).

[6] The author stresses the difficulty of applying blasphemy laws to political speech.

The balance between speech and religion becomes more problematic when the speech or attack is political, as in the recent Hebdo incident, and the European Court has suggested that there is little scope for restrictions on political speech[6] which was allegedly blasphemous (*Kunstler v Austria* (2008) 47 EHRR 5). This may lead to feelings on behalf of followers that religious views are largely unrecognised and unprotected, particularly as the Convention does not insist that domestic blasphemy laws apply equally to all religions (*R v Chief*

Metropolitan Stipendiary Magistrate, ex parte Choudhury [1991] 1 QB 1006; *Choudhury v United Kingdom* (1991) 12 HRLJ 172). Consequently, the state has discretion whether to enact blasphemy laws, and to choose which religions to protect under such laws. Indeed, to avoid this dilemma and inequality the English law of blasphemy was abolished by **s.78 of the Criminal Justice and Immigration Act 2008**.

This of course leaves *all* religious followers unprotected, although the position may be mitigated by the domestic law of certain race or religious hatred crimes.[7] These laws might indirectly protect individuals from racial and religious discrimination and protect their right to freedom of thought, conscience, and religion under **article 9**. For example, **ss.18–23 of the Public Order Act 1986** create a number of offences relating to the incitement of racial hatred—defined under **s.17** as hatred against a group of persons defined by reference to colour, race, nationality (including citizenship), or ethnic or national origins. These provisions did not apply specifically to religious groups, although some such groups (such as Sikhs and Jews) have been held to come within the terms 'race' and 'ethnic or national origins' (*Mandla v Dowell Lee* [1983] 2 AC 548). However, **s.1 of the Racial and Religious Hatred Act 2006** amends the 1986 Act and it is now an offence to use threatening, abusive, and insulting words or behaviour where that person intends to stir up religious hatred, or where such hatred is likely to be stirred up (**s.18** of the 1986 Act). This does not provide protection against offensive or insulting attacks per se and will require religious hatred to ensue. Moreover, it is a defence that the defendant did not intend his words or behaviour, or the written material, to be, and was not aware that it might be, threatening, abusive, or insulting (**s.18 (5)**). These qualifications protect true freedom of speech and under **s.7** of the Act no proceedings may be brought without the consent of the Attorney-General.

Further, racially, and religiously, aggravated public order offences were introduced via the **Crime and Disorder Act 1998**, which provided for increased penalties for certain public order offences. These provisions apply where at the time of committing the offence, or immediately before or after doing so, the offender demonstrates towards the victim of the offence hostility based on the victim's membership (or presumed membership) of a racial group; or where the offence is motivated (wholly or partly) by hostility towards members of a racial group based on their membership of that group. This principle was extended by **s.28 of the Anti-terrorism, Crime and Security Act 2001**, where the commission of the offence was activated on the grounds of religious hatred, including the victim's membership of a religious group (a group of persons defined by religious belief or lack of religious belief, **s.28(4)**). This gives greater protection than the old

[7] The author now explores other laws which may fill the gap left by the absence of a blasphemy law.

law of blasphemy, which only protected the religious observer from outrageous attack (*R v Lemon*), and which allowed the court to find that the object under attack was not religion, but other social matters, such as media morality (*R (Green) v Westminster Magistrates' Court* [2008] HRLR 12).

[8]The author explains the low tolerance of hate speech shown by the courts.

Domestic courts will be mindful of the need to uphold freedom of expression, although case law thus far suggests that the courts will show a limited tolerance to such speech.[8] Thus, in *Norwood v DPP, The Times,* **30 July 2003**, it was held that the display of a poster containing, in very large print, the words 'Islam out of Britain' and 'Protect the British People' constituted an aggravated offence under **s.5 of the Public Order Act 1986** of displaying an insulting sign likely to cause harassment, alarm, or distress. The appeal court held that the sign was plainly unreasonable, indicating a public expression of attack on all Muslims in this country as opposed to a temperate criticism against the tenets of the Muslim religion. This decision was upheld by the European Court of Human Rights (*Norwood v United Kingdom* **(2005) 40 EHRR 11**), which held that the speech was not protected by the Convention. This was because it was a general and vehement attack against a religious group, linking the group as a whole with grave acts of terrorism, and thus incompatible with the values of the Convention, notably tolerance, social peace, and non-discrimination. That reflects the Court's intolerance of hate speech (*Glimerveen and Hagenbeek v Netherlands* **(1980) 18 DR 187**) and thus provides some protection to the right of religious observance.

[9]The author concludes by stating that article 9 is inconsistent in its protection of such rights, although other laws may provide some protection.

In conclusion, **article 9** of the Convention offers a limited and inconsistent protection against blasphemous and other religiously offensive speech.[9] The absence in **article 9** of a positive right to defend one's religion and beliefs from verbal attack militates against full and effective protection in this field. Further, this situation is compounded by the absence of any specific domestic blasphemy laws in the UK. This is to an extent mitigated by the growth of racially and religiously aggravated offences, which at least outlaw unreasonable and insulting attacks against religion and religious followers.

➕ LOOKING FOR EXTRA MARKS?

▓ Show that you understand the importance of restrictive free speech laws on the enjoyment of religious freedom, together with the inherent dangers of restricting free speech.

▓ Appreciate the inevitable dilemma facing the law and the courts in recognising religious sensibility, together with the democratic problem of restricting free speech for such reasons.

▓ Use leading and topical cases and events (Charlie Hebdo) which highlight those dilemmas and which allow you to employ your critical skills to conclude on the central question.

QUESTION | 3

Critically examine the extent to which the European Court of Human Rights has safe-guarded the fundamental right of political association. In your opinion are domestic restrictions in this area compatible with the European Convention and its case law?

CAUTION!

- This question requires a very sound overall knowledge of article 11 and the right of association, but the answer should concentrate on the right to *political* association and the extent to which the European Court, and then domestic law, has safeguarded that right.

- The question employs the phrase *critical examination* in respect of the European Court's role, so you should take a critical approach having understood the importance of political freedom and association and the controversies inherent in restricting, or proscribing such groups.

- The second question refers to protection in domestic law, but it is permissible to use cases from the European Court as well as domestic decisions in order to examine how such decisions have impacted on the domestic courts' case law and have led to any legislative changes.

- Use cases—from both jurisdictions—which examine the legal and constitutional dilemmas faced by the courts in upholding and restricting the right of association, focusing on the control of terrorist groups.

DIAGRAM ANSWER PLANS

> Explanation of the theory and value of the fundamental right of association, including its relationship with democracy and other Convention rights

> ▼

> Consideration as to the extent and efficacy of the European Court's case law in the light of the democratic and other values that the freedom purports to uphold

> ▼

> Explanation of the conditional status of that right within the Convention and the need to limit that right in order to protect individual and collective interests

> ▼

> Explanation of various domestic laws restricting the right of association, and their rationale; especially with respect to terrorist groups

> ▼

> Consideration of the compatibility of relevant domestic law with the Human Rights Act 1998, supported by any relevant post-Act case law

Article 11 of the European Convention states that everyone has the right of association, expressly including the right to form and join trade unions. 'Association' includes political parties and in *United Communist Party of Turkey v Turkey* (1998) 26 EHRR 121 the Court recognised that such parties are essential to the proper functioning of a democracy. Further, **article 11** must be considered in the light of **article 10**, particularly in relation to political parties, because of their essential role in ensuring pluralism.[1]

[1] The author stresses the democratic importance of political association and of article 11.

The Court has attached special significance to the political views of the speaker (*Vogt v Germany* (1995) 21 EHRR 205). Thus, it will safeguard associations more vehemently where the group in question has a democratic mandate, as opposed to those forming for social purposes (*Anderson v United Kingdom* (1998) 25 EHRR CD 172) or for recreation (*Countryside Alliance v United Kingdom* (2010) EHRR SE6). The Court will subject any restriction on political association, particularly any form of proscription, to the closest scrutiny.[2] Consequently, proscription cannot be sanctioned simply because the group's views conflict with established political orthodoxy and any interference has to be based on compelling evidence. For example, in *United Communist Party of Turkey v Turkey*, the dissolution of a political party on the basis that it used the word 'communist' in its name was in violation of **article 11**. Although it had advocated a separate Kurdish nation, the group's dissolution because of the use of the word 'communist' was not necessary in a democratic society. Despite it advocating different views from the government on the Kurdish problem, there was insufficient evidence that it advocated division of the Turkish nation. This decision was upheld in *Socialist Party v Turkey* (1998) 27 EHRR 51, where the Court held that the same principles applied even if proscription was based on the group's activities after formation.

[2] The author points out that restricting political association will require strong justification.

The Court has also taken a robust approach with respect to measures that interfere with the individual's enjoyment of association. Thus, in *Vogt*, it held that the dismissal of a teacher simply because she had as a member taken part in the activities of the German Communist Party, violated **article 10**. There was insufficient evidence to support the necessity of the dismissal as she had never acted in a way that was inconsistent with the compulsory declaration of allegiance to the German constitutional order. However, in *Ahmed v United Kingdom* [1999] IRLR 188 the prohibition of certain local authority officers from holding political office was proportionate to the aim of securing public confidence in public officers and the performance of their duties.

[3] The author now explores cases where proscription might be justified.

There will be exceptional cases where the Court is satisfied that an organisation poses a sufficient threat to the values of that society to warrant proscription. In such cases it must distinguish such threats from those cases where the views of the group are simply unpopular or inconsistent with other, democratic, majority views.[3] Thus, **article 17** provides that nothing in the Convention gives any person or group any right to engage in any activity or perform any act aimed at the destruction of any of the rights and freedoms of others. This provision could be used to justify the proscription of groups whose purposes and activities are either violent, or incite violence, or are otherwise inconsistent with the enjoyment of others' Convention rights. Thus, in *Refah Partisi Erbakan Kazan and Tekdal v Turkey* **(2002) 35 EHRR 2**, the Grand Chamber of the European Court confirmed that political parties whose leaders incite others to use violence could not rely on the Convention to protect them from resultant sanctions.

[4] The author continues to explore the justification for proscription on grounds beyond the prevention of violence.

However, violence is not a prerequisite of proscription and an association may be restricted for wider purposes.[4] Thus, in *Refah Partisi*, the Court accepted that political parties who campaign for changes to the legal or constitutional structure are allowed the protection of **article 11**. However, it stressed that any such change had to be compatible with the fundamental principles of democracy. In this case, the dissolution of the applicant's party because it had become a centre of activities against the principles of secularism, was within the state's margin of appreciation. The party sought to institute a system of Sharia law and such a system was incompatible with the state's role as the guarantor of individual rights, and would infringe the principle of non-discrimination between individuals.

[5] The author now begins to examine the practice of proscription in domestic law.

In domestic law, proscription has been reserved for the most extreme groups who pose major threats to public order or the security of the state. Instead, domestic law attaches criminal liability to words or behaviour that cause, or are likely to cause, particular harm.[5] For example, with respect to right-wing groups with racist agendas, the law instead makes provision for specific offences that seek to protect individuals or groups. Thus, **s.18 of the Public Order Act 1986** makes it an offence to incite racial hatred, and **s.1 of the Racial and Religious Hatred Act 2006** contains a similar offence of inciting religious hatred. In addition, some public order offences, such as using threatening or abusive words or behaviour likely to cause alarm and distress, can now be committed in a racially (**Public Order Act 1986**), or religiously (**Anti-terrorism, Crime and Security Act 2001**), aggravated form. These provisions are enforced stringently by the courts (*Norwood v DPP, The Times*, **30 July 2003**). However, they do not make a person liable by association only, even though their views might not attract the protection of **articles 10 and 11** of the European Convention (*Norwood v United Kingdom* **(2005) 40 EHRR 11**).

Nevertheless, there are certain provisions that criminalise association with a particular group. For example, **s.1 of the Public Order Act 1936** makes it an offence to wear a uniform in any public place or at any public meeting that signifies association with any political organisation or the promotion of any political object (*O'Moran v DPP* **[1975] QB 864**). This provision overlaps with **s.13 of the Terrorism Act 2000**, and it is argued that its potential use against peaceful and lawful groups, such as animal activists, would be a disproportionate interference with **article 11**, although the consent of the Attorney-General is required for any prosecution.[6]

[6] The author highlights the potential arbitrariness of proscription in terms of its application to certain groups.

Further, **s.2 of the Public Order Act 1936** prohibits the formation of military or quasi-military organisations—those organised or trained to be employed for the use or display of physical force in promoting any political object. The provision covers organisations concerned with usurping the functions of the police or the armed forces. Thus, it makes it an offence for any person to take part in the control or management of that association, or, as a member of that association, to take part in the organisation or training of members. The provision was employed in *R v Jordan and Tyndall* **[1963] Crim LR 124** against an extremist right-wing paramilitary group and appears compatible with **articles 11 and 17** of the Convention, especially as any prosecution requires the consent of the Attorney-General.

The proscription of terrorist groups is now covered by the **Terrorism Act 2000**, and **s.3** identifies proscribed groups as those listed in **Schedule 2** of the Act. The Secretary of State has the power to add to that list if he believes that it is concerned in terrorism—that it commits or participates in acts of terrorism, prepares for terrorism, promotes or encourages terrorism, or is otherwise concerned in acts of terrorism. 'Terrorism' is defined under **s.1** as the use or threat (for the purpose of advancing a political, religious, or ideological cause) of action designed to influence the government or to intimidate the public or a section of the public, which involves serious violence against any person or serious damage to property, endangers the life of any person, or creates a serious risk to the health or safety of the public or a section of the public. This could cover environmental groups or animal activists, who represent a genuine and strongly supported cause. Such groups are subject to a range of public order offences, and the use of proscription powers might be an unnecessary restriction on the lawful activities of that group. Equally, the law does not accept the concept of freedom fighters so as to exclude groups who otherwise would come under **s.3** (*R v Gul* **[2013] UKSC 64**).

This wide power of proscription, although subject to parliamentary approval (under **s.123**), is not subject to judicial review. However, **s.5** establishes the Proscribed Organisations Appeal Commission, which hears appeals against the Secretary of State's refusal to remove an organisation from that list (*R v Secretary of State for the Home Department, ex parte Kurdistan Workers Party and others* **[2002] EWHC 644 (Admin)**).

Once a group is proscribed, **s.11** of the Act makes it an offence to belong, or profess to belong, to a proscribed organisation. Further, under **s.12** it is an offence to solicit support for, to arrange, manage, or assist in managing a meeting which he knows is to support or further the activities of a proscribed organisation, or to address any such meeting in order to encourage support for such. **Section 13** then makes it an offence to wear an item of clothing, or wear, carry, or display an article in such a way or in such circumstances as to arouse reasonable suspicion that the person in question is a member or supporter of a proscribed organisation. The provision might apply to a person who, for example, holds up a placard expressing views in agreement with that group and **s.1 of the Prevention of Terrorism Act 2005** creates the offence of directly or indirectly encouraging or inducing an act of terrorism.[7] Such encouragement could consist of an act which the public could understand as glorifying such an act, thus blurring the distinction between incitement to violence and lawful support.

> [7] The author highlights another possible weakness in this provision in so far as compatibility with human rights is concerned.

Although the state's margin of appreciation is narrow with respect to the dissolution of political parties and the enjoyment of the right of association, the European Court is willing to sanction proscription in cases where the association threatens democratic values.[8] The distinction between those cases, and ones where the ideology of the group is simply inconsistent with established orthodoxy, might be difficult to apply in practice. With respect to the UK, current laws appear to be consistent with the European Convention, although, the *potential* application of those laws to groups with a legitimate agenda, but whose members have employed violent means, might threaten **article 11**.

> [8] The author provides a neat conclusion summarising the Convention's approach and the probable compatibility of domestic law.

LOOKING FOR EXTRA MARKS?

▓ Show that you understand the scope and importance of the right of political association to democracy and freedom, together with the reasons such a right may have to be restricted.

▓ Appreciate the legal and diplomatic dilemmas facing the European Court in enforcing such rights, together with the difficulty of justifying restrictions on grounds of public safety and national security.

▓ Use leading and topical cases and dilemmas, such as the fight against terrorism and terrorist groups, to illustrate those dilemmas and which allow you to employ your critical skills to conclude on the central questions.

QUESTION | 4

'The Courts consistently stated that under English law there is no right to demonstrate.'

To what extent, if at all, would you qualify that statement in the light of post-Human Rights Act case law?

! CAUTION!

- This question requires a very sound overall knowledge of the right to demonstrate and articles 10 and 11 of the European Convention, but the answer should concentrate on the quote and the *extent* to which it reflects the true position in domestic law, particularly in the post-Human Rights Act era.

- The question does not employ the phrase *critical examination*, but nevertheless you should take a critical approach having understood the democratic importance of the right to demonstrate and its recognition and protection from unnecessary interference.

- The question refers to protection in domestic law, but it is permissible to use cases from the European Court in addition to domestic decisions in order to examine how such decisions have impacted on the domestic courts' case law or have led to any legislative changes.

- Use cases—from both jurisdictions—which examine the law's attempts to recognise, and restrict, the right to demonstrate and the dilemmas faced by the law-makers and the courts in recognising and restricting this democratic right.

DIAGRAM ANSWER PLANS

Explanation of the importance of the right to demonstrate and of the residual and insecure nature of that right at common law

⬇

Examples where courts and Parliament interfered or failed to secure the right to demonstrate, and examples where Parliament or the courts gave support and recognition to the right to demonstrate

⬇

Explanation of the impact of the European Convention and Human Rights Act 1998 on the right to demonstrate, including an examination of case law which displays either a traditional or more robust approach to protecting the right of demonstration

⬇

Conclusions with respect to the efficacy of domestic law protection of the right to demonstrate and the truth of the quote

Articles 10 and 11 of the European Convention guarantee, respectively, the rights of freedom of expression and peaceful assembly. Although freedom to demonstrate is a conditional right, the European Court has stressed that any restrictions must be clearly prescribed by law (*Hashman and Harrap v United Kingdom* **(1999) 30 EHRR 241**) and must not impose disproportionate interferences on entirely peaceful protest (*Steel v United Kingdom* **(1999) 28 EHRR 603**). Domestic law, must, therefore, ensure that the right to demonstrate is free from arbitrary regulation.

In *Hubbard v Pitt* **[1976] QB 142** Lord Denning stated that the right to assemble for the purpose of deliberating upon public grievances was not prohibited as long as it was done peaceably and in good order and without threats or incitement to violence or obstruction. However, the absence of a constitutional guarantee of freedom of peaceful assembly made the right to demonstrate a notional one, given the proliferation of public order laws that existed, and still exist, to ensure public safety and the enjoyment of private interests.[1]

Traditionally, the courts displayed reluctance to accommodate the right to demonstrate. For example, in *Arrowsmith v Jenkins* **[1963] 2 QB 561** it was held that the offence of obstruction of the highway might be committed without any specific intention to obstruct on behalf of the demonstrator. In that case, the obstruction had occurred because of her presence and the motive of the speaker was irrelevant. However, in *Hirst and Agu v Chief Constable of Yorkshire* **(1987) 85 Cr App R 143**, it was held that the courts needed to consider the reasonableness of the protester's actions and thus balance the right to protest with the need for good order.

Further, the courts allowed the police wide discretion in how they balanced public order and individual liberty.[2] Thus, in *Nicol and Selvanayagam v DPP* **[1996] Crim LR 318** the police were allowed to arrest demonstrators for disrupting an angling competition by blowing horns. This was because their conduct, although not unlawful, was likely to cause a breach of the peace as the anglers were on the verge of using force against the protestors. Police discretion was particularly prevalent in cases where the demonstrator was charged with obstruction of a police officer in the execution of his duty (now contained in **s.89 of the Police Act 1997**). Thus, in *Duncan v Jones* **[1936] 1 KB 218**, although a demonstrator might not have caused any obstruction, or provoked a breach of the peace, she might nonetheless be arrested for obstruction if she was prepared to take the risk that a disturbance would result from her conduct. This conflicted with the principle in *Beatty v Gillbanks* **(1882) 15 Cox CC 138**, that a person cannot be punished for acting lawfully if he knows that in so

[1] The author identifies that the lack of clear constitutional rights places freedom of assembly in a precarious position.

[2] The author points out that the courts were unwilling to interfere with the actions of the police, then offering case examples in illustration.

doing he will induce another person to act unlawfully. Further, the courts were reluctant to subject police discretion to any real substantive review (*Piddington v Bates* **[1961] 1 WLR 162** and *Moss v McLachlan* **[1985] IRLR 76**).

[3] The author identifies a potentially new test for challenging police powers under the HRA.

After the **Human Rights Act 1998**, courts are obliged to take into account the case law of the European Court (**s.2**) and have the power to declare legislative provisions incompatible with a Convention right (**s.4**).[3] In particular, restrictions have to be prescribed by law and necessary in a democratic society for the purpose of achieving any legitimate aim, such as public safety.

A number of decisions in the post-Act era appear to provide greater protection for freedom of assembly. For example, in *Redmond-Bate v DPP, The Times*, **23 July 1999**, the High Court restricted the effect of *Duncan v Jones* by insisting that a police officer would have to concentrate on the *source* of the potential trouble when arresting someone for obstruction. Also, speech was not actionable simply because it offended the audience. Lord Justice Sedley held that speech included the irritating, contentious, and provocative, provided it did not tend to provoke violence, and that freedom only to speak inoffensively was not worth having. Again, in *Percy v DPP, The Times*, **21 January 2002**, it was held that behaviour which was simply an affront to other people (desecrating a national flag) was not outlawed.

Further, in *DPP v Jones and Lloyd* **[1999] 2 All ER 257**, it was held that members of the public could have a right to use the highway for the purpose of conducting a peaceful assembly. However, this was provided that was a reasonable and usual activity and consistent with the primary right to use the highway for passage and re-passage. In this case, the defendants' activities (a silent roadside protest) were peaceful and non-obstructive and therefore not unlawful; see also *Westminster CC v Haw* **[2002] EWHC 2073**.

[4] Having given examples of a more proactive approach by the courts, the author now provides examples where the traditional approach still remains.

The courts took a less liberal approach[4] in *R (Brehony) v Chief Constable of Greater Manchester Police, The Times*, **15 April 2005**, where it was held that the police had acted lawfully under **s.14 of the Public Order Act 1986** when they moved the protest to another location to accommodate the Christmas shopping period. Further, the courts have offered the authorities a wide margin of appreciation when achieving public order. For example, in *R (Gillan) v Commissioner of Police of the Metropolis and another* **[2006] 2 AC 307** there had been no violation of **article 10 or 11** when the police used their powers of stop and search under **s.44(4)(b) of the Terrorism Act 2000** to search people who were on their way to attend an arms fair to take part in a peaceful protest. The threat posed by terrorism provided the necessary justification for any violation of the claimants' rights and there was enough evidence that the arms fair was an occasion that warranted the use of their powers. However, this approach was questioned by the European Court of

Human Rights in *Gillan and Quinton v United Kingdom* (2010) 50 **EHRR 45**. Here it was held that there had been a breach of article 8 of the Convention. This was because the procedure interfered sufficiently with the applicants' privacy and private life, and the nature and scope of the powers (and the lack of available judicial review of such powers) meant that the provisions were not prescribed by law.

[5]The author gives further examples of a more human rights friendly approach by the domestic courts under the HRA.

Outside the context of terrorism, a more generous approach has sometimes been evident.[5] For example, in *R (Laporte) v Chief Constable of Gloucestershire and others* [2007] 2 WLR 46 it was held that the police had violated **articles 10 and 11** when they prevented the passengers of a coach from reaching the site of a demonstration. The House of Lords held that no such power existed unless they anticipated a clear breach of the peace; and that, on the facts, no such belief was present as they were unable to identify which (if any) of the passengers were a threat. In any case, the police could have dealt with any threat at the place of demonstration. That decision casts doubt on cases such as *Piddington v Bates*, where almost unlimited discretion was provided to the police in keeping the peace. Nevertheless, the courts do show deference and police do still have a general power when they, reasonably, anticipate a breach of the peace.[6] Thus, in *Austin v Commissioner of the Police of the Metropolis* [2009] 1 AC 564, the House of Lords dismissed a claim under **article 5 and 11** and upheld the use of a power to detain ('kettle') demonstrators for seven hours. It was found that this was a proportionate way of dealing with a definite and imminent breach of the peace. This decision was confirmed by the European Court as consistent with the Convention in *Austin v United Kingdom* (2012) **55 EHRR 14**, perhaps displaying a recent trend of the Court to offer a wide margin of appreciation in this area. In that case, it held that given the seriousness of the actual and anticipated breach of the peace there had been no deprivation of liberty despite the applicants being detained for that period. Accordingly, given the context of the containment there had not been any loss of liberty as opposed to a restriction on freedom of movement. This approach was also taken in the recent Supreme Court decision in *R (Hicks) v Commissioner of the Police of the Metropolis* [2017] UKSC 9, where the police were allowed to exercise their power of preventative arrest against individuals protesting on the day of a Royal Wedding.

[6]The author now qualifies the previous statement by offering examples where the police are given more discretion when a breach of the peace *is* anticipated.

[7]The author continues to give examples of a hands-off approach adopted by the courts.

Such respect has been mirrored by the domestic courts in more recent years,[7] and in *R (Moos and others) v Commissioner of Police of the Metropolis* [2012] EWCA 12 it was held that the police had not acted unlawfully or breached **article 5** in 'kettling' peaceful demonstrators to protect them from violent protestors of another demonstration, who had hijacked their demonstration. The Court of Appeal held that it was reasonable for the officer in charge to anticipate a breach of the peace and that the measures taken were reasonable and proportionate.

Importantly, it stressed that the reviewing court should not ask whether it would have taken the measures. Rather, it should decide whether the officer was entitled to take those measures and in doing so had unreasonably interfered with the protestors' Convention rights.

[8] The author concludes by referring to the Joint Committee's observations on the likely compatibility of our law.

The Joint Committee on Human Rights has concluded that, in general, domestic law facilitates peaceful protest and is compatible with the Convention. In any case, it is difficult to gauge whether domestic law is compatible with the European Convention as the European Court has granted a wide margin of appreciation[8] to the state with respect to the enforcement of public safety (***Chorherr v Austria*** **(1993) 17 EHRR 358**). Despite this, laws must be clearly prescribed by law (***Hashman and Harrap***) and must not impose disproportionate interferences on entirely peaceful protest (***Steel v United Kingdom***). The domestic courts now have the power and duty to ensure that any restrictions on this right comply with the case law of the European Court, although cases such as ***Austin*** suggest that any assertion of a right to peaceful demonstration should be taken with caution.

LOOKING FOR EXTRA MARKS?

- Show that you understand the importance of the right to demonstrate in terms of democracy, liberty, and free speech, together with the practical and other reasons why it may have to be restricted.
- Appreciate the legal and practical dilemmas facing Parliament and the courts in upholding the right to demonstrate, together with the need for them to balance the right to demonstrate with others' rights and the need to secure public safety.
- Stress the need for both judicial activism and deference to the police and other authorities in this area and the guidance offered by the European Court in that balance.
- Use leading and topical cases on demonstrations which illustrate those dilemmas and which allow you to employ your critical skills to conclude on the central question of whether domestic law, in reality, recognises the right to demonstrate.

QUESTION | 5

Jack Morrissey is the head of a protest group called 'Rebels against Cruelty', concerned with the killing of animals for human consumption. Three weeks ago he and four members of the group were campaigning on a pavement in Leavington when they were confronted by local butchers, who started swearing at them. Several members of the group started chanting, referring to the butchers as 'murdering bastards'. A police officer arrived on the scene and asked the group to move along because they were causing an obstruction, and when they refused to move Jack was arrested for obstruction of the highway, and the other members for obstruction of a police officer.

ⓘ

The next day Jack distributed leaflets in Leavington with pictures of pigs with their heads cut off. The leaflet stated that the group intended to hold a silent protest outside a farmer's house in the Boventry countryside and the Chief Constable, on reading the leaflet, immediately applied for an order to prohibit the assembly of any persons on the land of the farmer, or on any adjoining highway. The group nevertheless proceeded to the lane outside the farm and lined up along the grass verge of the lane. When the police arrived, they were asked to move and when they refused to do so Jack, together with four other members of the group, were arrested for taking part in a trespassory assembly. In addition, other members of the group, armed with banners, were stopped en route to the farm and told to turn back. When they refused they were arrested.

Jack now wishes to organise a procession through the streets of Boventry to launch the group's 'Meat is Murder' campaign and applied to the police giving two weeks' notice. The police gave permission for the procession but imposed the following conditions: that the number of marchers is restricted to 200; that due to the busy shopping period the procession must circle and not enter Boventry shopping precinct; and that during the procession the protesters must not distribute leaflets likely to distress the public.

Advise Jack and the others as to the legality of the police action and whether they are likely to be found guilty of any offence.

CAUTION!

- This question requires a very sound overall knowledge of the right to demonstrate and its underlying values, but the answer should concentrate on the specific legal provisions which are engaged in the scenario.

- The question requires a methodical approach in identifying and interpreting the relevant legal provisions and applying the relevant case law in advising on the legality of the actions of the demonstrators and the police.

- The question requires a knowledge of domestic law and cases, but you also need to be aware of cases from the European Court in order to assess the likely decision of the domestic court in this scenario.

- Give practical and full advice on the facts, avoiding theoretical and political arguments surrounding the right to demonstrate unless they assist you in guessing the outcome of the challenge.

DIAGRAM ANSWER PLANS

Identify the issues	◾ The legal issues and the claims ◾ Various public order offences; compatibility with ECHR rights (judicial review/HRA)

Relevant law	◾ Outline the rules and cases relating to the scenario ◾ Obstruction of the highway; breach of the peace; s.14 of the Public Order Act; articles 10 and 11 ECHR

Apply	◾ Application of the rules on liability and defences to the facts

Conclude	◾ Conclude on whether the charges, or any claims under the HRA would be likely to succeed

SUGGESTED ANSWER

The Arrests in Leavington

[1] The author immediately states the ingredients of the first offence that they will advise on—obstruction of the highway.

Section 137 of the Highways Act 1980 makes it unlawful to wilfully obstruct a highway without lawful authority.[1] However, for the officer to arrest Jack the court must be satisfied that Jack had caused an obstruction, that it was wilful, and that the obstruction was unreasonable (**Nagy v Weston [1965] 1 WLR 280**). Jack's presence must interfere with the public's right to use the highway, which would include the pavement. Consequently, there would have to be some evidence that as a result of the protest and the altercation the public could not use the pavement effectively. The court would then consider whether that obstruction was unreasonable—for example, whether pedestrians were forced to use the busy road to walk on as opposed to using another viable route. The could also take into account the fact that Jack and the other members were taking part in a political protest (**Hirst and Agu v Chief Constable of West Yorkshire (1987) 85 Cr App 143**). Thus, under **s.12 of the Human Rights Act** the court must take into account Jack's (and the butcher's) freedom of expression[2] in determining whether that obstruction was unreasonable (**Westminster CC v Haw [2002] EWHC 2073**).

[2] The author stresses that the use of this power will be subject to scrutiny under the HRA.

Jack may be guilty of the offence even if he did not intend to cause an obstruction (**Arrowsmith v Jenkins [1963] 2 QB 561**) provided the obstruction occurs because of his presence. Therefore, he may be arrested even though his real intention is to protest. In the post-Act era, the police must discover the source of the trouble (*Redmond-Bate v DPP, The Times*, **23 July 1999**) and consider whether the butcher was at least partly to blame for the incident. The police must not, therefore, assume that Jack is to blame.

[3] The author now moves to the next offence, detailing its requirements before considering the relevant cases.

Under **s.89 of the Police Act 1997** it is an offence to obstruct a police officer in the execution of his duty[3] and it would be argued in this case that the officer reasonably apprehended an obstruction of the highway and that by refusing to move along they have obstructed their efforts to deal with it. Alternatively, the officer may have reasonably apprehended a breach of the peace and that by refusing to move, the members have obstructed that duty (*Duncan v Jones* **[1936] 1 KB 218**). A breach of the peace is an act or threatened act which either actually harms a person, or in his presence his property, or is likely to cause such harm, or which puts someone in fear of such harm being done (*R v Howell* **[1982] QB 416**). That covers the situation where a person is either inciting a breach of the peace by his conduct or words, or where such words or behaviour are likely to result in another person committing a breach of the peace. The officer must, therefore, reasonably believe that the members were about to use violence towards the butchers, or that the butchers were about to use violence.

Further, the words or conduct of the demonstrators must not interfere with the rights of others and be unreasonable (*Nicol and Selvanayagam v DPP* **[1996] Crim LR 318**). Consequently, the officer must be satisfied that he reasonably apprehended a breach of the peace, and also direct his attention to the source of the trouble (*DPP v Redmond-Bate*). In *Redmond-Bate* the source of the trouble was the actions of onlookers and not the protesters, although in our case both factions appear to be using inflammatory language. Although the words and conduct must be more than annoying (*Percy v DPP, The Times*, **21 January 2002**), calling people 'murdering bastards' would incite others to violence and might then justify the arrests.[4] However, the officer may have to have been present at the incident to draw such conclusions and for the arrests to be lawful.

[4] The author provides clear and informed advice to the parties on the basis of the facts and the words used in the scenario.

The Banning of the Trespassory Assembly

Section 14A(1) of the 1986 Public Order Act allows a chief police officer to apply to the local council for an order prohibiting the holding of all trespassory public assemblies in that area. **Section 14A(9)** defines an assembly as one of two or more persons. Assuming that there will be at least two demonstrators, the legality of this order is then dependent on the chief police officer's reasonable belief that such an assembly is intended to be held on land to which the public has no, or a limited, right of access. Further, the assembly must be either likely to be held without the permission of the landowner or to conduct itself in a way which would exceed that permission or the limit of such access. If the land outside is a public highway, their attendance would have to go beyond their right of access (*DPP v Jones and Lloyd* [1999] 2 All ER 257).

The group was to hold a silent protest 'outside the farmer's house', so the chief police officer must have contemplated that this was either on the farmer's land, or on the highway yet constituting an unreasonable use.[5] Further, there must be a reasonable belief that the assembly might at least result in serious disruption to the life of the community. This could include blocking a public highway if such an obstruction would seriously disrupt rural or community life. However, the meeting would have to seriously affect community life, rather than the rights of the landowner. At the very least the police must have evidence of potential trespass and disruption. For example, there must be a *reasonable and objective* belief that the demonstrators will not keep to their silent protest and might go onto the farmer's land, or into his house, and take part in other unlawful and disruptive activities.

[5] The author neatly summarises the requirements of lawful action by the police with respect to this offence.

The Arrests for Taking Part in a Trespassory Assembly

Section 14B(1) makes it an offence for a person to organise such an assembly knowing that it is prohibited by an order, and, under **s.14A(2)**, for a person to take part in such an assembly knowing that it is prohibited. Further, under **s.14B(4)** a constable in uniform may arrest without warrant anyone whom he reasonably suspects to be committing such an offence. Following *DPP v Jones and Lloyd* it is insufficient that they are simply in breach of the order,[6] whether that was made on reasonable suspicion or not. Thus, the question is whether lining up on a grass verge is in excess of their legal right of access.

[6] The author clearly states the relevant test as to whether the police arrest is lawful or not.

In *Lloyd* the police had arrested a group who had assembled on a grass verge on the roadside. The House of Lords held that the defendant's actions constituted a peaceful, non-obstructive assembly consistent with their limited right of access to the highway. Thus, in the absence of any evidence to suggest that this was causing an unreasonable obstruction of the highway, they would not be taking part in a trespassory assembly. Further, if the police had no reasonable evidence to suggest that they were taking part in a trespassory assembly, the arrests and subsequent detentions would constitute a violation of **article 5** of the European Convention.

The Arrests for Obstruction for not Turning Back

Under **s.14C** a police constable has the power to stop persons from proceeding to a trespassory assembly where he reasonably believes that a person is on his way to a prohibited assembly. The constable may stop that person and direct them not to proceed in the direction of the assembly. In such a case any person who refuses to comply with a direction which he knows has been given to him is guilty of an offence and a constable in uniform may arrest without warrant anyone he reasonably suspects to be committing an offence (**s.14C(4)**). This is in addition to the police's power to preserve the peace, which can be used to stop protesters from reaching particular destinations (**Moss v McLachlan [1985] IRLR 76**). This is subject to any detention not being unreasonable in length and there existing a reasonable apprehension that those arrested are likely to threaten the peace (**R (Laporte) v Chief Constable of Gloucestershire and others [2007] 2 WLR 46**). The police would have reasonable grounds to suspect that the protesters were on their way to the relevant area because they were holding banners and moving in the direction of the farm.[7] However, despite **Jones**, **s.14C** talks about *suspicion* that someone is on his way to an assembly prohibited under that section, without expressly requiring that the order is lawful. In all likelihood the officer is required to have a reasonable suspicion that the protesters were about to act in breach of that order by exceeding their right of access on the land. In addition, given the limited discretion afforded to the police with respect to anticipating and preventing a breach of the peace (**Laporte**), the courts would require evidence that the protesters were to exceed their right to be on the land or to act in breach of the peace (**R (Hicks) v Commissioner of the Police of the Metropolis [2017] UKSC 9**).

[7] The author uses the facts in the scenario as the basis of his advice on the likely effect of the protestors' actions.

The Legality of the Conditions Imposed on the Procession

Jack appears to have complied with **s.11 of the Public Order Act 1986**, which imposes a duty on the organiser of a procession to give advance notice to the police six days before the date when it is intended to hold the march. Despite that, the police have a further power under **s.12** to impose conditions on a procession. The conditions must be imposed by the chief police officer in the area. Further, that officer must reasonably believe that serious public disorder, serious damage to property, or serious disruption to the life of the community may be caused by the procession, or that the purpose of the assembly is the intimidation of others. The officer can have regard to the time, place, and circumstances in which the procession is to be held and may give to the organiser and those taking part such conditions which appear to him necessary in order to prevent such (**s. 12(1)**). This can prescribe the route of the procession and prohibit it from entering any public place specified in those directions.

Such powers are subject to judicial review and they must comply with the **Human Rights Act 1998** by being necessary and proportionate.[8] The courts have allowed a wide margin of discretion to the police under this section, and under **s.14** with respect to conditions imposed on public assemblies (**Broadwith v DPP [2000] Crim LR 924**). Thus, in **R (Brehony) v Chief Constable of Greater Manchester Police, The Times, 15 April 2005** it was held that the police must give basic reasons for their use. In our case, the police do not appear to have

[8] Again, the author stresses the need for any police action to be compliant with the HRA.

given any reasons for imposing the conditions and have not identified which of the statutory reasons is applicable in this case. Consequently, there appears to be no reason why the number of protesters should be limited and why the procession should not enter the shopping precinct.[9] Further, the condition that they should not distribute leaflets which are likely to cause distress to the public could be regarded as both insufficiently clear to be prescribed by law (***Hashman and Harrap v United Kingdom* (1999) 30 EHRR 241**). Equally, it may be a disproportionate interference with reasonable and peaceful protest (***Steel v United Kingdom* (1999) 28 EHRR 603**).

[9] The author offers a neat explanation as to why the police appear to have acted unlawfully in this aspect of the scenario, together with supporting case law.

LOOKING FOR EXTRA MARKS?

- Show that you understand the importance of the right to demonstrate and the need for the law and the courts to protect it from unnecessary interference.

- Appreciate the court's role in reviewing the use of the provisions in the light of human rights' principles in the ECHR and the HRA and any likely deference offered to the police and other public authorities.

- Use leading cases, domestic and European, which provide guidance on the likely outcome of the claims made by the protestors in the scenario.

TAKING THINGS FURTHER

- Joint Committee on Human Rights, *Demonstrating Respect for Rights? A Human Rights Approach to Policing Protest* 2008-09 HL 47/HC 320
  A re-examination of UK public order law as it impacts on the right to protest and the law's compatibility with human rights law

- Mead, D, *The New Law of Peaceful Protest: Rights and Regulation in the Human Rights Act Era* (Hart 2010)
  A comprehensive account of public order law as it impacts on protests and human rights law

- Oreb, N, 'The Legality of "Kettling" after Austin' (2013) 76 (4) MLR 735
  An examination of cases involving the control of demonstrations via 'kettling' and its compatibility with the right to protest

- Rainey, B, Wicks, E, and Ovey, C, *The European Convention on Human Rights*, 7th edn (OUP 2018) chs. 17 and 19
  A thorough and expert coverage of freedom of religion, and freedom of assembly and association, as covered under the ECHR

- Steinbach, A, 'Burqas and Bans: The Wearing of Religious Symbols under the ECHR' (2015) 4 (1) Cambridge Journal of International and Comparative Law 29
  A critical analysis of decisions of the European Court of Human Rights relating to the banning or restriction of religious dress in certain European states

Trispiotis, A, 'Two interpretations of "Living Together" in European Human Rights Law' (2016) 75 (3) CLJ 580
A further analysis of SAS with a critical discussion of the concept of 'living together'

Online Resources   www.oup.com/uk/qanda/

Go online for extra essay and problem questions, a glossary of key terms, online versions of all the answer plans and audio commentary on how selected ones were put together, and a range of podcasts which include advice on exam and coursework technique and advice for other assessment methods.

12 Skills for Success in Coursework Assessments

Achieving Success in Coursework Assessments in Human Rights and Civil Liberties

In Chapter 1, we looked at some of the challenges you may face in studying human rights and civil liberties. These related to the need to combine an awareness of human rights and political and social issues with knowledge of *the law* of human rights—the relevant statutes and treaties, the case law, and proposals for legal reform. It is not enough therefore to have an interest in human rights; you must approach human rights issues as a human rights lawyer; yet one who is aware of the social, political, and constitutional significance of addressing and resolving a human rights dispute—such as whether an individual has a right to die, whether celebrities have a right to privacy, or whether a prisoner should be able to vote.

Human rights assessments must therefore be approached from both angles—displaying a sound knowledge of the relevant law and an ability to appreciate the moral and other arguments surrounding the relevant disputes. Remember, judges and law-makers will be aware of both perspectives and students must show an appreciation of both to provide correct and convincing answers.

In addition your assessments need to be approached logically—displaying excellent and logical structure. Whether you are answering a problem question or an essay question, your task is to build up a convincing argument applying the 'evidence' from the relevant case law, statutory or treaty provisions, and the supporting academic arguments to the facts of your scenario or to an analytical essay. The reader needs to be taken through the relevant law—that, for example, governs the area of assisted suicide—and then needs to be introduced to the moral and other arguments with respect to criticism and possible reform of the law.

This chapter will look primarily at coursework essay questions, which normally form the basis of most of the questions you will be given in this module, and which require the greatest amount of research and critical skills; although some advice will be given with respect to problem question technique. For this type of assessment, examiners are looking for a combination of knowledge, accuracy, relevance, clarity, and, importantly, a depth of analysis and argument with respect to the various issues that we have identified earlier.

In terms of structure, content, and presentation, answering coursework questions in human rights is really no different to answering examination questions: you will still be expected to answer the question, address the law and other issues, and present the issues logically and in order (in terms of essays and problem questions, you can refer to the sections earlier in this book on examination success). The distinction between courseworks and examinations is primarily in the depth of the answer and in the way you are able to research and approach the question and present your answer. Remember, examiners are likely to be much *less* tolerant of mistakes, or failure to explain legal and other issues in-depth in coursework than they would be in an examination. The research materials are in front of you and you have been given time to research and refine your answers. As such, there are no excuses for basic errors, or poor presentation.

The marker will also expect a professional standard of academic writing and referencing; not perhaps to the standard displayed in academic journals and textbooks, but a style based on that type of academic paper. In coursework questions, unless you have been advised otherwise by your lecturer, it is crucial that you provide full references and citations for sources that you refer to. The recognised citation system for academic law writing is the Oxford Standard for the Citation of Legal Authorities (OSCOLA). It is worth getting to grips with this system early on in your course, as you will certainly need to use it when you tackle longer essays or pieces of substantial research, such as a dissertation or long essay.

Starting your courseworks: the 'blank page' syndrome

The most difficult thing about coursework is how to get started. Students have difficulties knowing how to begin their essay, and as a result there can be blank periods where days and weeks go by with nothing written, thus inducing panic. This is usually because the student does not fully understand the question and its scope: *What constitutional, moral, and legal issues have been raised by the recent prisoner voting case?* Take time, almost immediately after you receive the title, to think what the question is about and what it will require for you to answer it. In particular, what is the question (and the teacher) getting at and what do they expect from me?

In other words, instead of starting to write straight away, think about where you are in terms of this legal area: have you had lectures on it and do you understand the legal area and issues? This will determine the point at which you start your research—from the very basics or from a more advanced position—and once this research gets under way you will build up the confidence to tackle the question head-on. Do not simply go and locate and download relevant articles and cases and then wait until the writing stage to read and digest these sources. If you think about the question at an early stage these sources will make more sense to you when you come to read them and place them into your assessment. Note even at this early stage you can then start thinking of the issues and arguments you may cover: *statute law on voting, position of prisoner voting under the ECHR, political and public arguments against prisoner voting, arguments of equality, and rehabilitation in favour.*

Researching, planning, and preparing to write

As with an exam, for courseworks you need to undertake some revision of your existing knowledge; gathering all your materials and starting to consolidate them into a form from which you can start to fully answer the question. The first thing to do, therefore, is to gather all the material you have on the relevant topic, and ensure that you know and understand the law. Now is the time to iron out any problems, or areas you have not fully understood.

The next thing you should do is plan your answer: you can think of an initial plan the moment you get the question, but once you have undertaken your research you can then start to formulate a fuller, more informed, plan, ensuring that the different aspects of your answer are supported with cases and statutory provisions, and the appropriate academic and other arguments. Thus, before you start the writing process, you have a good idea what you are going to include, argue, and analyse, and you are confident that you are addressing the question. You may also want to write a draft introduction at this stage, outlining the central issues raised by the question and explaining how your answer will address those matters.

Critical analysis and evaluation

This is the difficult part of any coursework: for example, in problems this means applying the law to the facts in question and reaching a conclusion in a reasoned way. It is not enough to simply state the law, and this applies to essay questions as well: anyone can copy out chunks from texts, articles, and treaties and cases, but even if you are using relevant sources, you will be expected to take a *critical* approach based on your *understanding* of the law and issues. This will show your appreciation of the question and the legal and other dilemmas.

For example, with problem questions, when you state a legal rule, make sure you apply every part of that rule to the facts of the question: what does the rule (an obstruction of the highway must be unreasonable) mean for a political protestor charged with this offence? Are there any cases which suggest that the opposite conclusion may be drawn? Are there any particular facts, unique to this problem which you need to discuss? And, especially, in human rights' questions, what political, social, or constitutional factors might influence the judge's decision.

Critical skills are also expected in essays, where you are expected to understand the prevalent arguments and to formulate an argument, often for or against the particular assertion of the question—should prisoners be entitled to vote? This involves becoming familiar with the relevant arguments and academic opinion, understanding the various arguments, and considering the validity and strength of those opinions, along with your own personal (and informed) opinions. This does not necessarily involve criticising the law and current academic opinion, but you should at least show that you understand and appreciate the issues; if you have strong opinions, ensure they are tempered with counter arguments and are based on the law and sound legal arguments. The kinds of things that you may have to consider are whether there is a problem with this area of law, any gaps in the scope of the legislation, whether the cases conflict, whether the law is unclear or unfair to a particular group of people? In order to ascertain these points, you will need to refer to secondary sources of law, such as Command Papers, other consultation papers, and academic journal articles.

Thus, a good answer needs to show these skills: you should avoid discussing everything you know about a given topic (prisoner voting) and instead ask whether each statement you are making in the essay actually addresses the question. The essay should have a traditional introduction, main body (containing your arguments and analysis), and a conclusion, and you should ensure that each part addresses the question and assists you in providing the answer.

Relevance and sticking to the word limit

This is another common comment made by examiners on student work. For problem answers you need to select the correct legal rule for the scenario. Do not discuss all of the rules, only the ones which are relevant on these facts and for which the parties need advice. For example, if a party has been denied legal representation, advise on that part of **article 6 ECHR**, not **article 6** in its entirety.

Students often complain that the word limit for the piece of coursework is inadequate. Although word limits can be tight, it is an important legal skill to be able to stick to what is relevant and answer the question and it is often apparent that the student has included material which is in the general topic area, but which is not relevant to the question. In a problem question, this might be adding unnecessary facts of cases, or giving several examples of, say, breach of the peace cases, instead of just one. In courseworks, there is a temptation to include everything that you have read so as not to lose the benefit of your research. Again, think whether this information is relevant, and how much of it is necessary to make the point you are making; you can always include extra research or case names in footnotes to show off your research.

The word limit also becomes less problematic if you know the law before you start writing; it is difficult to issue-spot if you do not know which issues you are looking for, and more difficult to include relevant arguments if you do not appreciate the nuances of the law and the question. In terms of whether you are allowed to exceed the word limit at all, check with your tutor. Some law schools will allow, say, a 10 per cent leeway. You should try to stay as close to the limit as possible.

Referencing and citation of legal authorities

In coursework you are usually expected to follow the academic standard of citation, including providing a bibliography, footnotes, and proper citation of authorities. The reason for this is to encourage academic integrity and the avoidance of plagiarism. Any material which is not your own must be acknowledged in the body of your work in the form of a footnote and you need to provide a separate bibliography listing cases, statutes, and secondary sources. Some institutions also require a separate table of cases and a table of statutes. The recognised system for referencing academic work in law is the Oxford Standard for the Citation of Legal Authorities (OSCOLA).

Writing up, proofreading, and checking before you submit

A key part of any writing process is the checking and proofreading at the end. Ask yourself: does each point flow naturally to the next; does the essay flow or does it appear disjointed? Put your work through a spellcheck. When you are ready to write up, use your plan to help you structure your answer. Be sure to write a draft (or several drafts) before you submit the final work. As in all law assessments, you should adopt a formal written style and avoid personal opinions or journalistic language—see the answers in this text for guidance on how to get the style right—not too informal, yet clear and readable.

Checklist for Coursework in Human Rights law

- Do I understand the question and the relevant legal area?
- Have I produced a plan?
- Have I included sufficient and relevant cases and statutory or treaty materials?
- Does my work include—in the bibliography and footnotes—properly cited primary and secondary sources?
- In problem questions, have I considered the relevant law (and influencing factors such as politics or policy) in giving advice?
- In essay questions, have I understood and considered academic opinion in the form of learned journals, and evaluated the strengths and weaknesses of those opinions with reference to the question I have been given?
- Have I kept descriptions of the law and cases to a minimum, instead of concentrating on application of the law to the facts (problems questions) or evaluated arguments for criticism and reform (essay questions)?
- Have I stuck to the word limit and included relevant information (and excluded irrelevant information)?
- Have I followed the presentation and submission instructions?
- Have I proofread my work, put it through a spellcheck, and ensured that it is readable and convincing?

All this requires time and dedication, but it will be worth it.

Good luck!

COURSEWORK QUESTION

Below is a question on assisted suicide and human rights. It is a relatively popular area for assessment and the topic remains controversial, academically and as a matter for public and political discussion. The question is followed by advice on how to:

- Interpret the question and which aspects and wording to concentrate on
- Structure the answer in terms of dealing with the main issues
- Decide which approach to take in dealing with the controversial legal and moral issues
- Decide which primary and secondary sources to use in addressing and answering the question
- Include leading academic opinion and blend that opinion into your answer
- Conclude your answer in a way which highlights your views but leaves the issues sufficiently open-ended

The question

'The refusal of Parliament to change the law on assisted suicide has failed the victims of the current law,[1] which is both arbitrary and discriminatory.[2] It is time for the law and the courts to accept the human rights arguments for change, and to reject the arguments based on parliamentary and state sovereignty and judicial deference.'[3]

Critically analyse that statement[4] and consider the desirability of its call to change the law.[5]

Interpreting the question and its scope

The marginal notes on the question have identified the central focus of the question.

Thus, although the question is generally about assisted suicide and the human rights' arguments for challenging and changing the law, its wording suggests that there are more specific, constitutional and diplomatic, matters to be considered by the student. This is evident from the inclusion of words and phrases such as:

- Parliament's refusal to change the law
- Parliamentary and state sovereignty
- Judicial deference

[1] The question immediately focuses on Parliament's refusal to change the law on assisted suicide, thus concentrating on the political and constitutional dilemmas, which appear later in the question.
[2] The quote claims that the law is arbitrary and discriminatory; thus, you need to relate that to human rights claims such as individual liberty and autonomy and principles of necessity, proportionality, and non-discrimination which underpin such claims.
[3] You are now being asked to consider whether it is time, after a long line of cases giving deference to Parliament and the state on this issue, for the courts to put human rights' arguments first and to force legal change.
[4] Although the statement is clearly in favour of change, you need to consider that statement objectively, and from both sides, carefully considering the strength of both arguments—abandoning or maintaining deference.
[5] You are now required to consider the arguments contained in the statement for reform of the law, remembering that the counter arguments may be stronger than the ones made in the statement.

Therefore, although it asks you to consider the human rights arguments, and to consider the 'right to die' claim, it is clear that this should be considered alongside the constitutional and diplomatic considerations of whether it is Parliament, as opposed to the courts, who should effect any change in the law.

You must therefore be aware of this particular controversy as, so far, both the domestic and European courts have shown deference to Parliament and let it choose whether or not to change the law. You must, therefore, appreciate issues such as parliamentary sovereignty (legal and political), the separation of powers, judicial deference and the constitutional role of the courts, and the European Court's application of the margin of appreciation.

The quote also claims that the law is 'arbitrary and discriminatory'—this requires you to focus the human rights arguments on the claim that the law conflicts with principles of necessity, proportionality, and the principles of equality under the law.

Structuring the answer

- Because of the wording and angle of the question, your introduction should include a summary of the current situation—the courts' refusal to declare the law incompatible—and the range of human rights and constitutional and other issues which are underpinning this legal battle. This way you are identifying the main controversies and preparing yourself to tackle those issues when addressing the cases and other developments in the main body of the essay.

- You can then move to explaining the current law—common law and under the **Suicide Act 1961**—and it potential conflict with human rights' arguments based on liberty, personal integrity, and freedom from discrimination.

- You can then examine the case law in this area—both in domestic law and before the European Court—where the legislation and prosecution policy has been challenged. At this stage, you should highlight and analyse the human rights' claims (under **articles 2, 3, 8, 9, 14 ECHR**) and the courts' consideration of them. However, central to this analysis are the reasons for the courts' refusal to declare the law incompatible with the ECHR and their refusal to interfere with what they regard as an issue best dealt with by Parliament (or, in the European Court's case, the state's own legal system). This can also summarise the reasons provided by the state for refusing to change the law (preservation of life, protection of the vulnerable, public morality, and ethics).

- You should now review this situation and consider the essential issue—should the courts abandon deference in this case and declare the law incompatible on the basis that it is arbitrary and discriminatory (in that it applies in a blanket fashion to everyone irrespective of physical ability)? This requires a full appreciation of the clash between human rights and sovereignty and whether in this area the courts should abandon or qualify deference. At this point students can give examples of deference (prisoner voting rights) and more robust approaches (detention without trial).

- You are now in a position to draw a conclusion (possibly tentative) with respect to the desirability of changing the law. This will involve the desirability of the courts effecting any change, and any specific proposals that have been put forward for change. These can be considered in the light of principles of human rights (proportionality and non-discrimination) together with the reasons for keeping the law as it is.

Determining which approach and angle to take

As we have seen, the question focuses on a constitutional approach to the question. You need to be aware of the medical and ethical arguments against reform, and, of course, the human rights' arguments; however, these should be mentioned in the context of the wider issue of who should decide the law's compatibility and content in this area.

The above plan allows for consideration of all the issues, but clearly focuses on the constitutional and diplomatic clash between law makers and the judiciary (and the state and the Strasbourg Court).

Using primary and secondary sources to support your answer

You need to be aware of the primary legislation (**Suicide Act 1961**), the common law of murder/euthanasia, and the human rights which are being employed to challenge the law—**articles 2, 3, 8, 9, and 14 ECHR**. You also need to be aware of any legislative proposals in this area—most recently the Assisted Dying Bill.

The case law of both the domestic and Strasbourg courts is essential in addressing the question: *Pretty, Purdy, Nicklinson, and Conway*. These cases will identify all the relevant legal issues as well as the moral, ethical, and constitutional/political considerations addressed by the courts.

Using academic opinion to critically reason your answer

There has been a great deal of academic (and professional) commentary in this area and a number of journal articles have tackled all the issues raised by the question of the right to die. Much of this commentary has come from experts in medical law, who have considered the ethical issues surrounding the right to die. These are relevant to the issues raised by the question (in appreciating the medical/ethical objections to law reform), but they are not central to the constitutional arguments highlighted in the question and the suggested plan.

The employment of academic arguments which have considered the legal and human rights' issues are thus the most useful and appropriate. These articles will highlight the legal issues raised by the cases and the general challenge to the law on human rights' grounds. More specifically, those articles which concentrate on the constitutional battle between the courts and Parliament will identify the central arguments, both for law reform or retaining the status quo. Students may wish to look at these articles:

- Steve Foster, 'The Right to Die and Private Autonomy Versus the Sanctity of Life' (2017) 22(2) Coventry Law Journal 71
- Nataly Papadopoulou, 'From Pretty to Nicklinson: Changing Judicial Attitudes to Assisted Dying' [2017] 3 EHRLR 298
- John Adenitir, 'A Conscience-based Human Right to be "Doctor Death"' [2016] PL 613

The student can also refer to a number of academic case comments that have outlined and analysed the decisions in the leading cases; many of these may be contained in weekly or trade journals which provide useful coverage of developments in this area.

Reaching a logical, interesting and cogent answer

Having examined the law, the case law, and other developments, and having appreciated the arguments for and against law reform (in the context of the constitutional and other concerns), you are now ready to reach a conclusion. As this is a complex moral and constitutional area, your conclusions should to a great extent be qualified and tentative (appreciating the arguments for reform and the counter arguments). Ensure that you summarise the fundamental arguments for and against, which you should have identified from the judgments, political opinions, and academic articles. You can then finish with a final recommendation as to whether the law should be changed, or whether the status quo is maintained.

Index

F